THE HERO'S CLOSET

THE HERO'S CLOSET

SEWING FOR COSPLAY AND COSTUMING

GILLIAN CONAHAN

Photographs by
KAREN PEARSON

ABRAMS | NEW YORK

CONTENTS

INTRODUCTION

It was almost inevitable that I would get into cosplay. I love to make things, and I grew up on a steady diet of science fiction, fantasy, comics, anime, and video games. I started sewing way back in elementary school, first by hand and then on a sewing machine and serger. With practice and experimentation, I learned to work with a variety of fabrics, fit patterns to my body, and sew clothes I wanted to wear. I spent years learning to manipulate patterns—eventually, I learned to make my own. But the fact is, sewing everyday clothes can get pretty boring. I wanted to make something exciting, something elaborately embellished and full of interesting shapes and details, even if I didn't generally wear that sort of thing. Some people might start in on an outrageous evening gown at this point. But for me, costumes were the answer. Long before I knew cosplay was a thing, I cherished Halloween as an opportunity to re-create my favorite characters. Now, with more experience and better tools at my disposal, I can make things that would once have been pure fantasy. As a creative person and a nerd, it's hard to imagine a better feeling.

As my costume collection has grown, I've found that sometimes I enjoy the crafting process even more than I like wearing the result. It turns out I'm at least as much of a sewing geek as I am any other kind of geek. But although my stack of sewing and drafting texts now rivals my science fiction stash, I can safely say that none of the writers had elves and superheroes in mind. Most of that I had to puzzle out myself—and now I want to share it with you. Maybe you picked up this book because you're brand-new to cosplay, or perhaps you're a seasoned pro sick of pouring money into costumes that fall short of your exacting standards. For whatever reason, you're interested in sewing costumes yourself. Awesome! But even if you're brand-new at this, and not convinced you'll get into sewing just for the joy of it, I still think that every cosplayer should learn to sew at least a little bit, if only to open the door

to new and more ambitious costume projects. Here are just a few reasons why DIY might be a good option for you:

You need an item that isn't commercially available.

While it's possible to find commercial costumes for many recognizable characters, the character you love might not be among them. Even if you can find part of your costume in a store, there may be other components that are harder to track down. If that's the case, you'll have to find something similar and modify it. An even better solution? Make it yourself! It's often much simpler to add the distinctive features that make a costume shine—like piping, collars, sleeve cuffs, or ruffles—if you're starting from scratch rather than altering an existing garment.

You want something unique.

Maybe you've picked a popular character to cosplay, and you've managed to find the costume in stores or online. Great! But when you arrive at the convention, there's a good chance that someone—or lots of someones!—will be wearing the exact same costume. While you should definitely high-five and maybe take a goofy picture together if this happens, sometimes it's nice to be able to put your own spin on a character and know that no one else is going to have anything quite like it. You can pick a less common costume variant, create character mash-ups, transport your character into a different time period or an alternate universe, or invent your own character for a truly unique costume.

You want total control over the materials, color, style, and details.

If you cosplay, you probably sweat the small stuff. You know that attention to detail can make or break an outfit, and maybe you've been disappointed with purchased costumes in the past. If you sew your costume yourself, you have total control over each piece from beginning to end. You can choose exactly the right fabrics and trims, and accurately replicate details like sleeves and collars. No settling for someone else's interpretation, or for something that's "almost right." And if it doesn't turn out as well as you'd hoped, at least you can be certain that the next one will be better!

You want a custom fit.

Off-the-rack clothes are made to a standard body size and shape, and chances are that body is at least a little bit different from yours. If you're petite or tall or have proportions that differ from the standard, you might not be able to find the pieces you need at all. Actors have their costumes custom-fitted to look flawless, and you can do the same if you make your costume. Fitting your garments to your exact specifications means you'll end up with an outfit that's comfortable, won't pull or gap, and makes you look amazing.

You're on a budget.

It's true, you could pay someone else to sew you a custom creation. But honestly, how many people have the budget to do that all the time? If you have time to create a costume for yourself, you don't have to pay for someone else's labor. If you shop around for your materials, you can find a price that fits into your budget—or find a less expensive alternative. And, once you've got a few costumes under your belt, you can even start offering your services to wealthier friends!

You enjoy that smug "I made this" feeling.

If you're not already convinced, consider the satisfaction of wearing a knockout costume that you put together all by yourself. For bragging rights, that's pretty hard to top!

A handmade costume is also a common prerequisite for participation in masquerades and costume competitions, so sewing skills are essential if you have any affinity for official accolades and shiny trophies.

The Hero's Closet is intended to give beginners a strong foundation in sewing for cosplay and costuming, but I also want to provide direction for more adventurous sewists who may want to combine patterns, alter pattern pieces, or perhaps eventually begin to design their own patterns in order to more accurately replicate a character's look. I've started with patterns for eleven basic pieces, and then have combined, altered, and adapted them to create nine costumes so you can see how to build a character's look out of these simple parts. If you've never done this before, I've also included a warm-up project that will help you get comfortable with the basics while adding some geeky flair to your wardrobe. Along the way, I'll walk you through planning a costume and choosing a pattern and fabrics, and share my most-used sewing techniques and construction tips. There are step-by-step instructions provided for each of the basic pieces, and directions for the costumes as well.

I think a lot of people have the idea that sewing is hard, or scary, or for professionals only. And yet most of these people drive cars, use computers, and exercise all kinds of specialized technological skills without a second thought. A sewing machine is just another tool, and one that anyone can master with enough practice. To start making your own costumes, all you need are some simple sewing skills, such as threading a needle and tying a knot. Familiarize yourself with the basic operation of your sewing machine: threading, winding bobbins, starting and stopping. Start with one of the simple patterns, be patient and meticulous, and follow the directions carefully while you're learning. After that, the sky's the limit!

GETTING STARTED

RESEARCH AND PLANNING

We all know that choosing which character to cosplay isn't always a rational decision. If you're going to put your time, money, and creative energy into a costume, the most important thing is to choose a character—and an outfit—that you're in love with. If you're really excited about your work, it won't matter if you have to spend hours and hours sewing, adjusting a pattern, or setting rhinestones. If you're not enchanted with the project, it's not worth it—even if you can throw it together in a weekend—because you won't enjoy wearing it. ⇒ That said, it does help to consider a few practicalities as you're setting out: skill level, time constraints, access to materials, and budget. If you're brand-new to sewing, you may not want to tackle a tailored jacket right out of the gate. (Beginners, you'll learn about all the techniques used in this book in Chapter 3, Costume Sewing Basics, page 43.) If you're on a tight budget, you may not want to choose a ball gown that requires 10 yards (9 m) or more of fabric (unless you're willing to make some serious compromises on the quality of that fabric). And if the convention is next weekend, this really isn't the moment to start an outfit with extensive hand embroidery. Look for a project that speaks to these criteria. The goal is to challenge yourself, but not to set yourself up for frustration. Although you may run into some hitches along the way, if you're realistic from the outset, you should still be able to power through and end up with a successful result. Not actually sure what you're ready for? Read on! First, I'll help you figure out what goes into the research for and planning of a potential costume. Once you have a good idea of what the making of your costume will involve, you'll be able to decide whether to scale back your ambitions or reach for the stars. Here's how to get started, in five easy steps.

STEP 1

Gather References

Whether you're sewing, commissioning, or assembling your costume from found pieces, the first step in most cosplay projects will be gathering references. Keep in mind that you're not just looking for cool pictures, but for images that show you how the costume comes together in as much detail as possible. In order to accurately replicate a character design, you'll want to have clear views of the front, sides, and back of your outfit. Try to get some pictures of the costume in motion as well, since this will help you to determine what kind of fabric you're looking at, how much fullness you need in the skirt or sleeves, and other useful information that might not be obvious from a basic static pose. Beginning on page 14, we'll discuss the specific design elements and construction techniques you need to understand in order to transform 2-D art into a real wearable garment, but for now, just think about collecting as much information (and inspiration) as possible.

As cosplay grows more widely recognized, some creators are making detailed reference images available for their characters. If you've picked one of these, collecting the necessary information can be as simple as an Internet search. Often, though, you may need to be a little more creative to get the most useful material. Screenshots from games and animated TV shows can be a good starting point, but since the visuals in these media are often simplified for better performance or lower production costs, you may find more detail in promotional posters, art books, strategy guides, figurines, or other peripheral materials. If you're working from a movie or live-action show, you may find that behind-the-scenes photos make great references since they're less likely to be obscured by dramatic angles and lighting.

STEP 2

Consider Its Parts

Once you've collected your references, you'll need to study them to find out how your costume is going to come together. Break the outfit down into its component parts and look at each item individually, as in the illustration at right. Even very complicated costumes are often composed of several familiar garments layered together, so as far as construction is concerned, you'll want to consider each item independently. The Pirate (page 185) is a good example of building an outfit from separate pieces: the Tunic pattern (page 121), the Pants pattern (page 137), and the Coat pattern (page 149) are put together to create the entire costume.

In addition to the main garments, look at any accessories or add-ons and decide which can be made and which would be better to buy. You'll most likely need to buy shoes, but making shoe covers are an option if the style is unusual or a difficult color (see page 170). You may also need gloves, hats, bags, belts, or other pieces to complete your outfit. Many of these can be made yourself, and making is the best option if you need the pieces to match exactly, but be realistic about how much time you can spend on them. Gloves in particular can be fussy and time-consuming to sew, so they might be overwhelming if you're new at this. Even if you have to buy some pieces of your costume, you can still customize them with your own details and embellishments.

Next, take a good look at the information in front of you. Where are the seams? This tells you how the item was constructed. What fabrics are used—are they stretchy, drapey, or stiff—and how are they embellished? How does the character get into his or her outfit? If the answer to that question is

"It gets sprayed on with a magical costume hose," where can you add an unobtrusive zipper? This is one practical detail you can't overlook, because you do have to wear it! Does the costume need to shape and support the body inside it, as a corset does, or do parts of it need to stand up on their own, like a big theatrical collar or body armor? Start thinking about what materials you might need, including fabrics and embellishments as well as linings and any necessary structural support. If you're fairly new to sewing and are not sure what to look for, take a look at Chapter 2 (see page 25) for an overview of fabric and other materials that help build your costume.

If you're puzzled by how an item might be constructed, try looking for similar garments in your closet, in stores, or online. This may give you some ideas about how the pieces are sewn together or how the desired silhouette is achieved. If you've got an old garment you can dissect, so much the better—just make sure you take notes about how it was originally put together, lest you find yourself with a useless pile of scraps. Get in the habit of looking at garment tags, or at the descriptive text if you're looking at things online, and pay attention to what materials the clothes are made from, since this will help you when you start shopping for fabric.

Keep a folder or inspiration board full of images you find useful, either because they help to pin down the details of your intended costume or because they give you hints about materials and construction. Also make note of any particularly useful search terms in case you need to look for more information later. Jot down accessories from your reference images that you may need to source elsewhere—hats, gloves, shoes, crowns, and so forth—so you can keep an eye out for those items while you gather the rest of your materials.

Finally, at some point you may have to make some educated guesses. If you're working from a TV or movie costume, your refs should give you a good idea of where the seam lines are and how each item of clothing is shaped. But if you're working from a graphic novel, animation, or game, there may be more room left for interpretation based on the style of the artist who created the image. Seams in clothing are often subtle enough that individual artists may choose to omit them, so even for a relatively straightforward outfit, the art might not give you the whole picture. Some art styles are better at communicating fabric drape and texture than

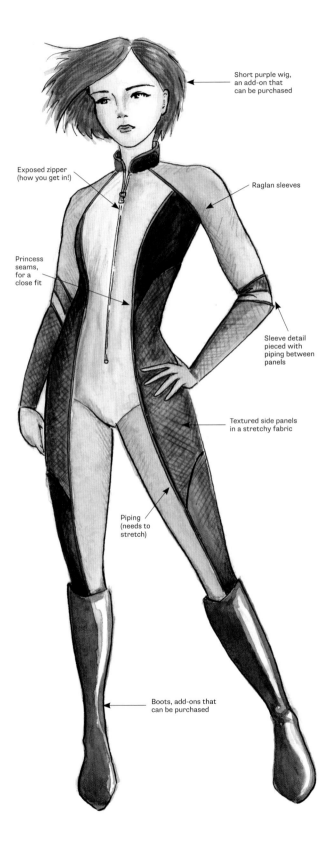

Short purple wig, an add-on that can be purchased

Exposed zipper (how you get in!)

Raglan sleeves

Princess seams, for a close fit

Sleeve detail pieced with piping between panels

Textured side panels in a stretchy fabric

Piping (needs to stretch)

Boots, add-ons that can be purchased

others, and a real-life costume will frequently need more detail than the animated version in order to look convincing. Some artists cheerfully design costumes that make no physical sense, and you'll have to judge for yourself whether to attempt an approximation or just make something up. This is where your creativity and a little knowledge of fabric and how clothing is constructed will serve you well, because you'll be able to visualize what *should* be there even if the artist doesn't spell it out for you.

STEP 3

Make a Map

Since you'll most likely be gathering information from multiple reference images, you may want to create your own sketches to keep track of everything you've learned. Use these drawings to take notes as you render the key details of each garment—the placement of seams and darts, whether a skirt is gathered or pleated, the shape of the collar or sleeve, and the length of the coat or dress. If the costume has multiple layers, draw each piece individually. Even if part of a piece will be hidden when you wear it, you need to know how the unseen areas will be constructed.

Achieving the correct proportions can be one of the trickiest parts of replicating a costume, so refer back to your reference images and look for landmarks that will help you get the relationships right. How wide is the skirt compared to the waist? Does the jacket end halfway down the thigh, or more like a third? Where does the sleeve end relative to the hem?

Multilayered costumes also require a little thought to make sure the pieces will fit together nicely. Remember that garments worn over other garments will need to be a little looser, and that the proportions between the pieces need to be correct in addition to fitting the proportions of your body. Later, you'll be able to compare all these observations to the measurements of your patterns to determine if you need to make alterations (see page 73).

If you're not comfortable with drawing, or if you're in a hurry, you may want to use a croquis to give you a starting point and create a consistent look between sketches. A croquis is a plain line drawing of your body, shown in a simple standing pose from the front, back, and sometimes the side (see opposite). Fashion designers use them to save time when sketching, because they allow you to focus on drawing the clothes and not worry about drawing out the whole body every time.

You can find croquis online to download and print, but you'll mostly see stylized fashion model shapes that won't be as useful for people with differing body types. Instead, you can make your own custom croquis by tracing around a photograph of yourself like I did for the croquis on the next page. Get a friend or use a timer to take a straight-on picture of you from each side, holding the camera around torso height to avoid distorting your proportions. Wear close-fitting clothing and stand against a plain background so you can see the outline of your body clearly. Then, trace around the outlines of your body using your favorite image editing software or a sheet of tracing paper on top of the printed photos. You may want to put front, side, and back figures on the same page for the sake of efficiency, but make the figures nice and big so you can draw in fine details if you need to. Make sure you can see where your waist, hips, knees, and elbows should be, and add reference marks if necessary. Then print or photocopy the croquis so you can draw over the top of it.

These sketches will be your map for your whole project, so make them on sturdy paper and put them up where you can see them as you work. Take them with you when shopping for materials and accessories, and as you decide on fabrics and trims, you can draw them in or attach swatches. Once you have clear references and a good plan, you're ready to start creating a convincing costume.

STEP 4

Identify Design Elements

After you've done a bit of research and have made a map, you may be tempted to rush right out and buy fabric. But don't! If you were just sewing clothes for yourself, you might pick out a pattern you like and then choose fabric, or start with a gorgeous fabric and come up with a project to suit it. But the process for creating a costume is different: you're

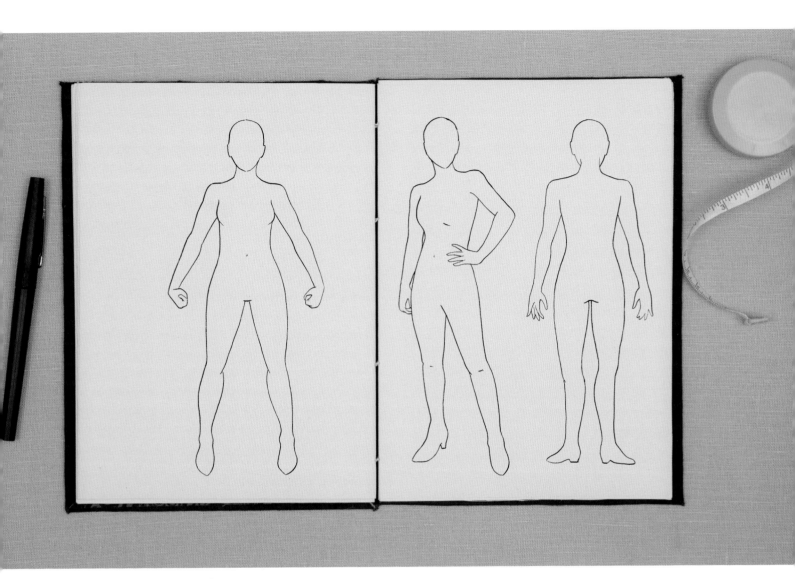

picking a character to cosplay, then identifying the pattern (or patterns) to help you make that character's costume, based on the design elements in the outfit. Once you're confident that you can find patterns for the pieces you need—or create your own patterns if your skills allow—then you can shop for fabric, materials, and embellishments that will work with the underlying shape of the costume. So understanding a bit about design and construction is the key to choosing the patterns that help you build a successful costume.

Here's how you might translate the drawing you made of your character's clothing into a costume. Suppose your character wears a school uniform like the one on page 179. When you break it down it consists of two garments: a blouse and a skirt. The blouse has a loose fit with side darts to give it a little shape, and long set-in sleeves that gather into cuffs. The neckline is V-shaped, with a sailor collar (natch). There is trim around the collar and the cuffs, and an accent scarf in a contrasting color. What are the defining elements of the skirt? It's a bit simpler, featuring evenly spaced pleats and a basic waistband. If this happens to be one of your favorite constumes, you're in luck, because you can find the patterns right inside this book. But if you need to construct the

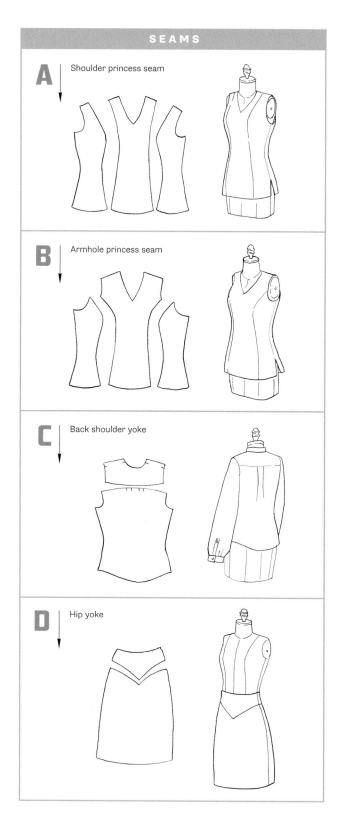

SEAMS

A Shoulder princess seam

B Armhole princess seam

C Back shoulder yoke

D Hip yoke

costume on your own, this example shows you how easy it is to identify the major elements of an outfit.

The illustrations in the Glossary of Style Elements on pages 198 to 202 present an overview of design elements to help you choose the appropriate patterns for practically any costume. These elements include neckline, collar, sleeve, skirt, dress, and pant styles. Remember that there are 11 basic patterns (see pages 96 to 153) to help you get started, and these can be easily supplemented by commercial patterns to customize individual pieces. You'll learn all about working with patterns in Chapter 3, page 48, but start with recognizing these features from your costume map.

Some basic construction techniques are used to bring a design into 3-D, and to faithfully replicate a costume, you will need to recognize these as well. The most basic technique is the seam itself, which joins two pieces of fabric. Darts allow flat fabric to conform to the body's curves and are essential to making a fitted garment from woven fabric that has no inherent stretch. Other features you may see in your reference costumes (some seen in the design elements above) include pleats, gathers, flounces, godets, gussets, ruching, and shirring. Here's some basic information about each of these construction essentials to help you identify them:

SEAMS. Most artists will at least suggest where a clothing item has seams, as seam placement is one of the main ways to define a garment's style. Look for solid lines crossing the garment, clear breaks between colors or textures, and details like piping or decorative topstitching that may have been added to highlight the garment's construction (read more about these decorative details in Chapter 5, page 87). Sudden changes in shape can also indicate the presence of seams, as when a narrow sleeve suddenly becomes very wide and full or a fitted bodice blossoms into a voluminous skirt.

When looking at your reference images, you'll want to determine whether the seams are just for show (a style line) or if they contribute to the fit of the garment (a shaping seam). The latter (also called a dart-equivalent seam) helps mold the garment to a body. You're probably familiar with a common vertical shaping seam, the princess seam, that originates at the shoulder or armhole and passes vertically near the bust point and down to the hem (**A, B**). Horizontal seams,

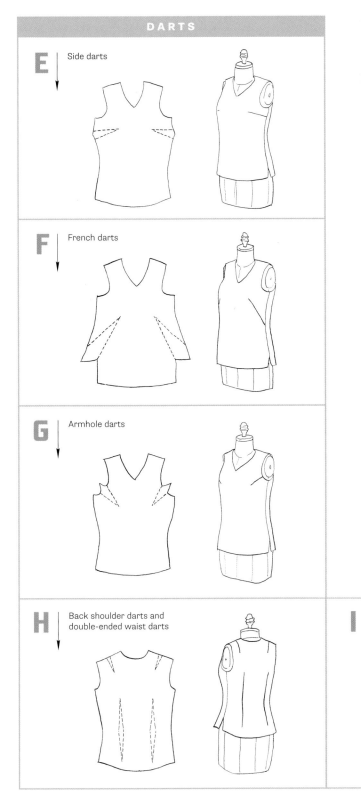

DARTS

E | Side darts

F | French darts

G | Armhole darts

H | Back shoulder darts and double-ended waist darts

I | Waist darts on a dress bodice and skirt

or yokes, can also add shape to a garment: the back shoulder yoke on a menswear-style shirt often adds a little shape in lieu of a shoulder dart, and the back yoke on jeans, hip yokes on skirts and dresses, and most low-rise waistbands incorporate at least some shaping, partially or completely replacing waist darts (**C**, **D**).

DARTS. On reference art, darts are usually drawn as a simple line with an abrupt end, but you will probably find many artists who don't bother to draw them in. Unless you deliberately emphasize them, they tend to disappear into the surrounding fabric, especially when viewed from a distance. This means that they can be a good choice for unobtrusive shaping in situations where the source material doesn't specify a method. Darts always point to a "peak" of the body, such as the tip of the breast, the widest part of the hip, or the curve of the butt. You may also find darts on the back shoulders of jackets or fitted tops, where they help the fabric curve over the shoulder blades; on sleeves to account for the natural curve of your arm; and anywhere else you want to add shape to a garment (**E**-**I**).

A relaxed blouse may have a bust dart but no waist darts, and a loose-fitting shirt may have no darts at all. Men's clothing uses fewer darts than women's because men's clothes don't fit as closely, and generally men don't have the curves that most women do, but you'll still see back darts on some fitted shirts and on tailored garments like suit coats and trousers. You'll also need more shaping if you're making a historical style that's meant to be closer-fitting than modern menswear.

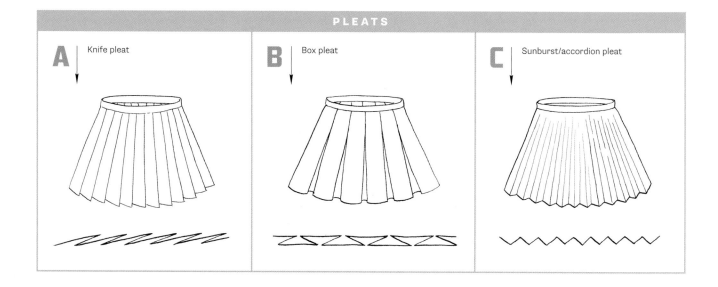

A | Knife pleat

B | Box pleat

C | Sunburst/accordion pleat

PLEATS. Pleats can help shape a garment, and in many cases they're a key design element. In simple form, a pleat is a fold in the fabric that may be anchored with a few stitches at one or both ends. A reference image may have pleats in a variety of forms. Knife pleats, often used in skirts and trims, are a series of equally-sized Z-shaped pleats that all point in the same direction (**A**). In art, they look like a series of parallel lines with a zigzagging lower edge. Box pleats are symmetrical, created with pairs of folds that go in opposite directions (**B**). You may find them alone at center front or back, in pairs to replace darts on a skirt or other item, or placed around an entire garment. Individual box pleats can be formed inward or outward, with the paired folds pointing toward or away from each other. An inward box pleat is sometimes called an inverted box pleat. Drawings of box pleats will show how the paired folds come together at the top edge and spread out as they go down, with the "valley" of the pleat falling into shadow. You'll also see the symmetrical fold pattern along the lower edge—the part of the pleat that falls to the outside usually has a convex curve along the hem, and the inside will have a concave edge. Cartridge pleats are deep and regular, sewn perpendicular to a seam, and can take up very large amounts of fabric. They're especially common in big historical gowns.

Some types of pleats are not sewn in place, but simply creased. Accordion pleats are formed from a simple back-and-forth folding of the fabric. A variation of this is sunburst pleating, in which the accordion pleats radiate outward from a central point as in a circular skirt (**C**). You can identify this type of pleat by the regular zigzag of the lower edge and the regularly spaced pleat lines that disappear before reaching the waistband or seam where they're attached. Broomstick pleats are narrow and haphazard, formed by wrapping the fabric around a pole (the "broomstick") and crushing it into tiny folds. Mushroom pleats are similar but slightly more regular, and usually permanently molded into the fabric by a machine. These very fine pleats may resemble gathers in an illustration, but will cling closer to the body because the shape is creased into the fabric. Complex patterns can be formed by pleating the fabric in two dimensions, creating repeating patterns like an Escher print.

GATHERS. Gathering is a very common method for attaching skirts to bodices, but it might be seen anywhere that a large volume of fabric is condensed, like when a puffed sleeve is collected into an armhole or cuff. Gathers are often used instead of darts in soft shirts or blouses. Unlike pleats, which shorten a length of fabric by a fixed amount depending on the depth of the folds, gathering can be made loose or dense depending on the type of fabric and the desired look. The downside is that it can get very bulky in the real world, so dense gathering is usually only appropriate when using lightweight fabrics.

Ruching and shirring are both variations of gathering that can be used to add texture to a garment. Ruching is an overlay of gathered fabric on a fitted under-layer that creates a wrinkled effect, often used to add detail on fitted bodices (**D**). Shirring is composed of multiple regularly-spaced rows of gathering, nowadays often created by sewing with elastic thread (**E**). It creates a deeply textured panel with an orderly look, and elastic versions are commonly used in the back of fitted bodices to make the fit more forgiving. (You may own or have seen a sundress that uses this technique.)

In art, it can be difficult to distinguish gathering from some kinds of pleating, but the most obvious difference is that gathering will generally be more irregular and random-looking, having curved lines instead of straight. You can see examples of how these elements are commonly drawn in the illustrations at right (**F**, **G**).

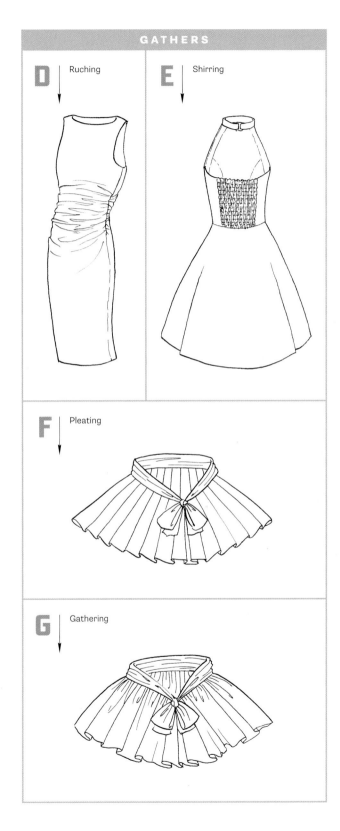

GATHERS

D   Ruching

E   Shirring

F   Pleating

G   Gathering

RUFFLES. Gathering is also used decoratively to create ruffles, a long strip of fabric that's gathered or pleated and attached to the garment. They are commonly seen in Edwardian and steampunk styles, and as an accent on corsets, shirt fronts, or sleeves (**A**, **B**).

FLOUNCES. A flounce is a piece of fabric cut in a curve and attached to a garment along the inside edge of the curve. Because the outside edge of the flounce is longer than the inside edge, it falls into graceful cone-shaped folds. The simplest type of flounce is a partial or full circle, which falls into evenly spaced folds all the way around. One example of this is a circle skirt, which consists of a very large circle with a waist-sized opening in the center, usually attached to some kind of waistband. Narrow flounces are often used decoratively, placed horizontally or vertically to adorn skirts, shirt fronts, and sleeves (**C-E**). Though decorative flounces and ruffles are often used in similar ways, you can distinguish them visually by the way the folds fall. A flounce will be smooth along the attaching seam and fall into loose ripples at the hem, whereas a ruffle has tight gathered folds along the attaching seam that relax toward the edge.

GODETS. A godet is a wedge-shaped panel of fabric that's inserted into a seam or slit in the garment. If your reference image has a trumpet or mermaid-style skirt, godets are one way to achieve this silhouette that is narrow through the hips but flares out into a luxurious, swishy hem. Generally, godets are used in garments made of lightweight fabric, so they collapse into soft folds (**F**).

GORES. A gore is a panel of fabric that's shaped to create a certain silhouette—usually narrow at the top and wider toward the bottom. For example, a mermaid skirt might be constructed from several narrow gores that all flare out toward the hem (**G**).

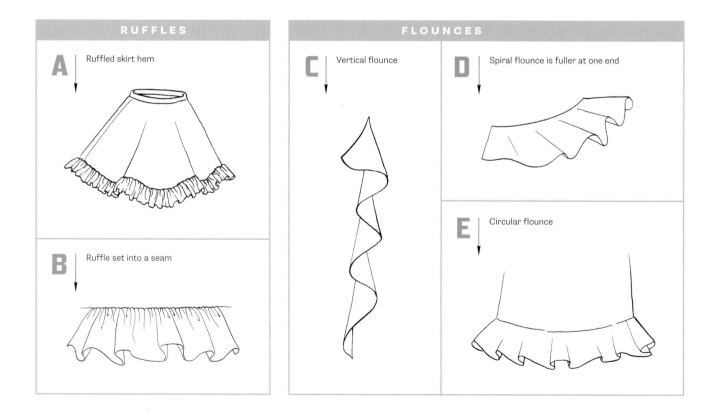

RUFFLES

A | Ruffled skirt hem

B | Ruffle set into a seam

FLOUNCES

C | Vertical flounce

D | Spiral flounce is fuller at one end

E | Circular flounce

F | Godet set in a center back seam

G | Multiple similarly-shaped gores create a flared skirt shape

H | Underarm gusset adds more room to raise arms

GUSSETS. These are small panels of fabric that are inserted at high-stress locations like underarms and crotch seams to improve the range of motion. You may have seen these in purchased tights or leggings, and they're often used in costumes for dance and theater. Though not obvious when the garment is worn normally, this is another real-world consideration if your costume is meant for vigorous activity, so look for them in a pattern. The Seamless Super-Suit (see page 117) has a built-in gusset to allow for movement (**H**).

EASE. In identifying the major construction elements of your garment, don't forget to look at the overall silhouette. The technical term for the difference between the garment measurements and body measurements is ease. This encompasses both wearing ease—the amount of ease needed to make a garment comfortable and mobile enough for its intended purpose—and design ease, which accounts for the difference between a tailored blouse and a billowing pirate shirt. Some garments even feature negative ease, because they are actually smaller than the body measurements; these pieces either stretch into shape to help accentuate the body or they pull the body in, as a corset does. Remember also that garments intended to be worn over other garments, like jackets and coats, will need more wearing ease in order to avoid binding and restricting your movement. Your reference map should help you see how closely the costume should fit, which has a lot to do with how a garment behaves when you are actually wearing it. Your fabric choices will also contribute to the amount of wearing ease needed in your costume. (Much more about the qualities of fabric in Chapter 2, page 25.)

Loose-fitting garments drape over the body instead of following its every curve, so they are often composed of simple, blocky shapes with soft pleats and gathers instead of shaped seams or darts. On the other hand, a close-fitting garment will need to be precisely fitted to your body in order to lie smoothly, perhaps with strategic darts and seaming. A body-hugging garment with no obvious darts or other shaping construction elements must be made of stretch fabric to allow it to mold to the body and move with it.

STEP 5
Pick a Pattern

Now that you've identified the features you want in your costume, it's time to pick the pattern (or patterns) that you'll make it from. Ideally, you want to find a pattern that has the same general shape, fit, and design elements as your reference costume. This book includes patterns for several basic pieces in Part 2 (see page 96), designed to be a useful foundation for a variety of cosplays. Several patterns include variations, so you can pick and choose the elements you want for your cosplay, and in Part 3 (see page 154), you'll see examples of how the basic pieces can be combined to form more elaborate costumes. If you don't see the exact details you want, some fixes are very simple: skirt and sleeve lengths are easy to adapt, and you can add more seams or change the shape of a neckline without too much difficulty. I detail these alterations in Chapter 4 (see page 73). Changing collar and sleeve shapes is a little more involved, but doable with a bit of experience (or a lot of trial and error); swapping out pattern pieces to switch up a look is also explored in Chapter 4. Commercial patterns can complement those provided in *The Hero's Closet* to give you more options and variations; find out more in the sidebar on the opposite page.

CHOOSING YOUR SIZE

Sewing pattern sizes are different from store-bought clothing, so always use your actual body measurements to choose your size. Stand naturally and have a friend measure you for the most accurate results. When measuring, wear your normal undergarments (the style you plan to wear with your costume) and a leotard or close-fitting top and leggings, if you want them for modesty. Measure your bust/chest and hips around the fullest part of each, and your waist at the narrowest point. If you have larger breasts, measure your upper chest (over the breasts and under your arms) as well. For all measurements, the tape should be parallel to the ground, flat against your body, without squishing or flattening anything. Take each measurement a few times and average them for the most accurate results.

Check the measurement chart on page 188 and refer to your measurements to choose your size. Coats, tops, and dresses will be sized by your chest or upper chest measurement; pants and skirts will be sized by the hip or sometimes the waist, if it's a men's size or a very full style that doesn't touch your body at the hips. Women's patterns are almost always sized for a B cup, which means the pattern will assume a 2" (5 cm) difference between the upper chest and the fullest part of your bust. If you measure more or less than that, you should use your upper chest measurement to pick a size and plan to adjust the pattern (see page 78).

The pattern is the key to the construction of your costume. Now that you've mapped out basic structure and identified patterns, it's time to start learning about fabrics.

Commercial Patterns

For a wider selection of patterns, check out the offerings at your local fabric store or online. (Most pattern companies sell through their websites, and you can find out-of-print styles on Etsy and eBay.) Browse the catalogs for available styles, but don't limit yourself to costume patterns! Many characters wear costumes based on common clothing. Note the brand and number for your selection so you can request it (or locate it yourself if the store has self-serve pattern cabinets). Check what size combinations are available so you can get the right one for your measurements; see "Choosing Your Size," opposite, for tips.

Once you have the pattern envelope in hand, flip it over and take a look at the information on the back. The photos or illustrations on the front of the envelope might not look exactly like what you want for your cosplay, so look for a line drawing that shows the "bones" of the pattern to see if it works for the design you've mapped out. The back of the envelope should also tell you what fabrics are appropriate, how many yards you need to make each size, what other supplies are necessary, and sometimes the finished measurements. Taken together, all this information should give you a good idea of whether the pattern will work for your project. It also serves as a shopping list for when you're gathering materials.

Companies will use certain phrases to indicate how the garment is supposed to fit. A "close-fitting" or "fitted" garment should skim close to the body, while a "loose-fitting" garment will drape and fall away from the body. There are specific standards for how much ease corresponds to each category, and you can find a guide in the pattern catalog or on the company website. Even so, it can be difficult to picture what 6" (15.2 cm) of ease looks like, so try measuring some of your own clothes to determine how much ease you prefer for each type of clothing and adjust your chosen size accordingly.

If you unfold the pattern tissue, you may see the garment's finished measurements printed on the front or side front piece. If not, you can measure the pieces yourself, remembering to subtract seam allowances (the amount of fabric taken up when sewing a seam). These measurements will usually be larger than your body, to allow for wearing ease and the design of the garment, but if you're making a corset or using a stretch fabric, you may want the measurements to be the same or even smaller than yours. The difference between the finished measurement and the body measurement is the amount of ease in the pattern, and it should be the same as the amount described on the envelope (though you can adjust to your preference if you want a looser or tighter fit than the designer intended). Refer back to the description of ease on page 21 if needed.

CHAPTER 2

FABRICS AND MATERIALS

Now that you've mapped out the basic structure of your costume and have selected the patterns you need, it's time to start looking for fabrics. Choosing the right fabric isn't just about finding the color or pattern your character wears. You'll also want to keep in mind the things you've learned about the shape of the costume and how it will ultimately fit, so you can match the characteristics of your costume up with fabrics that have the appropriate properties. The pattern instructions in the book give you suggestions for appropriate fabrics, and so will a commercial pattern. And if you're just starting to sew, don't worry! This section will go over some of the different types of fabric you might encounter, so you can determine what's right for you and your project. ➡ Fabric will be the largest expense for most sewn costumes. We all have budget constraints, so it's important to know your needs and your limits before you hit the fabric store. Bad fabric can spoil the entire costume—it might be too flimsy, shiny, or wrinkly to give the effect you're looking for, or it might be scratchy, hot, and uncomfortable to wear. If you don't buy enough fabric, you might end up kicking yourself when it's the night before the convention and your costume has no sleeves or only half a skirt panel. But at the same time, you don't want to let fabric eat up your entire budget—you want to leave some room for wigs, accessories, and the rest of the pieces that will make your costume come together. So it's all about striking a balance and finding materials that will look good in person and in photos without spending your entire paycheck.

Understanding Fabric Types

Fabric is created in two ways: it is woven on a loom or it is knit with a series of loops. Exceptions exist, but most knit fabrics are intrinsically stretchy and wovens not so much, although they can have some stretch based on the type of fibers they're made from. It's important to understand the differences between woven and knit fabric, because the fabric is a huge factor in the functionality of your costume, and the characteristics of the fabric also allow you to faithfully re-create your reference garment's qualities.

WOVENS

Woven fabrics are composed of two perpendicular sets of threads, the warp (along the length of the fabric, the direction it unrolls from the bolt) and the weft (across the width of the fabric, parallel to the cut edge). The structure of the fabric comes from the crossing of these threads over and under each other, and the result can be very plain or very intricate, depending on the type of weave. Woven fabrics have a straight grain, which runs parallel to the warp threads, and a cross grain, which runs parallel to the weft (**A**). The selvage (the tightly woven border along the edges) is along the warp edge; it helps you quickly identify the direction of the grain of the fabric. This is important when you are laying out and cutting your pattern pieces (see page 48); because the warp threads are usually a little stronger than the weft, items cut on the straight grain (with the warp running vertically) will

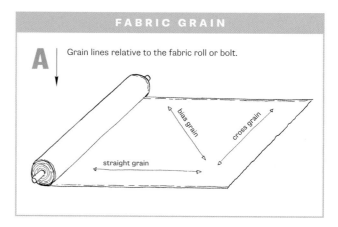

FABRIC GRAIN

A Grain lines relative to the fabric roll or bolt.

bias grain

cross grain

straight grain

tend to fall more softly while garments cut on the cross grain will be a little stiffer and more voluminous. The bias grain runs at a 45° angle to the straight and cross grains, and usually has more give or stretch. You might cut pieces on the bias when making slinky, drapey gowns, or for making historical leggings and hose where you need a stretch fit without anachronistic spandex (see page 31).

Woven fabrics are made from all kinds of fibers in all weights. Although they share some general traits, there are infinite exceptions. For example, many woven fabrics are prone to fraying, because the threads run across the fabric in a roughly straight line and so can be pulled out individually. But if the threads are textured, felted, or otherwise entangled with each other, as with many wool coatings, they can resist fraying very well. Most wovens do not naturally stretch, but often they will have some amount of "give," which can cause sagging in tightly fitted garments. And if spandex or another stretch fiber is incorporated in the woven fabric, it can have stretch and spring on par with many knits.

Types of Weaves

The weave of a given fabric can have a large impact on its suitability for a particular piece of your costume, sometimes more so than the type of fiber it's actually woven from (more about fiber content on page 29). See below for illustrations of some common weave patterns.

> **Plain** weave has a simple pattern of alternating over/under threads in each direction (**B**). Traditional cotton or cotton-blend fabrics like muslin, broadcloth, poplin, voile, batiste, gauze, and quilting cottons are woven this way. A plain weave is also often used for linen, both in the fine handkerchief weight and the more substantial bottom-weight versions used for skirts or pants, and for some silk fabrics including organza, habotai, and dupioni. Some wool suitings are plain weaves as well. Plain weaves tear more easily than other weaves and are more prone to wrinkling, but in general they're a good choice when you want a plain, neutral fabric type.

> **Twill** fabric is created when the threads pass over and under multiple threads in a staggered pattern (**C**). This results in a faint diagonal texture, sometimes broken up into a herringbone pattern. Fabrics of this type are often simply called twill, but also include denim, gabardine, serge, drill, and the herringbone coutil designed for corset making. Twills are often basic, rugged fabrics good for uniforms and casual pieces, but they can also be very fine.

> **Satin** weaves have long "floats," threads that cross over many more threads than they cross under, giving them a smooth, slippery surface (**D**). The most lustrous satins are made from silk or synthetic facsimiles, but more subdued wool and cotton sateens can be lovely for dresses and jackets because they look dressy but don't read as "shiny" on

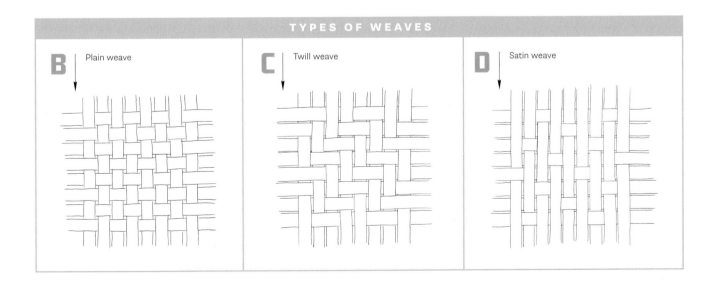

TYPES OF WEAVES

B | Plain weave

C | Twill weave

D | Satin weave

camera. Duchess satin, characterized by a heavy weight and low-key sheen, is also excellent for costumes that call for deep colors, a smooth texture, and lots of body (magical girls and princesses, take note).

➤ **Patterned** weaves may be simple or very elaborate. Jacquard weaves are one major family, including brocades and a variety of other all-over woven designs. These fabrics are wonderful for creating a rich look if you're cosplaying someone royal or otherwise important, but you probably won't find the exact pattern your character wears. If you're very particular about this, you'd be better off re-creating the design with embellishment or a custom print.

➤ **Velvet** and **velveteen** are woven with a pile, which is an additional set of threads that stick straight out of the surface like a carpet. You can find inexpensive versions made from polyester, or more costly and luxurious versions made from rayon and silk. Velveteens are often cotton, and somewhat easier to sew than the others, because true velvets require careful handling to avoid crushing and a lot of basting to prevent the layers from creeping as you sew.

KNITS

Just like a knitted sweater, knit fabrics are made from a continuous length of yarn that forms a series of interlocking loops (or sometimes multiple interlocking yarns). Many knits have inherent stretch, and are sometimes enhanced with the magical spandex (see page 31) to give them power stretch, which means that they stretch and spring back vigorously when released. It's the kind of fabric you want for leotards and bodysuits. Others have minimal stretch and can be treated more like wovens. Stable knits more or less hold their shape while you work, making them a good choice for beginner projects. Very stretchy or drapey knits may stretch and sag out of shape or wiggle and slink while you cut and sew them, so tackle them after you've finished a few projects.

When picking knit fabrics, the most important properties are the stretch and recovery. Stretch allows the fabric to expand to fit your body, and gives you more flexibility and freedom of movement. Recovery is the fabric's ability to spring back after being deformed, which makes for a consistent,

TESTING STRETCH

A Fold the fabric and grip two points. Stretch as far as it will go, then divide the stretched length by the unstretched length, subtract 1, and multiply by 100 to get the percent stretch.

100%
75%
50%
25%

body-hugging fit. Fabrics with no spandex content may still have stretch due to their structure (this is often described as "mechanical" stretch) but will mostly have less recovery. Much like with wovens, a small percentage of spandex in a knit can help to improve recovery and prevent sagging.

Knits may stretch horizontally, vertically, or both, and in varying degrees. You can test the stretch of a knit following the formula in (**A**). Patterns designed for stretch fabrics, like many in this book, will indicate how much stretch is required, with a percent difference between the relaxed and stretched lengths or a printed gauge that you can use to measure your fabric directly.

Confusingly, a fabric that has significant stretch in both horizontal and vertical directions is sometimes called four-way stretch, and two-way stretch may mean a fabric that has significant stretch in one direction and minimal stretch in the other. Make sure you know which you're looking for—as a general rule, bodysuits and leggings require four-way stretch.

Types of Knits

Just as with a woven fabric, the specific characteristics of a given knit can make it right (or wrong) for your costume.

➤ **Activewear knits** are nylon/spandex or polyester/spandex knits available in a variety of weights, with shiny, matte, or foil finishes. These are the default fabrics for swim and dance wear, bodysuits, and leotards, and are less common in fashion because of those associations. They're a great choice for skintight superhero outfits, because the stretch and recovery are reliably good, so you can even order them online without too much risk. Just note whether the stretch is two- or four-way and how the specific store defines those terms.

➤ **Cotton/spandex jersey** is available with varying amounts of stretch; small amounts of stretch are most appropriate for T-shirts and dresses, while stretchier cotton knits can make very comfortable bodysuits.

➤ **Double knits** are more substantial than single knits, and are generally stable and easy to sew with. Ponte di Roma is one popular type, made from blends of rayon, polyester, nylon, and spandex. They may have generous stretch and recovery or very little. Use them for dresses, jackets, pants, or structured jumpsuits.

➤ **Mesh knits** include illusion and glissenette, stretch mesh, athletic mesh, fishnet, and powernet. They're used to add breathability, inconspicuously support cutouts and other details, or layer over other fabrics to add texture. Firmer nets such as powernet can also be used to line garments for a built-in shapewear effect.

➤ **Rayon/spandex jersey knits** are extremely soft and comfortable, but may be too clingy and unstable for bodysuits. Use them for projects that benefit from the light weight and lovely fluid drape.

➤ **Rib knits** are used for bands at the neck, wrists, and waist of sweatshirts and jackets. They're often available in narrow pre-cut cuffs and bands as well as full-width yardage.

➤ **Scuba** and **spacer knits** are thick, spongy, springy knits often confused with neoprene, but are actually made from nylon or polyester. They have a futuristic look that works well for bodysuits or structured garments, but the amount of stretch varies, so choose carefully.

➤ **Slinky knits** are named for the way they drape and cling to the body. These extremely stretchy, fluid knits aren't usually stable enough for bodysuits or leggings, but are great for clingy, sexy gowns and skirts.

➤ **Sweater knits** are loosely knit from chunky yarns for a hand-knit look. They're a great solution if your costume calls for a sweater and you don't have the time or inclination to knit one, but they can be hard to source.

Fiber Content

Many of the properties of a fabric are determined by the type of fiber it's woven or knit from. They fall into two broad categories: natural fibers that are derived from plant or animal sources, and synthetic fibers, which are produced by physical or chemical means from base materials. While there are some traits that are broadly applicable within each category, there are also innumerable variations.

NATURAL FIBERS

Natural fibers are used in some of the oldest types of fabric, since the technology to produce them in one form or another has been available for hundreds or even thousands of years. That makes them a sure bet for historical costuming, and for historically inspired fantasy settings. They also age and fray beautifully, as a general rule, so they're a great choice for projects that need distressing (see page 95). They tend to be more breathable than synthetic fabrics, and they have a range of other properties derived from their plant or animal origins that determine what projects you may want to use them for.

❶ COTTON is a plant fiber, known for its strength, breathability, and versatility. It's one of the least expensive natural fibers, though you'll pay a bit more for very high-quality cottons. Lightweight cottons are very comfortable for summer wear, especially when sheer, and heavier weights are great for structured dresses, jackets, and uniforms because they're crisp and hold their shape well. Beware of low-cost cottons, especially if they're marketed for quilting, as they can look papery and cheap (which they are).

❷ LINEN is derived from the flax plant, and is available in very light "handkerchief" weights all the way up to heavy canvas. It's been used for thousands of years, so it's an ideal choice for many historical costumes. It's also one of the most comfortable fibers to wear in hot weather. Linen wrinkles easily, which is great if you're aiming for a weathered or rumpled look, but expect a lot of ironing if you want it crisp.

❸ WOOL fabric is made from the fleeces of sheep and other animals, and comes in various weights from sheer, floaty gauze to crisp, formal suitings to cuddly-soft coat

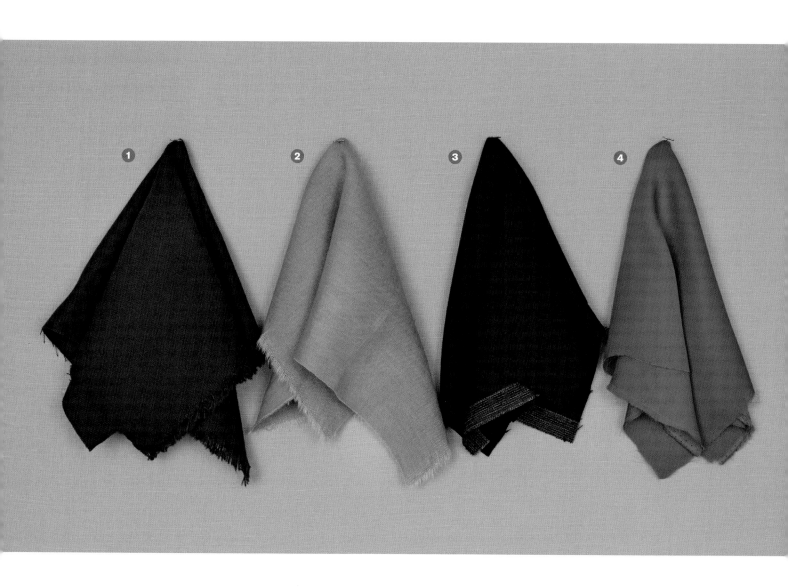

fabrics. It's also one of the easiest fabrics to work with. The downside is that it often needs to be dry cleaned, or at least hand washed, and it can be hot to wear.

④ **SILK** is synonymous with luxury, but it's also a very useful and versatile fiber that comes in a plethora of vivid colors. It's derived from silkworm cocoons, which are individually unspooled to create extremely long, thin, strong fibers. This gives silk a high sheen in fabrics like satin, and allows it to be woven into very thin, delicate-looking fabrics. It takes dye well, and is sometimes easier to work with than synthetic alternatives. Heavier-weight silks are generally very expensive, but make beautiful gowns and coats.

SYNTHETIC FIBERS

Synthetic fibers are often less expensive than natural fibers, and many of them resist wrinkling. They can form permanent creases, which is great for items like pleated skirts, but they may melt if your iron is too hot! They are also more prone to static cling. While synthetics have a reputation for poor breathability, microfibers and other high-tech fabrics designed for performance clothing can be excellent for hot weather. That said, there's evidence that some synthetic fibers absorb and retain body odors more readily than natural fabrics.

⑤ **RAYON**, or viscose, is a manufactured fiber, but since it's made from cellulose (the material that gives plants their

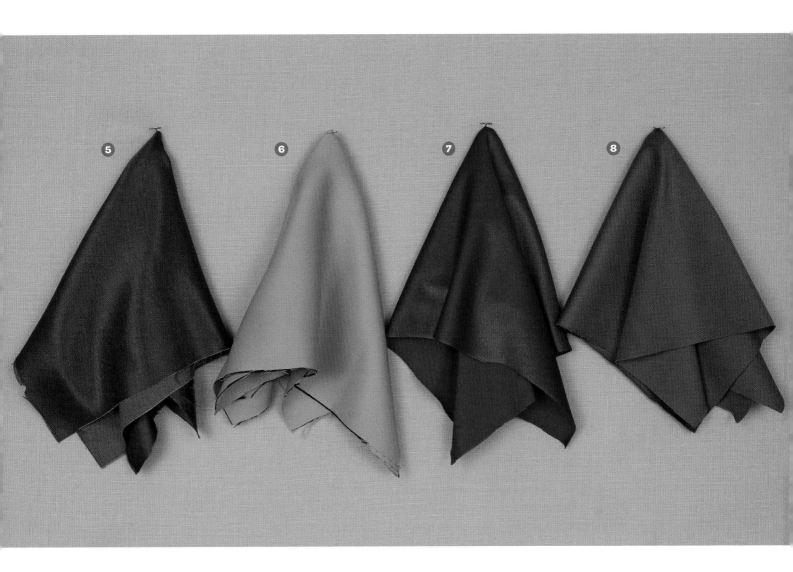

structure) it's absorbent and breathable in much the same way as plant fibers are. Rayon usually has a soft, fluid drape, and is often blended with other fibers. It is a popular choice for suitings, blouse and dress fabrics, and knits.

6 POLYESTER can simulate everything from cotton to wool to silk at much less cost. It's often blended with other fibers to make them more economical and easier to care for, as it's very durable and resists wrinkling. Negatives are static, pilling, low breathability, and a tendency to stain and retain smells. It's also difficult to dye and requires special dye formulations, so it's best to buy the exact color you need, rather than try to dye it yourself.

7 8 NYLON is a very strong synthetic fiber that is commonly blended with spandex (see below) to create stretch knits, or used in rigid woven form. Wool/nylon blends are usually cheaper than pure wool, and may be stronger and easier to care for. The downside is that you might see more pilling (little balls of fiber). **SPANDEX**, or elastane/ Lycra, is basically magic. Alone, it's capable of stretching up to seven times its original length and recovering more or less completely, but it's usually blended with other fibers to give them stretch, wrinkle resistance, and recovery. Above, you can see two examples of nylon/spandex blends: a lightweight shiny spandex and a heavyweight matte moleskin.

Materials and Supplies

In addition to fabric, there are other important materials and supplies you need to sew your costume. Each of the Patterns (see page 96) and Costumes (see page 154) in this book include a complete list of all the supplies required to make each garment. Here's a bit about these other essentials, many of which you'll also find where you shop for fabric.

STRUCTURAL MATERIALS

Often, the base fabric for a garment needs a little extra support or reinforcement to achieve the desired effect. Knowing how to effectively use interfacings, boning, and other structural materials in your costumes will improve the fit, help them to look crisp and neat all day, and make them more durable besides. Most commercial patterns include suggestions for interfacings and notions to achieve the look on the envelope, but use your best judgment for choosing what will give you the effect you want.

Interfacing

Interfacing is a fabric or fabric-like material that's inserted behind your outer fabric in areas where you need it to be firmer or have more body. It's used on collars and cuffs to make them crisp and smooth, on waistbands to prevent them from collapsing and wrinkling, and on neckline facings to prevent them from crumpling and stretching out. Interfacing is also used on areas where you'll be making buttonholes or inserting a zipper to prevent the fabric from rippling, and on areas that will be heavily embellished or embroidered to help support the weight and tension of the thread. Tailored coats and jackets may have multiple layers of interfacing and use different types in different areas.

Some interfacings are made from a non-woven bonded material, while others are made from woven or knitted fabrics. Woven interfacings have very little stretch, but give a little bit along the bias. Knit interfacings are good where you need the result to be more pliable. Weft-insertion interfacing is a great hybrid of knit and woven interfacings that is very substantial and is often used in tailoring. Non-woven interfacings

are very stable in all directions, with no grain, and the heavier craft weights can be useful for stiff, exaggerated, armor-like structures like you see in a lot of anime-style costumes.

Many interfacings are fusible, which means that they're coated on one side with a heat-sensitive glue that you activate with an iron. Fusibles are great because they bond permanently with the fabric, so you won't have to worry about keeping the layers lined up when you sew. If you make a lot of costumes, it's a good idea to keep a selection of your most-used interfacings on hand, so you'll always be ready if you decide a project needs some extra oomph.

Make sure you're buying good quality interfacing, though, as the cheap stuff can ruin your garments by shrinking, peeling away, and forming bubbles over time. Also, try fusing a sample of interfacing to a scrap of your fabric first, because the fused interfacing and fabric may be much firmer than you'd expect from either material alone, and wash it to see how it will wear over time. Always follow the package directions for fusing to ensure a good bond, and make sure you place the interfacing on the fabric with the coated side down so it doesn't stick to your iron. Use a protective press cloth between the interfacing and iron to help avoid getting gunk on your iron and workspace; I always trim the interfacing a little smaller than the piece I'm fusing it to so it doesn't spill over the edge. On the bolt, interfacing is generally narrow—about 20" (51 cm)—but fortunately it's easy to overlap and piece together to avoid buying more than you really need.

Sometimes you may want sew-in interfacing, especially if you're making a historical garment or using velvet or a sheer fabric. In these cases, you would baste the interfacing to the outer fabric, sewing within the seam allowances so the stitches don't show, and then treat the two layers as one for the rest of construction. You can either buy sew-in interfacing or use an extra layer of the outer fabric for this purpose. Or, in some situations, you may want to use a lightweight cotton or silk organza in a matching color.

Structural Materials: 1. Weft-insertion interfacing **2.** Knit interfacing **3.** Batting **4.** Spiral steel boning **5.** Spring steel boning **6.** Wire

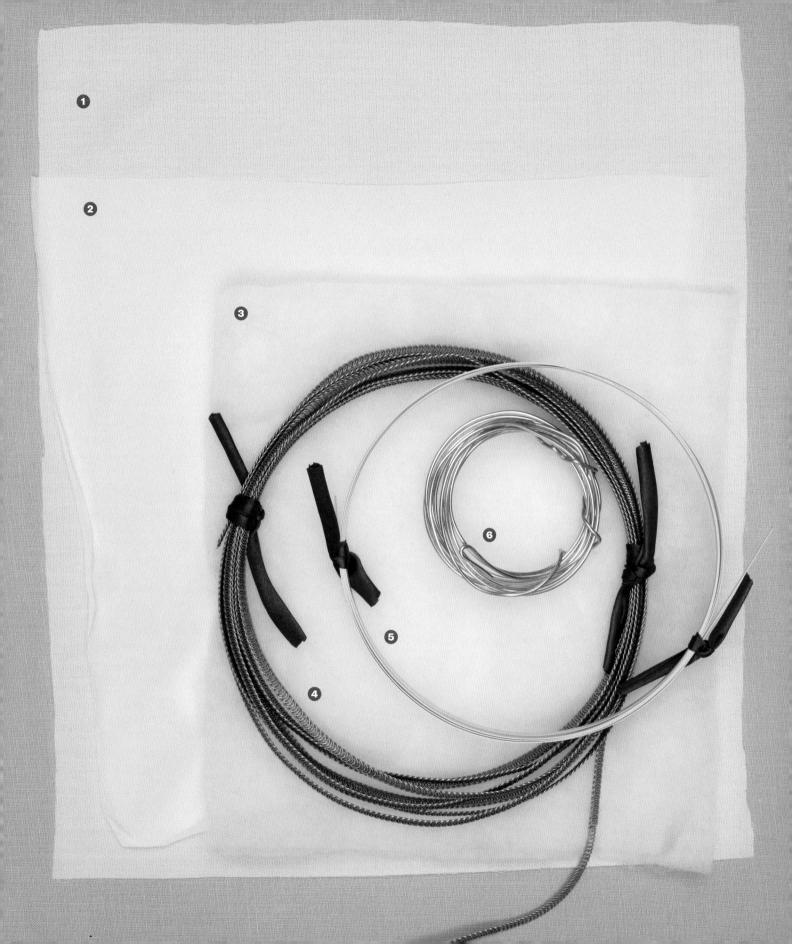

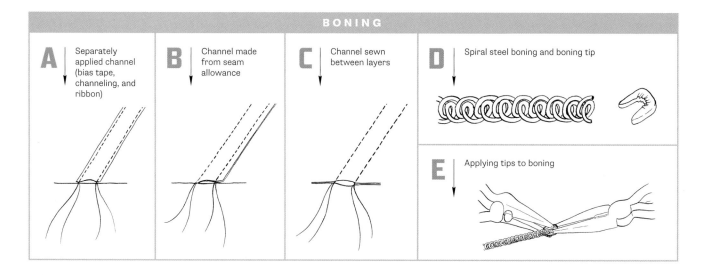

A | Separately applied channel (bias tape, channeling, and ribbon)

B | Channel made from seam allowance

C | Channel sewn between layers

D | Spiral steel boning and boning tip

E | Applying tips to boning

Boning

No, it's not made out of bones! The original "whalebone" used in corsets was actually the whale's baleen, but now boning is made of plastic, steel, or nylon. Boning is an essential component in fitted bodices, corsets, and other tight-fitting, structured clothing; most often, the strips of boning are inserted into casings or channels that are sewn into the garment (**A-C**). The main purpose is to prevent the fabric from wrinkling and collapsing, especially when the garment is strapless; the Dress (see page 143) has boning in the bodice. You can also use it to support large standing structures like collars or fins, and heavier-weight boning is used for hoopskirts and bustles.

The number and type of bones you need to use will depend on the project. On a dress bodice that you'll be wearing with separate undergarments, you might just want boning at the side seams to help it stay nice and smooth. If the bodice is strapless or needs to support you all by itself, you'll probably want more than that. On a corset, you may want bones every 2" (5 cm) or so to keep the fabric smooth and taut as it molds your body.

Rigilene, a woven tape containing wiry strands of plastic, is the most common and least expensive boning. It's convenient because you can sew through it, so you don't have to worry about casings and it won't twist or slide around in your garment. However, it's not very durable and can buckle and warp over time, making it a poor choice for corsets that

will be worn often or will be under a lot of strain. Plastic boning, often sold with a pre-made fabric casing, is a little sturdier and similarly inexpensive and easy to find, but still best for bodices and corsets that will be lightly stressed or worn infrequently. Plastic cable ties, sold in hardware stores, are an inexpensive and durable alternative.

For serious corsets that reduce your waist, most costumers insist on steel. Steel boning comes in two types, flat and spiral. Spiral boning flexes from side to side as well as front to back, and is great for curved seams. Flat (spring) steel flexes in only one direction, and is used where rigidity is needed—especially on lace-up panels where you really don't want any sideways flex. Steel boning is available in pre-made lengths or in larger rolls (but note that you'll need special tools, like wire cutters, to cut it). Steel-boned garments require careful cleaning to avoid damage and rust.

If boning is cut or trimmed to size, it's important to finish (or "tip") the ends so they don't tear through the garment and potentially injure the wearer. Plastic boning and Rigilene can be rounded with scissors or melted smooth with a candle or lighter, and the ends wrapped in a scrap of fabric or interfacing for extra insurance. Steel bones of either type should be filed smooth; spiral steel boning should be tipped with little metal caps that are applied with pliers (**D**, **E**), while flat steel boning should be wrapped in plumber's tape or dipped in a special liquid plastic coating.

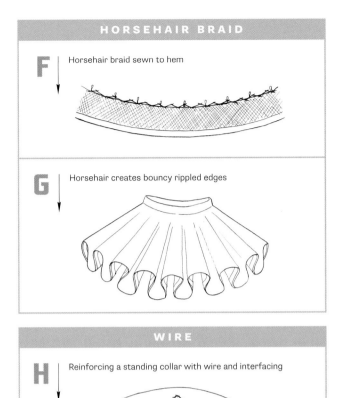

HORSEHAIR BRAID

F | Horsehair braid sewn to hem

G | Horsehair creates bouncy rippled edges

WIRE

H | Reinforcing a standing collar with wire and interfacing

Additional Structural Materials

Costumes often involve exaggerated shapes that you don't see in ordinary clothing. To achieve these effects with fabric, you may need to get a little more creative with your structural materials. Although not all of these materials were used in the book, they are important to keep in mind as your costume-making skills advance.

➤ **If you want to create a thick, pillowy effect,** fiberfill and batting are the materials you need. Fiberfill, or stuffing, is the loose, fluffy fiber used to stuff soft toys. To use it, you'll sew the area to be stuffed first, leaving a small opening to insert the fill, and then close it up afterward with a hand stitch (see page 50). Batting comes in a flat sheet that may be less than ¼" (6 mm) thick or well over 1" (2.5 cm) thick, but is usually thin enough to sew through. Use it for quilted effects, or build it up in layers to create soft structured shapes.

➤ **If you want to create soft armor, dramatic collars and headpieces, masks, and props,** Fosshape and heat-moldable craft stabilizers are the textile answers to thermoplastics like Worbla (used in armored costumes and props). These materials look like a thick interfacing or batting and can be sewn through, but become sculptable when heated with an iron, steamer, or hot air (heat) gun. Some are coated with fusible adhesive on one or both sides so it's easier to cover them in fabric.

➤ **If you want to make full skirts and ruffles with wide springy ripples,** use horsehair braid. Wider braid will give a more pronounced effect, but will also be more visible. To apply, simply trim your hem allowance down to ½" (1.3 cm), then align the braid with the cut edge on the outside of the fabric. Sew ¼" (6 mm) from the cut edge, then roll the braid to the inside so the fabric wraps around the edge of the braid. Use the gathering thread included on the top edge of the braid to pull it into a gentle curve, matching the curve of the hem, then secure by hand or machine (**F, G**).

➤ **If you want to create a lot of volume, like in petticoats and inside puffed sleeves,** use net, organza, or crinoline. Typically, you'll do this by gathering multiple layers of material to create a stiff, poufy ruffle that helps to support the fabric on top (see gathering instructions on page 58). Some nets can be scratchy to wear, so bind the edges or add a lining to your garment (see page 69) to keep them away from your skin.

➤ **If you want to support large standing collars, wings, and other features,** use wire, especially when combined with buckram (a stiff cloth product) or heavy craft interfacing. To add wire for structure, first cut your shape out of one or more layers of buckram or interfacing. Arrange the wire on top or between the layers, then zigzag stitch over the wire to secure it, being careful not to hit it with the needle. Finally, insert the whole piece between the layers of fabric that make up your special feature. The result is a solid-but-invisible internal structure that can be easily molded into your desired shape (**H**).

FASTENERS AND CLOSURES

Closures can be totally functional, mostly decorative, or somewhere in between. Since not all artists have the best grasp of how clothing works, you might have to get a little creative when deciding how you want to get into your costume. Hidden zippers, hooks, and snaps are good fallbacks, if there are no visible closures or if the given closure methods are unnecessarily cumbersome (unless wrestling with laces on the back of a bodice or fiddling with a hundred buttons helps you to get into character). Otherwise, you may want to think about which fasteners would be appropriate for your character and setting, especially for historical-type costumes where a prominent zipper might spoil the effect. Laces, ties, buttons, and hooks-and-eyes are better choices if you're looking for a period effect, though of course all bets are off when you get into steampunk. Here is an overview of fasteners and closures; you'll learn how to install them in Chapter 3 (see page 60).

1 **BUTTONS** are functional, easy to add, and fun to shop for. Additionally, they are historically accurate for many period costumes. They can also be purely decorative, and you can fasten them in a variety of ways. Learn to make buttonholes and loop closures for buttons on page 63.

2 **ZIPPERS** are secure, versatile, and quick to sew. It pays to use them thoughtfully, as the type of zipper you choose and the insertion method can affect the overall feel of your garment. An invisible zipper is the most neutral option, since it more or less disappears into the seam. Centered and lapped zippers are also fairly unobtrusive, but they need to be topstitched for security, so they give your project a slightly more structured look. Exposed zipper methods make the zipper into a decorative feature, so you can show off glittery metallic teeth or use one of those giant chunky plastic styles you see on JRPG (Japanese role-playing game) characters. (Giant zippers can be ordered online if you can't find them locally.) Standard zippers can be made of metal or plastic. Smaller sizes fasten with a continuous nylon coil, while some heavier zippers have individual plastic teeth. Invisible zippers are made so that they curl inward when fastened, pulling the fabric together and concealing the join (see the top zipper at

right for an example). A separating zipper is the familiar type often used on jackets and coats.

3 **GROMMETS AND EYELETS** are often used in the lace-up features common on historical costumes, for attaching leathery armor, and of course on corsets. In most situations, a sewn or metal eyelet is enough to prevent the fabric from tearing at the lacing point if the lacing just needs to support the weight of a garment and hold up to ordinary wear and tear. Corsetry is a special case, because the lacing actually needs to pull the body in and is under a whole lot more strain as a result. For a corset designed to reduce your waist, you should always plan to use two-part grommets and place boning (optimally spring steel boning) on either side of the grommets to prevent the lacing panel from buckling.

4 **SNAPS** might not always be the most authentic choice, but they make a great all-purpose costume fastener. They're excellent when a piece needs to be easily removable for convenience or performance purposes, they're easy to conceal, and they work on heavy layers that are too thick for buttonholes. Sew-on snaps are the easiest to find in fabric stores, and are available in a range of sizes from very small (3⁄16" / 4.8 mm) up to over 1" (2.5 cm) across. Other types of snaps have two parts to each side, the actual snap portion and a claw or rivet that passes through your fabric to grip it. These come with a variety of decorative faces for the claw side, and have a nice professional look but need to be applied with a special tool. Magnetic snaps, often sold for bag making, are an interesting variation that are great for quick-release pieces. These are usually a clamp-in style with a special washer for the back to prevent the snap from pulling out, but they may or may not require special tools for insertion.

5 **HOOKS AND EYES** are among the oldest fastening methods, useful for an unobtrusive closure on everything from historical gowns to modern jackets. They're also available in a whole range of sizes—use a tiny one at the top of a zipper to keep it from coming undone, or a big chunky one to close a heavy coat or cape. Trouser hooks like the ones shown here, are made from a flat piece of metal instead of bent wire, and are good where you need a very sturdy hidden fastener.

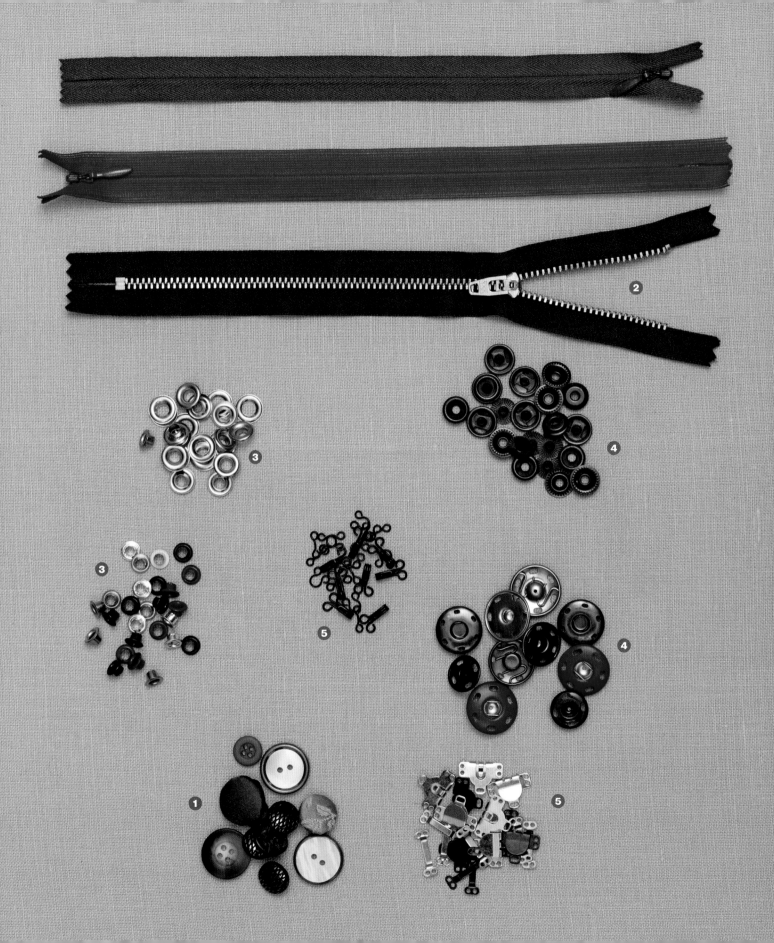

Specialty Fasteners

There are some additional fasteners that may be appropriate for your costume. A busk is a heavy-duty metal fastener used in corsetry. Each half of the fastener is assembled on a rigid metal base, available in 1" (2.5 cm) length increments to match the opening of your corset. Insert so that the posts are on your left when worn, loops on the right. Swing hooks are heavy metal clasps used as an alternative closure for corsets.

A frog is made from looped cord, with a decorative knot on one side and a loop on the other. These are common on jackets and cloaks. You can buy these pre-made or make them yourself from cord. A toggle is similar to a frog, but it's anchored with a large oblong bead instead of a knot; they're mostly used on heavy coats. Finally, a rivet is a permanent fastener that's also sometimes used for reinforcement. You've probably seen them on your jeans, and they're great for straps and leatherwork.

STICKY STUFF

Adhesives definitely have their place in sewing, but it's almost always in a supporting role—for example, to hold an appliqué in place while stitching (see page 89). Fabric glues can be very tempting in the craft store, promising easy no-sew solutions for a variety of situations. Unfortunately, they're almost certain to disappoint if you try to use them to replace needle and thread. Fabric is too porous and too flexible to take glue well, so the amount of glue necessary for a good hold will stiffen the fabric to an unappealing cardboard texture.

Fabric glues are available in liquid, glue stick, and aerosol forms. If you intend to sew through the glue for a permanent bond, make sure you pick one that won't goo up your needle. Some fabric glues are permanent, while others are designed to dissolve when your project is washed.

Fusible web is the same stuff that coats fusible interfacing, minus the fabric backing, and is available in sheets or tapes of various widths. Cut as much as you need, iron over the paper backing to transfer the fusible to one fabric surface, then remove the paper and iron again to stick it in place. You may even find fusible thread, which can be used in your machine's bobbin to sew out a precise line of sticky stuff on the underside of your fabric.

Wash-away tape or basting tape is a double-sided tape used when you want a temporary hold and a little extra stability, but don't want to permanently stiffen your fabric. It's great for securing hems while you stitch, and also handy for temporarily tacking appliqués and trims (see Chapter 5, Trims and Embellishments, page 87).

MISCELLANEOUS MATERIALS AND SUPPLIES

Depending on your costume, you may need some assorted supplies you can also find at the fabric store or online. For example, single- or double-fold bias tape, seam binding, and hem tape are often used to finish raw edges; twill tape helps stabilize areas of a garment; and fray stopper, a liquid seam sealant, is helpful to prevent edges from fraying. Elastic is used in many costumes; it's available in a variety of widths to suit almost any purpose. There are many supplies and gadgets that might appeal to you if you browse through the store while you're shopping.

Shopping for Fabric and Materials

Finally, time to shop! Each of the patterns and costumes in the book specify all the materials you need, including thread, elastic, and so on, so take your entire materials list with you when you go to the fabric store.

When choosing fabrics, your eyes and fingers are your best guide. Get used to groping the fabrics; the feel of the material in your hand is a good indicator of how it will feel on your body. Scrunch it up and see if it wrinkles; hold it up and try to see your hand through it to gauge opacity. Unwind a bit from the bolt or roll, and compare the drape to your reference materials. (Remember, some garments need a soft, fluid drape, while others call for crisp fabrics that will hold a crease.) If you need stretch fabric, check both the stretch percentage and the recovery. Consider the weight and how warm it will be to wear. Be cautious when choosing fabrics that are glossy or shiny; they tend to look much more so in photos, and construction imperfections tend to be magnified

Additional Costume Considerations

In addition to aesthetic concerns, your material choices have some practical implications for your costume. Before making your purchases, consider:

VENUE AND TEMPERATURE. Consider the setting and choose fabrics that will breathe in hot weather or keep you warm in air-conditioned convention centers.

MOBILITY. Even if your costume doesn't technically require stretch, you may want some for freedom of movement in tight-fitting bodices, jackets, or pants.

ENTRY/EXIT. Don't be that person who takes years in the restroom. Choose closures that will let you get into and out of your costume as needed.

WASHABILITY. Convention days are long, and you'll probably want to clean your costume after wearing it a few times. Plan for this.

as well. Make sure that the weft is exactly perpendicular to the warp for woven fabrics (see page 26 for a refresher on fabric weave), and if your fabric has a printed design, you should make sure it's correctly aligned with the grain (which you can find by folding the fabric along the cross grain so the selvages align on each side). If the grain is skewed or the print is crooked, this is usually a sign of poor quality, and it can cause problems in cutting out your pattern. Finally, check the end of the bolt for vital information like the fiber content and care instructions, and write these down or snap a photo of the label for future reference.

Once you've selected your fabric, take it to the cutting table. Buy the amount of fabric specified in the book's pattern instructions (or on the envelope of a commercial pattern). Note that most stores won't take fabric back once it's cut, so consider the cutting table your point of no return. Before you leave the fabric store, it's a good idea to pick up items like zippers, threads, trims, and embellishments in corresponding colors to your fabric so you can work without interruptions once you get home. If you can't find an exact match, pick something a shade darker than your fabric.

ONLINE SHOPPING

If you don't have a brick-and-mortar fabric store near you or can't find a good selection of what you need there, online shopping is unbeatable. Online retailers are great for several reasons: they offer more rare specialty fabrics, have expanded color options, and often feature good deals on fancy designer remnants. A store with a good search function can save you time, since you'll be able to filter down the options and see if they have what you need. The downside is that you can't feel the fabrics, so it pays to have a good understanding of the different fabric types and qualities before you make shopping online a regular habit.

Good online fabric stores will provide clear photos of the fabrics, including a ruler or other object to help indicate the scale of the print or pattern. Multiple photos are even better, especially if they show the fabric scrunched or draped so you can see how it hangs. Also look for a description that indicates the fabric weight, the hand, and amount of stretch. (See the box on page 26 to review important fabric qualities.) Some stores will suggest garment types that a fabric would be appropriate for, or even specific patterns that would work well. While your project may not be on the list, you might see something similar. For instance, if the fabric is described as being suitable for a winter coat, you might reconsider using it for your summer convention outfit.

But even the best descriptions can't take the place of holding the fabric in your hand, especially if the shop's idea of a "lightweight" or "crisp" fabric doesn't match up with yours. To get around this, many online stores allow you to order swatches. Sometimes there's a small charge associated with this, and you have to wait for shipping, but it's a lifesaver if you need a specific fabric quality or if you're concerned about getting a good color match.

You also have the option to get fabric custom printed. There are several different companies, including Spoonflower and Fabric on Demand, that will accept image files and print them on the fabric of your choice. Check the companies' websites for fabric options, pricing, and image guidelines, and order samples first, if possible, to avoid disappointment.

FABRIC PREPARATION AND CARE

When you get your materials home, you'll probably want to whack into the project right away. But resist that impulse (sorry!). First you need to prepare the fabric, so that your project will be easier to care for in the long run. If you don't pre-wash the fabric, your finished costume might shrink the first time you wash it, resulting in too-tight, too-short, or distorted garments. If you will have a mix of light and dark colors in a washable garment, you want to get rid of excess dye so the colors don't bleed the first time it's laundered. It's also helpful to remove sizing and stiffeners that may have been added during manufacturing, as they can affect how the fabric handles and drapes, and may irritate sensitive skin. Finally, it's nice to get rid of any dust and other gunk the fabric might have picked up during storage and transport.

Different fabrics call for different kinds of pre-treatment, depending on the fiber content and sometimes on the weave or structure. As a general rule, you want to pre-treat the fabric in the same way you intend to launder it in the future, so that there won't be any surprises once the project is finished. (This advice holds for sewing regular garments as well.) See the sidebar opposite for specific recommendations for different types of fabric.

Always check the care instructions for your specific fabric before pre-treating, as certain dyes, finishes, and effects might require special handling. If the appropriate care for a fabric is in question, try a swatch before you throw your entire piece in the washer. You'll be able to compare the washed sample to the original fabric and decide whether the results are acceptable. If pre-washing three or more yards (m) of fabric, you may find it helpful to fold the length in half and machine baste the ends together to help prevent twisting and tangling. Iron thoroughly after washing to remove wrinkles.

Preparing Fabric for Sewing

Here are some suggestions about pre-treating specific fabrics before sewing.

COTTON AND RAYON are usually washable, and prone to shrinkage, so your first step after getting them home should be to throw them in the washer and dryer unless the care instructions indicate differently. Cotton fibers are actually stronger when wet, but rayon weakens, so handle soggy rayon fabric with care and lay it flat to dry if you want to be extra careful.

WOOL is a little bit trickier, because you want to avoid future shrinkage, but soap and agitation can cause it to felt. Pre-treat it by steaming it thoroughly with an iron, soaking it in cool-to-lukewarm water and air drying, or sending it to a dry cleaner to be steamed. Never use bleach on wool, as it deteriorates the fibers.

LINEN also shrinks somewhat, but it can be pre-treated in a couple of ways depending on how you plan to use it. For a crisp, refined look, you may want to dry-clean it to preserve the finish. For a more lived-in effect, wash it in hot water and dry it on high a couple of times to soften the fibers.

SILK might be hand washable, but check the care instructions and wash a test swatch first, because some types (including dupioni and taffeta) may lose their luster and crispness after getting wet. If the silk is washable, stick with cool water and a gentle soap or shampoo. If not, make sure to dry-clean only.

NYLON AND POLYESTER generally don't shrink, so you can pass on pre-washing them if you wish. Some fabrics, especially knits, may actually be easier to work with before washing, because the manufacturers may have treated them to make them more stable or reduce curling. If you do wash them, be careful not to get too hot with the washer or dryer or you might end up with permanent creases. If you don't wash the fabric before sewing, you might want to wash the finished garment before wearing it to remove any treatments that might irritate your skin.

SPANDEX is sensitive to heat, and the fibers can stiffen and deteriorate over time, so use a gentle cycle for your stretch fabrics and never put them in the dryer if you want them to last.

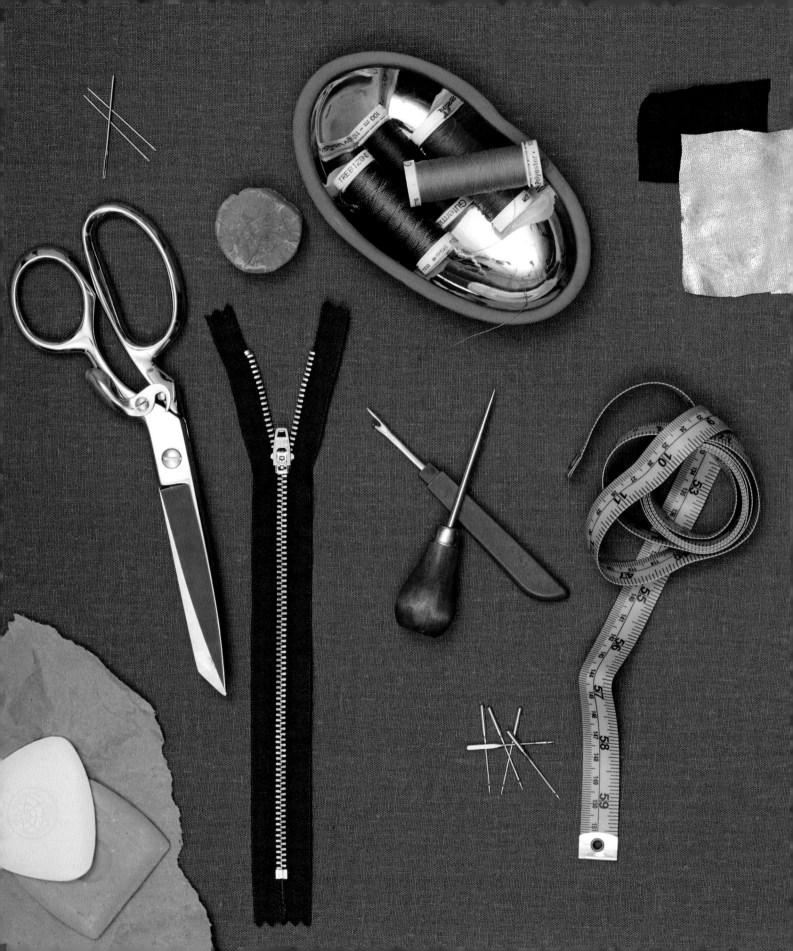

CHAPTER 3

COSTUME SEWING BASICS

Now that you've planned your project, broken it down into parts, and selected your materials, you're ready to start cutting out your pieces and sewing them together. You can do this by hand—after all, people did it that way for thousands of years—but for most people it's more convenient and more fun to get friendly with a sewing machine. For the dedicated, especially those who work with stretch fabrics on a regular basis, a serger (see page 52) may also be a valuable addition to your arsenal. You'll also need a few other tools and assorted supplies, which I'll detail in this chapter. ➡ The instructions for the costumes in this book give you detailed directions for completing a project. As your skills grow, you might make your own decisions about what order to use in assembling the pieces, how to sew and finish particular seams for the best results, and how to incorporate trims and embellishments (see page 87). Store-bought patterns may or may not offer suggestions on these topics, but with a little practice, you'll be able to judge for yourself what the best method for a particular fabric and situation might be.

One great way to learn about how garments go together is to take a few of your well-loved, but old, items apart. Dig up that worn, holey top and carefully snip the threads to see what the individual pieces look like. If you're careful to keep all the pieces intact, you can even iron them flat and then use them as a pattern for a new garment. When making a new or unfamiliar style of garment, try to find something similar in a thrift store that you can dissect for research purposes. Even master tailors sometimes take apart old jackets to study how other craftspeople did their work, and it's a great way to pick up new ideas and techniques.

Sewing Essentials

You'll need to gather up a few tools and supplies before you can get started making your own costumes; you should have these items on hand if you intend to make any of the garments in this book. You'll find these tools and supplies at local stores and online, too. See page 203 for a list of my favorite suppliers.

SEWING TOOLS

You may be able to find a basic sewing kit at the drugstore, but for your cosplay toolbox you'll want something a little more robust. Let's take a look at some of the supplies you should have on hand:

1 SCISSORS. Ideally you want at least two pairs, one for fabric and one for everything else. The fabric scissors should be the nicest, sharpest pair your budget allows, and if you don't let anyone use them to cut any other materials, they'll stay sharp for a long time. The other pair will be the ones you use for paper, cardboard, thermoplastics, foam, or other non-fabric materials, so they don't need to be anything special. If you have room for a third pair, consider a small pair for trimming and clipping or a set of pinking shears to help prevent your cut fabric edges from fraying.

2 NEEDLES. Grab variety packs of hand-sewing needles for versatility. Sewing machine needles are sold by size and style for different types of fabric. Be sure to buy extras, as it's best to replace them often.

3 PINS. Pins are available in assorted shapes and sizes, but fine, sharp silk pins are good for most garment sewing. Thick craft pins should be reserved for very heavy fabrics. Sometimes weights or clips may be used instead of pins (see pages 49 and 70).

4 THREAD. Get good-quality thread if you don't want to spend all your sewing time fighting with breakage and knots. Cotton-wrapped polyester or 100% polyester all-purpose thread is good for most basic sewing, and jeans or upholstery thread works for heavy fabrics and topstitching.

5 THREAD SNIPS. Use these instead of your big shears for trimming the thread tails at seam ends.

6 SEAM RIPPER. Ripping out work is, unfortunately, a part of sewing. Minimize the pain by dropping a few dollars on a good seam ripper, which has a sharp point for picking up stitches, a small, curved blade for fast ripping, and a ball on the other point to prevent damage to your fabric.

7 BEESWAX. Waxing your thread will help to prevent knots and tangles when hand sewing. After waxing your thread, fold it inside a press cloth and run an iron over it to melt the wax into the fibers.

8 MARKING TOOLS AND SUPPLIES. I like to keep a couple different colors of chalk on hand for marking different colors of fabric. Dressmaker's tracing paper and a tracing wheel are nice for marking seams, darts, and pleat lines, and a white gel pen is helpful for dark-colored fabrics and surfaces that don't take chalk well. Test any marking tool first to make sure the color can be fully removed from your fabric. Some chalks and inks get much harder to remove if they're heated, so try not to iron over any marks that could be visible.

9 RULER. Useful for marking seam allowances, measuring hems, laying out pattern pieces, and more.

10 MEASURING TAPE. For taking your measurements, making alterations, and checking proportions while you work.

11 ROTARY CUTTER. Makes quick work of cutting any long, straight edges. Also great for cutting out slippery sheers, stretch fabrics, and difficult-to-pin materials like leather. Use in conjunction with a cutting mat.

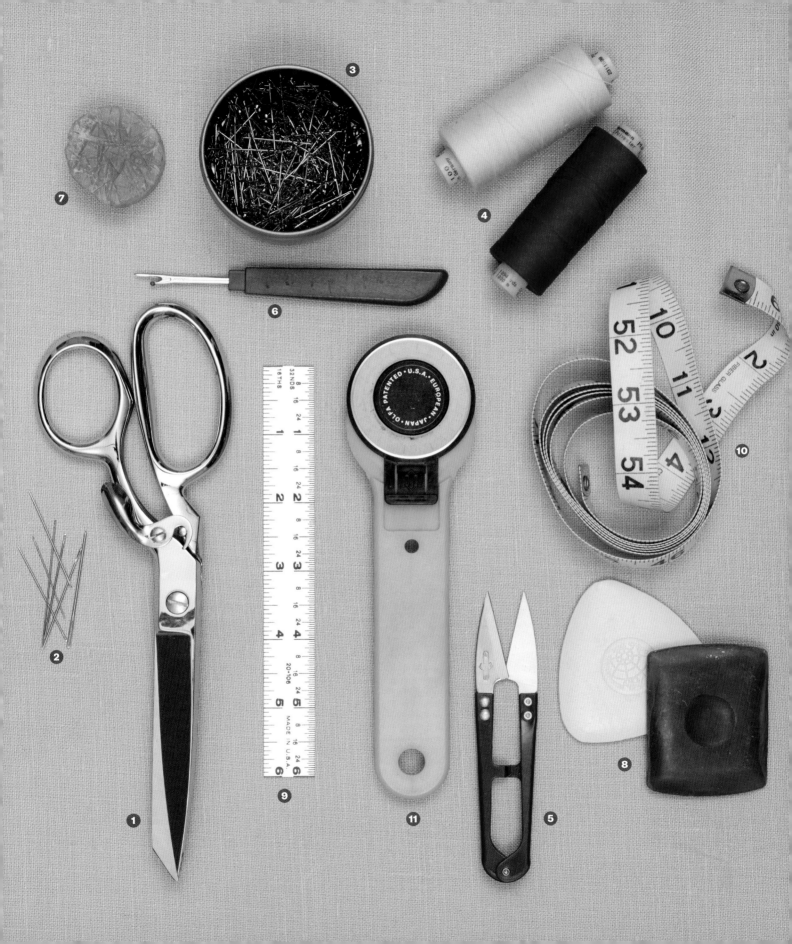

PRESSING TOOLS

Pressing is an essential part of sewing. A steam iron and ironing board will get you started, but a few extra tools will make pressing easier and the results more professional. See the sidebar below for tips.

1 PRESSING HAM. A rounded pillow stuffed with sawdust, used to support curved seams for more accurate pressing. A rolled-up towel works in a pinch.

2 SEAM ROLL. Slip a seam roll inside sleeves, pant legs, and tails to press seams without creating unintentional creases. A chunk of dowel will do the same thing.

3 CLAPPER. A pricey, smooth block of hardwood used to whack seams after pressing to get a sharper crease. Feel free to substitute a smooth block of generic hardwood.

4 POINT TURNER. A pointed wooden tool used to turn out and press sharp corners like collars.

PRESS CLOTH. A piece of lightweight muslin or silk organza used as a barrier while pressing. Keeps fusible goo off your iron, and protects delicate fabrics from excessive heat.

CARDBOARD. A thin piece of cardboard can be useful to slip under pleats, facings, and so forth so they don't leave indentations in the outer fabric when pressed.

Pressing

You may not think of your iron as a sewing tool, but you should start. The iron is used to remove creases, meld stitches into the fabric, create crisp and unobtrusive seams, flatten pleats, fuse interfacing, and shape the fabric. If your ironing board isn't already in your sewing room, appropriate it, because running back and forth will prevent you from getting anything done!

Pressing a seam is a little different from ironing a shirt. Use an up-and-down motion instead of gliding the iron from side to side, so that you don't stretch the fabric out of shape. It's a good idea to use a protective cloth between your work and the iron for certain fabrics, especially wool (which can develop a shine from overpressing) and synthetics (because they don't tolerate heat well). This can be a scrap of muslin or even an old white t-shirt; some people swear by silk organza because it protects your work but you can still see through it.

You should press every single seam you sew, once flat (exactly as you sewed it) and once with the seam spread open. If both layers of the seam need to be pressed to one side, do that as a third step. If sewing a French or flat-felled seam (see page 54), you may need to press after each sewing step for the best finish. Pleats, hems and edges, collars, and cuffs need to be pressed for a clean, sharp edge, and darts (see page 57) should be thoroughly pressed over a curved surface to prevent unfortunate bubbles of fabric at the tip.

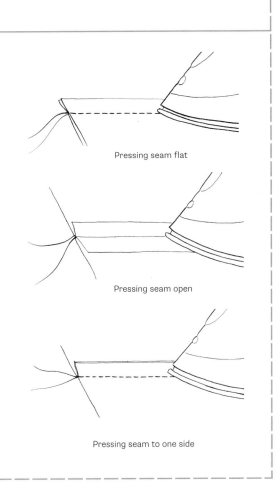

Pressing seam flat

Pressing seam open

Pressing seam to one side

Preparing to Sew

One of the things you'll discover about sewing is that even tiny changes can make a huge difference in the finished look and fit of your projects. It's important to be precise in your cutting and sewing—it's the key to success for a beginner. When you're still figuring out how clothes are put together, it's useful to start with a simple pattern with easy instructions for assembly. From there, you can learn to make the adjustments you need for fit and style, many of which are detailed in Chapter 4 (see page 73). The pattern is your guide

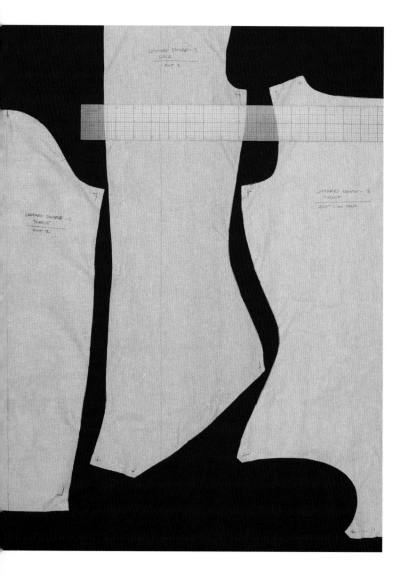

for cutting out the various pieces of your costume and sewing them together. Later, as you get used to the process and develop a sense for how the pieces look in 3D, you can dive into making your own patterns for a fully custom look.

LAYOUT AND CUTTING

When using the patterns in this book, you'll need to trace the pieces onto a new sheet of paper so you can cut them apart. Choose a paper you can see through to make this easy on yourself—tracing paper or tissue paper will work, or you can get rolls of thumbnail sketch paper from an art store. Alternatively, you can use carbon paper and a tracing wheel to transfer the outlines to paper laid underneath the pattern sheet. (Commercial patterns are printed on tissue paper and tightly folded to fit into the envelope. Refer to the instructions to figure out which pieces you need, and roughly cut around each one to separate them.)

The cutting layouts on pages 189-193 provide has diagrams indicating how the pieces should be laid out on the fabric, including how the fabric should be folded. If your fabric has a bold print or design that needs to be carefully placed, or if your fabric has flaws that you need to cut around, it's better to cut in a single unfolded layer so you can see everything.

Each pattern piece will have an arrow indicating the grain of the fabric, which determines how each piece should be oriented as you lay it out. Treat the grainline as law, because cutting off-grain can cause the finished item to twist (ever had a pair of jeans that liked to migrate around your legs?) or hang unevenly. Use a ruler to make sure that both ends of the arrow are exactly the same distance from the selvage before you pin the pieces to your fabric. If the piece is supposed to be cut on the fold, the pattern will assume the fold line is exactly along the grain as well.

Most patterns are multisized, with the outlines dotted in different patterns to show which line corresponds to each size. To avoid confusing them as you cut or trace, it may help to go over the line for your size with a highlighter. If you're different sizes in different areas, you can allow for this by drawing a gradual curve that connects the appropriate size

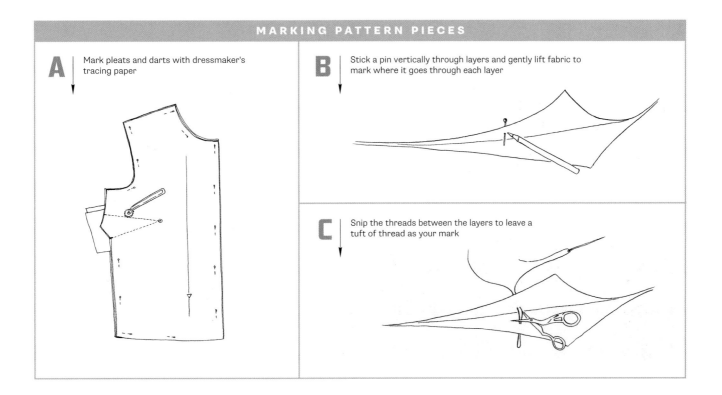

A Mark pleats and darts with dressmaker's tracing paper

B Stick a pin vertically through layers and gently lift fabric to mark where it goes through each layer

C Snip the threads between the layers to leave a tuft of thread as your mark

lines. If you're tall or petite, you may need to add or remove length from the pattern. We'll talk about this in more detail on page 74.

Pins are the traditional way to secure the pattern to the fabric, but many people prefer weights, as they distort the fabric less. This can be especially helpful for stretchy or slippery fabrics, or for materials like leather that show pin-holes. Use good, sharp scissors or a rotary cutter to cut out your pieces, and be as accurate as you possibly can, as even a fraction of an inch (cm) can make a huge difference in the fit when multiplied across several seams.

Notches are placed along the cutting lines to help match up seams, and these should be marked as you cut—snip inward for speed, or cut a triangle outward if you think you might need to make adjustments to the seam. Dots, triangles, and other symbols help to align the pieces and indicate placement for darts, pleats, pockets, and other features. These should be marked on all layers of fabric, which you can do with dressmaker's tracing paper (**A**) or by sticking a pin vertically through all the layers and gently lifting the fabric to mark where it goes through each layer (**B**). For fabrics that

that are difficult to mark, use simple tailor's tacks: thread a hand needle with unknotted, doubled contrasting thread, and take a loose stitch straight down and back up. Leave long thread tails, gently separate the layers, and snip the threads between the layers to leave a tuft of thread as your mark (**C**).

Once you're done cutting your pieces and transfer-ring the pattern markings to your fabric, you'll be ready to assemble your garment. Read through the instructions first and check the glossary on pages 195-197 if you need to revisit any terms or techniques.

A couple of final notes to commit to memory before the sewing actually begins: Follow the order of the instructions when you sew, and always press your seams open before sewing another seam that crosses or intersects them, because pressing after the fact is usually less effective (see the Pressing sidebar on page 47 for specifics). Finishing seams is also easier to do as you go, so that you don't have to work around complicated seam intersections. While seam finishes are technically optional, as they won't be visible from outside, they will make your costumes more durable. See page 54 for more information about finishing seams.

Sewing 101

Once you have your fabric pieces cut, it's time to put them together. A basic knowledge of hand stitches is important for finishing work and other assorted sewing tasks—and although it would be time-consuming, you could technically make your entire costume by hand—so let's begin there.

HAND SEWING

When sewing by hand, whether for construction or embellishment, you should begin by cutting the thread about as long as your arm. Longer threads won't save you any time, since they take more effort to pull through each stitch, and they're more prone to twisting and knotting.

To start a hand seam, you can knot the thread or simply take a couple small stitches in place. I prefer the latter, as it tends to be a bit flatter and less likely to break or work itself loose with wear. Here are some essential hand stitches:

RUNNING STITCH is useful for decorative effects, applying ribbons and trims, and seams that don't need to bear much strain, such as a collar or cuff. It is a simple up-and-down stitch through the fabric, with several stitches picked up at a time.

BASTING is like running stitch but with longer stitches. This stitch is not intended to be permanent, and it's used to attach pieces before you stitch them together to ensure more accurate seams, or to temporarily assemble a garment so it can be fitted. It may seem like a lot of trouble, but it's more accurate than pinning.

BACKSTITCH is a strong, secure seaming stitch. If you don't pull it too tight, the back-and-forth nature of the stitches makes it an effective option for stretch knits. To make a backstitch, bring the needle up through the fabric and back down a stitch back, then up again one stitch forward from the starting point. Insert the needle back at the end of the first stitch, and continue on in this way.

CATCH STITCH/HERRINGBONE STITCH is my go-to stitch for hems, tacking structural elements in place, and securing seam allowances. It can also be used decoratively. If you pick up just a few threads with each stitch, it should be nearly invisible from the other side of the fabric. Catch stitch is worked from left to right in a zigzag, with a small stitch in the upper row followed by a small stitch in the lower row, both in the opposite direction the stitch is traveling.

WHIPSTITCH is good for finishing seams to prevent fraying, and to seam pre-hemmed pieces or fabrics that don't ravel. Bring each stitch up through the fabric in the same direction, wrapping the thread diagonally around the fabric edge to return to the underside each time. Avoid pulling so tight that you dimple the edge.

PICKSTITCH is a decorative variation—the backwards stitch is shortened, so it looks like a small, widely spaced running stitch but retains all the strength of the backstitch.

SLIPSTITCH is handy for invisible hemming and other situations where you're securing a folded or clean-finished edge to a single layer of fabric. Take a tiny stitch (as small as two or three threads) in the single layer of fabric and then through the folded edge, working right to left.

STAB STITCH looks identical to running stitch but instead, you stick the needle straight into the fabric and pull it through before you make the next stitch. This stitch is better for thick or stiff fabrics.

FELL STITCH is used to invisibly secure bindings and linings. Bring the needle up through the very edge of the lining or binding, then into the bottom fabric just opposite. Run the needle a short distance under the lining or binding edge, then back up to form the next stitch.

BUTTONHOLE STITCH is used for buttonholes and eyelets, and also to secure hooks, eyes, and snaps. With the needle inserted from the wrong side of the fabric a short distance from the edge, grab the thread behind the needle and wrap it clockwise under the point. Pull through to form a small knot.

LADDER STITCH is used to invisibly join pieces and close openings in stuffed objects and linings. You'll need to turn the edges under or line the pieces first so the stitch has something to grab. Work this stitch back-and-forth through the layers, catching a small stitch in one layer at a time.

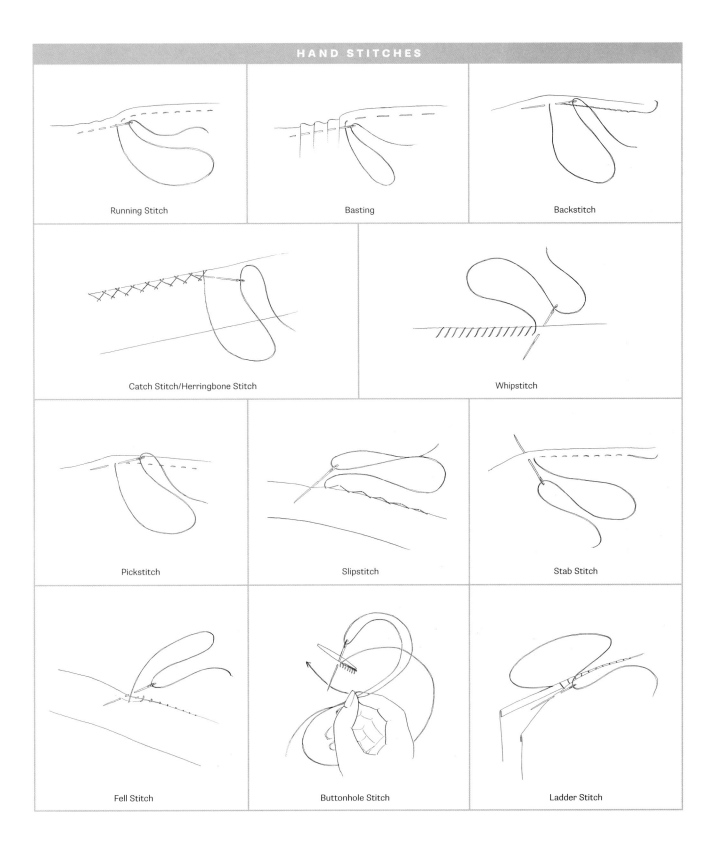

Running Stitch

Basting

Backstitch

Catch Stitch/Herringbone Stitch

Whipstitch

Pickstitch

Slipstitch

Stab Stitch

Fell Stitch

Buttonhole Stitch

Ladder Stitch

MACHINE SEWING

Although humans got by without sewing machines for thousands of years, clothing also used to be a lot more difficult and time-consuming to make. Hardcore historical re-enactors aside, pretty much anyone who has a serious interest in sewing will want to invest in a sewing machine (and possibly a serger, see below). A basic mechanical machine will serve the vast majority of costuming needs, and you can get a solid, reliable one quite inexpensively if you do some research. That said, you should probably walk on past the bottom-of-the-line budget models if possible, as they tend to be flimsy and frustrating to use. If you need to pinch pennies, a vintage machine is the way to go—most of them are much more robust than modern machines. Try to find one that still has its original feet and accessories. If the manual is missing, you can often find a PDF online by searching the model number.

Your machine will have a variety of adjustments to accommodate different situations and types of fabric. Start with a medium stitch length of 2.5 to 3 mm, and adjust to suit your fabric and project—longer stitches are suitable for thicker fabrics and basting; shorter stitches are best for fine fabrics, tight curves, and intricate seaming. Most likely, your machine will offer you a variety of stitches to do all sorts of interesting things, but you'll get the most use out of a zigzag stitch, especially if you plan on sewing with stretch fabrics. Read more about sewing with stretch fabrics on page 56.

Once you've spent some time sewing and have decided you want to stick with it, you may want to invest in a serger as well. Sergers are sewing machines that sew, trim, and finish a seam in a single pass, which can save a lot of time, and the seams have an inherent stretch that makes them particularly good for sewing knits. Most sergers have a differential feed feature that makes them very good at handling bias edges and difficult fabrics like chiffon, and they'll do a rolled edge that's the single fastest way to hem lightweight

or sheer fabrics. If you sew a lot of stretchy costumes, have limited sewing time, or see yourself taking on commissions at any point, a serger is probably worth the investment.

There are just a couple of things you need to know about handling a sewing machine before you begin. First, don't ever yank the fabric through the machine as you sew. Press the pedal gently, and the machine will feed the fabric through by itself. If you pull, you might bend the needle or cause other problems. To keep the seam straight, make sure you're watching the edge of the fabric instead of the needle as you sew—the needle will do its thing; your job is to keep the layers of fabric aligned correctly. Second, it's best to avoid sewing over pins. Pause and remove them before they're carried under the presser foot, so they don't snag on the machine or cause the needle to break.

Sewing a Seam

A standard straight seam joins two pieces of fabric with the right sides facing each other, so that the seam allowances will be hidden on the wrong side when complete. To sew a seam, align your fabric pieces so that the seam allowances match and the cut ends are even. Pin at each end and at intervals along the length to keep the layers aligned. (Or baste, if you prefer.) Drop the presser foot and lower the needle into the fabric before you hit the pedal, then hold the thread tails as you begin. Take a few backstitches at the beginning and end of each seam to prevent it from coming undone. (Refer to your machine's manual to learn how to engage backward stitching and to adjust any other functions referenced in this chapter.) Use both hands to control and guide the fabric.

Most standard patterns include a seam allowance of ⅝" (1.5 cm), which means the stitching line is ⅝" (1.5 cm) from the cut edge of the fabric. In this book, some seam allowances are ⅜" (1 cm) instead; this is done on small pieces like collars that require particularly accurate sewing, and on stretch knits because the fabrics will not fray and the narrower allowance is easier to sew on a serger. Any narrower-than-usual seam allowances will be indicated in the pattern and instructions. Most machines have guidelines marked in ⅛" (3 mm) intervals, so all you have to do is follow the correct line as you sew. Give each seam a good press

Machine Stitches: 1. Four-thread serged edge **2.** Straight stitch **3.** Zigzag stitch **4.** Three-step zigzag stitch **5.** Triple stitch **6.** Blind hem stitch **7.** Short length/wide width zigzag (good for attaching elastic) **8.** Short length/narrow width zigzag (good for delicate topstitching on stretch fabrics) **9.** Long length/narrow width zigzag (good for seaming stretch knits) **10.** Very short length/medium width zigzag (good for stretch appliqué)

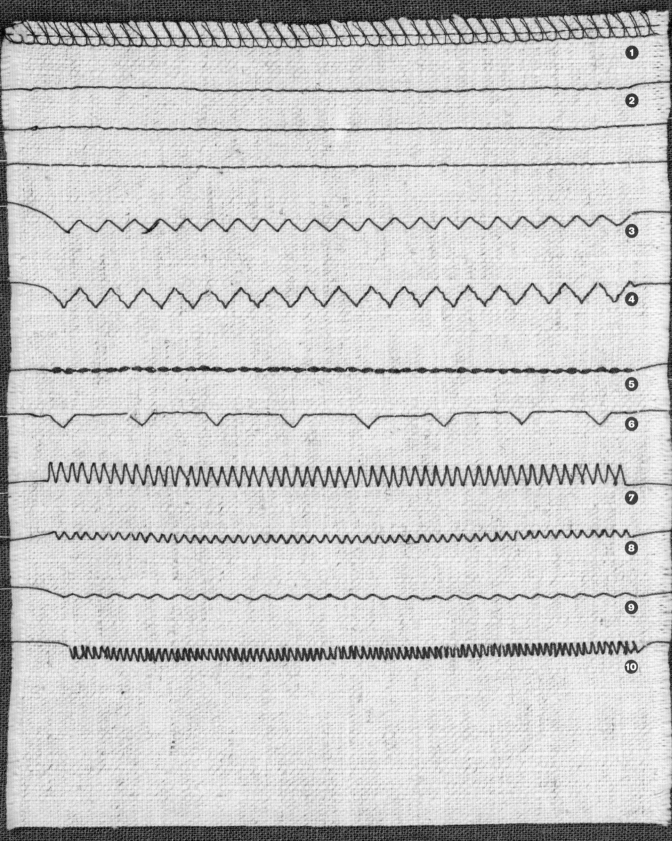

when you're done (see page 47). Occasionally, you may be directed to sew a line of staystitching before a seam is sewn. Staystitching helps prevent stretching, and it's often used in curved areas that need to be clipped before being sewn (see page 58). To staystitch, stitch in the seam allowance ⅛" (3 mm) outside the seam line.

Finishing a Seam

If you're using a fabric that frays at all, which could include many woven fabrics, you'll need to finish the seam allowances to prevent them from raveling. This is important for the durability of your garments, and will also make your projects look more professional. For most woven fabrics, it's a good idea to finish any seam that won't be covered by a lining. The simplest seam finish, common on vintage clothing, is to trim the seams with pinking shears. The zigzagging edge will resist fraying, and no bulk is added to the seam. Whipstitching the edges by hand is another very lightweight option, but time-consuming (see page 50). For medium-weight and heavier fabrics, a zigzag stitch right on the edge of the fabric is a good solution. If you have a serger, go with that (see page 57).

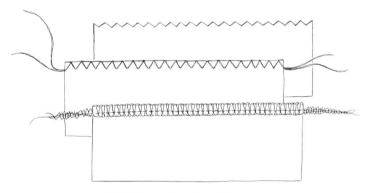

Pinked, zigzagged, and serged edges

SELF-FINISHED SEAMS

Some types of seams have finished edges when they are completed. A couple are described here, with each instruction based on taking up a standard ⅝" (1.5 cm) seam:

> **French seams** are great for lightweight fabrics, especially sheers, since they make a pretty, low-profile seam.

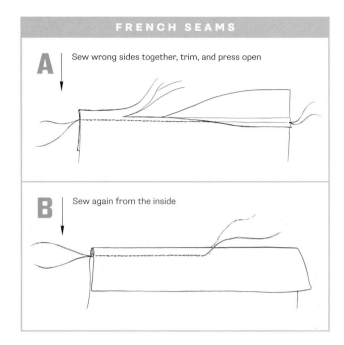

FRENCH SEAMS

A Sew wrong sides together, trim, and press open

B Sew again from the inside

Sew the fabric with wrong sides together using a ⅜" (1 cm) seam allowance, trim the seam to ⅛" (3 mm), and press it open (**A**). Then turn the garment inside out, press the finished seam closed, and stitch again with a ¼" 6 mm) seam allowance to seal the raw edges inside (**B**).

> **Flat-felled seams** look finished inside and out, and are good for tough, sporty pieces and crisp or heavy fabrics. You often find them on jeans, men's shirts, and casual jackets. To make a flat-felled seam that is centered over the original seam line, offset the cut edges ¼" (3 mm) (**C**) and stitch ¾" (1.9 cm) from the longer edge. Trim the longer edge to ⅝" (1.5 cm) and the shorter edge to less than ¼" (6 mm). Fold the longer edge down, then over to enclose both raw edges, and edgestitch (**D**).

GRADING A SEAM

An enclosed seam, like you might find on a collar or waistband, doesn't need to be finished per se. Instead, think about reducing bulk so you don't have a lot of extra fabric crammed in where it's not needed. Grading the seam—that is, trimming each layer to a different width so they don't all end at the same place and create a lump—is one way to do this; hold the scissors at an angle as you trim (**E**) or simply trim each piece

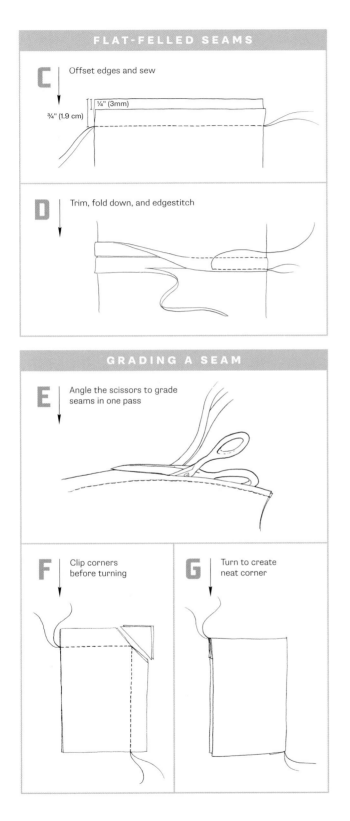

C Offset edges and sew

¼" (3mm)

¾" (1.9 cm)

D Trim, fold down, and edgestitch

GRADING A SEAM

E Angle the scissors to grade seams in one pass

F Clip corners before turning

G Turn to create neat corner

Topstitching and Edgestitching

TOPSTITCHING is the term for any line of stitching that's done from the right side of the fabric, and is intended to be visible in the finished garment. Although often decorative, topstitching also has a number of practical functions: to flatten seam allowances in bulky fabrics; to prevent linings and facings from rolling to the outside; and to add structure and rigidity to the garment. You can make your topstitching more prominent by using heavyweight or decorative threads, by using a double thickness of all-purpose thread, or by using a triple stitch, which sews back and forth over each stitch. You can also topstitch by hand using heavyweight thread, usually with a backstitch, pickstitch, or stab stitch (see page 50).

EDGESTITCHING is a variation of topstitching that is worked very close to an edge, usually ¹⁄₁₆" to ⅛" (1.5 to 3 mm) away. If you have trouble keeping your edgestitching straight, try using a special edgestitching foot for your machine that has a built-in guide.

to a different length. Trimming the edges with pinking shears to soften the line is another approach. You may also need to clip corners to make them turn out neatly (**F**, **G**).

CLIPPING AND NOTCHING A SEAM

Not all seams are straight. When you're sewing curved pieces, you'll need to treat the seams a little bit differently so they lie flat. Outward curves need to be notched by cutting out a little triangle of fabric, while inward curves need to be clipped. See page 58 for an illustration and instructions on stitching curved pieces.

Unsewing

A seam ripper is designed so that you can insert the ball end in a seam and "zip" the ripper along the stitches to remove them in one fell swoop. This is also a good way to cut gashes in your fabric if you're not careful, so I'd reserve the technique for tough, stable fabrics like cotton twill. The more cautious method is to use the point of the seam ripper to cut a stitch every ½" (1.3 cm) or so along the seam, which should allow the opposite thread to pull out in one piece (**A**).

To undo serger stitches (**B**), first cut the tails off both ends. Zip the seam ripper along the looper threads at the edge, angling the blade so you cut the loopers on just one side. This should loosen the needle threads enough that you can pull them out in one piece, and the remaining looper should pull out easily as well. Clean up stray thread fragments with a rubber eraser or piece of tape.

Stretchy Seams

Yes, you can sew spandex, or otherwise stretchy, nontraditional fabrics even on a standard sewing machine! If you're going this route, it's important to build stretch into your seams so the threads don't break. Use polyester all-purpose thread, as it has more give than cotton, and stretch needles to eliminate skipped stitches. Here are some of the most useful stitch options for sewing stretch fabrics:

> **Straight stitch.** Using a stitch length of 1.5 to 2 mm, loosen your needle tension slightly, and stretch the fabric gently as you sew by placing one hand in front of the presser foot and one behind. Be careful to apply even tension on both sides, and avoid yanking the fabric through the machine. The seam may look a little wavy when you're done, but you should be able to steam it back into shape. If not, lengthen your stitches a bit more or try a different stitch. This technique is best for fabrics with slight or moderate stretch.

> **Narrow zigzag stitch.** Use a zigzag stitch with a short stitch length and a narrow (1 to 2 mm) stitch width. Wider zigzags will have more stretch, but the seam won't look as smooth from the outside.

> **Triple straight stitch.** Some machines have a stitch that sews back and forth multiple times along the same

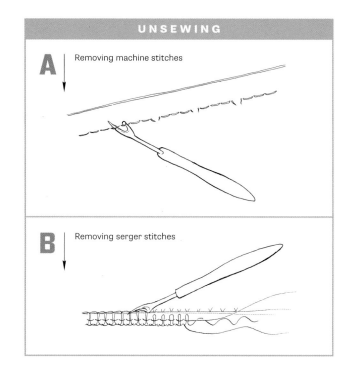

A Removing machine stitches

B Removing serger stitches

line, creating a very strong, stretchy seam that's great for high-stress areas and decorative topstitching. However, this stitch is very slow, it uses a lot of thread, and is difficult to remove if you make a mistake.

> **Lightning stitch.** The machine stitches back and forth in tiny jags for a fabulously stretchy seam that looks nice and neat from the outside. This stitch isn't available on all machines, but if you're choosing a machine for cosplay, you might want to look for one with this option.

> **Double-needle stitch.** This can be done on most standard machines, but you'll need to buy a special needle that has two shafts on one base. These are available in various sizes and point types with narrow and wide options for different looks. Thread the machine with two threads at once, put one through each needle, and sew a straight stitch. (Don't use zigzag, as the double needle can miss the opening in the needle plate and break.) You may need to loosen the tension slightly, or use stretch thread in the bobbin to prevent the stitches from "tunneling." The result looks like two parallel rows of straight stitching on top, with a connecting zigzag underneath, that is perfect for hemming and topstitching.

USING A SERGER

All that said, the serger is by far the most common way to sew stretch fabrics in ready-to-wear clothing, and with good reason. Serger seams have intrinsic stretch, and they work beautifully with stretchy woolly nylon thread if you want the extra insurance. If you have a serger, stick with a four-thread overlock stitch for most seaming, and for hemming you can use a blindstitch (your serger may even have a blindstitch foot), a zigzag or double-needle stitch from the standard sewing machine, or a coverstitch (available on high-end convertible sergers or as a separate machine). Consult your serger's manual for more information about its capabilities.

If you don't want to buy three or four spools of each thread color, pick a thread that matches your fabric for the leftmost needle as that's most likely to show through at the seams. You can use whatever color you like for the rest, since they're only visible on the inside.

Serged seams are sewn, trimmed, and finished in a single pass through the serger. Leave about 2" (5 cm) of thread chain at the beginning and end of the seam, and use a yarn needle to thread them back into the stitches afterward. Finishing edges is a serger specialty—choose a two, three, or four-thread stitch depending on your machine's options and the weight of your fabric (fewer threads for lighter-weight fabrics; more for heavyweight or very ravelly fabrics). Use a wider stitch setting if your fabric is prone to raveling, and a narrow one if your fabric is thin or doesn't fray much.

SEWING STRETCHY SEAMS BY HAND

If a serger isn't in the cards, and you're not happy with the stretch stitch options on your sewing machine, hand sewing is a totally viable option for stretch fabrics. Use a small backstitch for seaming, a backstitch or whipstitch for attaching appliqués and embellishments, and a catch stitch or other hemming stitch for edges (see Hand Sewing on page 50). These stitches should have enough stretch to avoid popped seams, though you'll want to use a heavy-duty thread or doubled all-purpose thread for durability.

Constructing Your Costume

In addition to joining pieces with a basic seam, there are a variety of other construction techniques you will use to make your costume. Each of these techniques is used in the Patterns (see page 96) and Costumes (see page 154) sections of *The Hero's Closet*.

MAKING A DART

Darts are the most basic way to add shape to clothes, but you'll need to use a bit of finesse to make them accurate and smooth all the way to the point. To begin, fold the dart down the center and match the marked stitching lines and baste or stick a pin through to keep them aligned as you sew. Backtack and start sewing from the widest point (**C**). When you're about ½" (1.3 cm) from the end, shorten your stitch length to 1 mm and slow down. Don't backtack at the tip, as that will make the dart tip pucker. Instead, sew a stitch past the edge of the fabric at the point and lift the foot. Clip the threads and tie a knot by hand to finish (**D**).

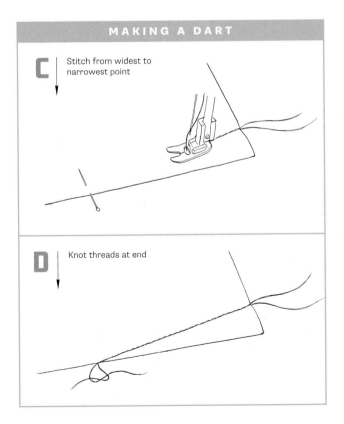

MAKING A DART

C | Stitch from widest to narrowest point

D | Knot threads at end

SEWING CURVES

When you sew princess seams and other curved pieces, you'll often be sewing a concave edge to a convex one. Although the stitching lines will match, one cut edge will be a lot longer than the other. The easiest way to sew such a seam is to staystitch both sides ⅛" (3 mm) from the stitching line, then clip into the seam allowance on the shorter (concave) side (**A**). The sharper the curve, the more frequently you'll need to clip to make it smooth. The clips allow the seam allowances to open up so they match the other side, and the staystitching prevents the fabric from stretching or tearing.

To prevent the convex edge from rippling when you press the seam, you'll want to notch that side. Trim out a little wedge with each clip so that the excess fabric doesn't make your seam look lumpy. After pressing your seam flat, you can finish it (see page 54) or leave it be if it'll be covered by a lining (see page 69).

When sewing low-stress seams on fabrics that don't fray excessively, you can trim the seam allowances to between ⅛" and ¼" (3 and 6 mm) instead of clipping (**B**). On most fabrics, you can then press it flat without trouble. This may give you smoother curves than the clipping method, especially for tight arcs like on a scalloped edge. For very tight curves, sew with a short stitch length to give the smoothest shape.

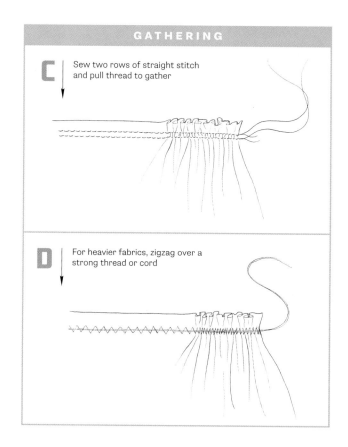

GATHERING

C | Sew two rows of straight stitch and pull thread to gather

D | For heavier fabrics, zigzag over a strong thread or cord

GATHERING

Gathering is a technique that allows a much longer piece to fit a shorter one; think puffy sleeves or a super-full skirt. You can gather fabric by hand, on a sewing machine, or on a serger. Two rows of gathering stitches (one on each side of the stitching line) make for tidier, more even gathers. For unstable fabrics or materials with a lot of body, sewing three rows of gathering stitches instead of two may help you to control the fabric.

To gather by hand, pick a strong thread and a longish needle. Sew two lines of basting stitches, one on each side of the stitching line, and pull up the thread to gather. This method can be used for fabric of any weight, especially if you use heavy-duty thread or a doubled all-purpose thread for strength.

On the machine, loosen your needle tension a notch or two and lengthen the stitch length to 4 to 5 mm. Sew without backstitching, then pull on the bobbin thread to gather

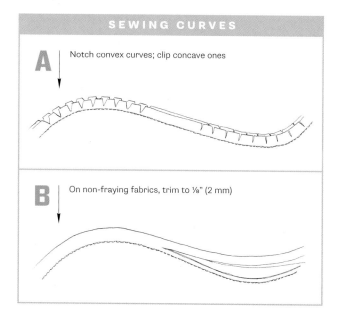

SEWING CURVES

A | Notch convex curves; clip concave ones

B | On non-fraying fabrics, trim to ⅛" (2 mm)

the fabric (**C**). This method works well for light and medium-weight fabrics, but if the fabric is thick you may find it hard to gather without breaking the threads. Again, two or more rows of gathering will give you more control over the fabric and make for neater, more even gathers once you've sewn them in place.

For heavier fabrics, you can zigzag stitch over a strong cord and pull the cord to form the gathers (**D**). Button thread is good for this; some people like to use dental floss as a substitute. The cord can be removed once the gathers are stitched down, as long as you're careful not to sew through it.

For all of the above methods, once you've pulled the fabric up to the appropriate length, matching the shorter piece, you'll knot the threads, thoroughly pin the gathered layer in place, and adjust the gathers until they're even. Stitch between the rows of gathering to secure, then remove the gathering threads.

Gathering on the serger is slightly different, and works best on lightweight fabrics, but is the fastest method for quickly gathering large quantities of fabric (like if you're making a garment with lots of ruffles). To do it, turn your differential feed and stitch length to maximum. Stitch a test strip of fabric to determine if the finished length is correct, and adjust the tension on the needle threads to produce more or less gathering. If you need to adjust the density of the gathers after stitching, you can slide the fabric along the needle threads to make them looser or tighter (make sure you've left enough length in the threads). If your serger has a gathering foot, you can actually gather your ruffle and attach it in a single pass. Gathering feet and ruffler attachments are also available for many sewing machines.

Easing a Sleeve

If you compare the top of a sleeve to the armhole it's supposed to be inserted in, you'll often see that the sleeve is slightly longer than the piece it fits, even if the sleeve is not designed to be gathered. This slight bit of fullness helps to round the sleeve over the shoulder, so it has a nice curve. The technique is very similar to gathering (see opposite page), in that you'll sew one or more rows of basting stitches on the longer side and draw them up until the lengths match. If done correctly, though, the layers will join smoothly with no visible gathers or puckers. You may have to steam the eased area to get it to cooperate. You may also find eased seams used elsewhere in the garment, where the easing functions almost like a small, invisible dart. Note that soft or loosely-woven fabrics ease more readily than very crisp ones, and on some fabrics you may have to reduce the ease by trimming down the longer side.

MAKING STRAPS OR TUBES

These pieces are essentially the same—a rectangle of fabric that is folded, stitched together with right sides facing along the long edges, and turned inside out through one of the open ends. Some are made from fabric cut on the bias (see Cutting Bias Strips on page 66 for details), while others are cut on the straight grain. Here are a couple of ways to turn them right side out—that's the tricky part! The first works if you have left both ends of the strap or tube open, while the second works if you leave only one end open.

1 Tie a piece of string or yarn to a safety pin and thread it through the strap, then secure the pin inside the far end. Use the pin and string to pull the strap right side out, then remove the pin. Flatten the strap with the seam in the center of one side and press (**A**, page 60).

2 Sew around one short end and along the long edges of the strap, leaving only one end open. Then use a dowel or the eraser end of a pencil to poke the short end through the strap and turn it right side out. Flatten and press (**B**, page 60).

If neither of the these options appeals to you, there's a simple way to make straps or tubes by just folding in the seam allowances (**C**, page 60), bringing the folded edges together, and edgestitching along the folded edges (**D**, page 60).

Finally, skinny bias tubes to use for spaghetti straps, button loops, decorative ties (as in the High-Collar Blouse Variation on page 135), and embellishments call for some special handling.

1 Start with a 1" (2.5 cm) bias-cut strip of very lightweight fabric. Slippery materials like charmeuse and habotai are easiest to turn out. Cut the strip at least 2" (5 cm) longer than you need, tie a knot in a piece of heavy thread or cord, and wrap the bias strip around the thread lengthwise.

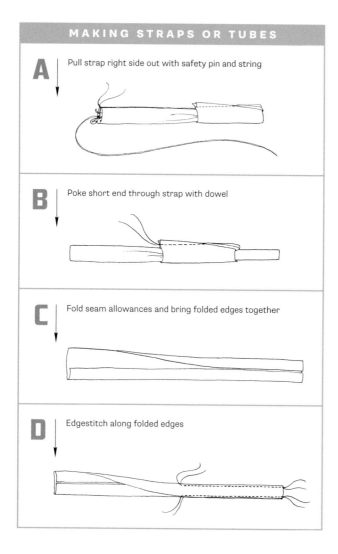

A Pull strap right side out with safety pin and string

B Poke short end through strap with dowel

C Fold seam allowances and bring folded edges together

D Edgestitch along folded edges

2 Sew across the end of the strip to secure the knot, then sew along the strip ⅛" to ¼" (3 to 6 mm) from the fold, depending on the width of the strap you need, being careful not to let the needle catch the string. Use polyester thread and a short stitch length so the finished strap will have enough give.

3 After sewing the entire length, pull on the string to turn the tube inside out, then clip off the end with the knot (the rest of the string can be reused). Pin the tube to your ironing board and gently pull on it while steaming to stretch out the bias, making the tube longer and narrower. If you need multiple tubes of the same size, it's best to sew a single long tube and then cut it into the lengths you need, as it can be difficult to precisely replicate a tube once it's sewn and stretched out.

ADDING CLOSURES AND FASTENERS

Many of the costumes you make might include one or more of the techniques described in this section. Even if you don't use them right away, having a sense of what's out there will help you to plan and execute future projects.

Sewing Zippers

To sew a zipper in, you need a special presser foot for your sewing machine that's open on one side and allows you to stitch right next to the teeth. Generally, they come with your machine. Some types are adjustable, so you can move the foot back and forth and stitch at varying distances on either side (**E**). Others are fixed but have two attachment points, so you can stitch on the left or the right side of the foot (**F**). If your foot only has one position (**G**), it will still work fine, but you'll need to adjust your technique so you're always stitching on the same side—sew top to bottom on one side of the zipper, and bottom to top on the other.

In addition to the foot, check to see whether your machine allows you to adjust the needle position to the left or right. If so, you can finesse the stitch so it lands exactly where you want it, especially if you're using a two-position or fixed-position foot.

STANDARD ZIPPERS. To insert a standard zipper, first sew the lower part of the seam up to the base of the zipper; you may also want to baste the zipper portion of the seam closed. Align the zipper behind the seam, baste or pin it in place, and topstitch it along either side. Start at the top with the slider partway undone so it doesn't get in the way. Sew for about 2" (5 cm), then stop with the needle down and close the zipper so you can sew the rest uninterrupted. Pivot at the bottom and sew across the base of the zipper, being careful not to hit the metal stopper. If your zipper foot allows you to stitch on either side, it's a good idea to start the other side back at the top to avoid skewing the layers or ending up with one side longer than the other (**H, I**).

SEPARATING ZIPPERS. These zippers are the easiest to sew of all. Place the zipper face down on the right side of the fabric, with the teeth ⅛" (3 mm) inside the center line of the opening.

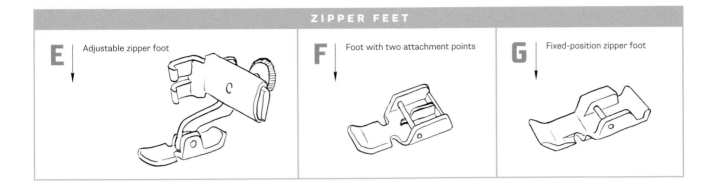

E Adjustable zipper foot

F Foot with two attachment points

G Fixed-position zipper foot

Stitch, pausing partway down to move the slider out of the way, and repeat on the other side. If you prefer to cover the zipper teeth, you can also use a centered zipper application as described for the standard zipper. To install a separating zipper in a lined garment, see the Dress (see page 143).

INVISIBLE ZIPPERS. Invisible zippers are usually sewn before the rest of the seam, and they need to be fully open while you sew them so you can unfurl the coiled teeth as you stitch. Using the appropriate invisible zipper foot for your machine model makes it very easy—you can get them at most fabric stores, sewing machine dealers, or online. The foot holds the curl open, and guides the zipper so your stitching is the correct distance from the teeth. However, you can also sew an invisible zipper with an ordinary zipper foot. Just iron some of the curl out of the tape before you begin, but be careful not to melt the teeth.

With the seam unsewn, place the zipper tape along the seam lines, right sides together, and baste along both sides (**A**, page 62). Open the zipper. If using an invisible zipper foot, lower the groove over the teeth and stitch from the top edge to the zipper pull along one side of the zipper; if using a regular zipper foot, uncoil the teeth with your fingers, adjust the needle position so it lands about a needle width away from the zipper teeth, and stitch (**B**, page 62). Repeat for the other side of the zipper. After the zipper is sewn in, stitch the rest of the seam using a zipper foot so you can get in next to the zipper bulk (**C**, page 62), first moving the zipper pull out of the way. Stitch about 1⁄16" to 1⁄8" (1.5 to 3 mm) farther from the edge than the zipper stitching to give the fabric room to roll over the zipper teeth.

Here are some additional tips about invisible zippers. The bottom 1" (2.5 cm) or so of an invisible zipper is unusable because the pull gets in the way of stitching any farther, so you should buy a slightly longer zipper than you need. Most invisible zippers have one standard tooth size, and they can feel a little flimsy if your costume is bulky or heavy or if the zipper goes across a seam. If you hunt a little, you can find the heavy-duty version used in bridal gowns. These are usually only available in black and white, but since most of the zipper is concealed when in use, you really only need to worry about the pull tab. You can cut the attached tab off and replace it, or simply paint it with nail polish to get the color you need.

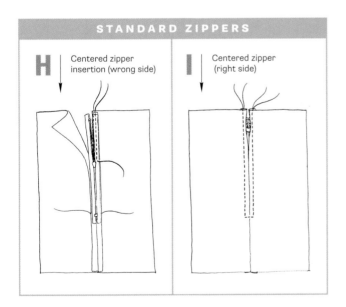

H Centered zipper insertion (wrong side)

I Centered zipper (right side)

A Baste both sides before starting

C Close the rest of the seam below the zipper

B Uncoil and stitch with invisible zipper or standard zipper foot

D Sew facing to right side and stitch box for zipper opening

E Slash down opening and clip into corners

F Turn facing to inside

G Baste zipper to facing only

H Stitch on garment side of facing seam

I Topstitch or edgestitch

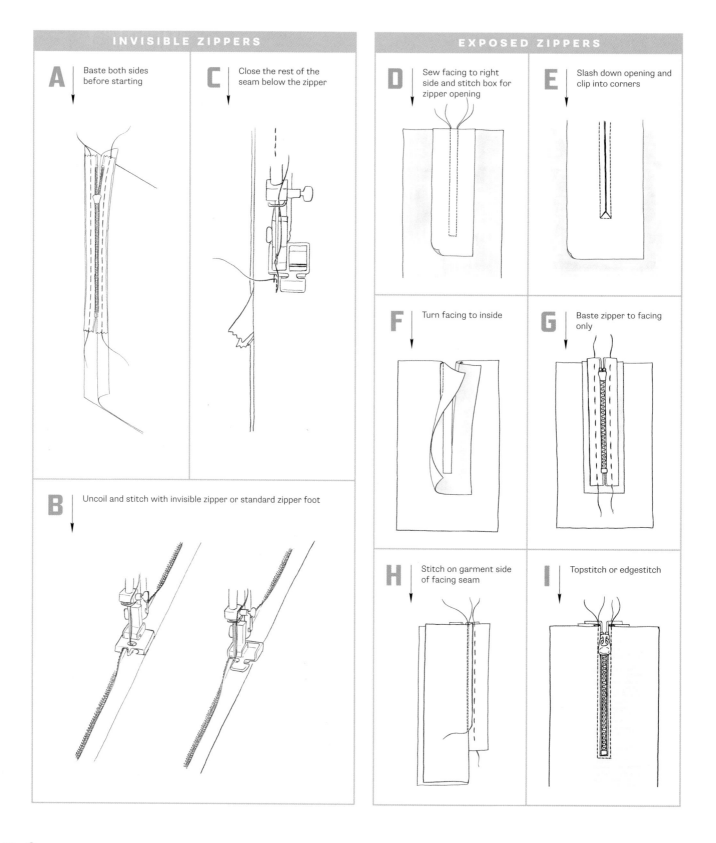

EXPOSED ZIPPERS. In addition to being decorative, exposed zippers are convenient because you can put them anywhere—you don't have to insert them in a seam. This makes them great for front or back closures on bodysuits and dresses that don't have a center seam, as well as for pocket openings.

On very stable fabrics like doubleknit or faux leather, you can simply interface (see page 32) the back of the zipper area, staystitch a box where you want the zipper to go, clip along the length and into the corners, and press the edges to the inside. If you're using a lightweight or woven fabric, create your opening with a facing. I like to use a strip of woven fusible interfacing cut 2" (5 cm) longer and wider than the zipper opening. Place it on the right side of the fabric with the fusible side facing up (baste it in place down the center line if the fabric is slippery). Sew a box for your zipper opening, the same length as the zipper and about ⅜" (1 cm) wide (**D**). Cut through both layers down the center of the box and diagonally into the corners (**E**). Flip the facing through to the inside (**F**). Position your zipper behind the opening and baste it to the facing only (**G**), then fold the fabric back and sew the zipper tape to the fabric, stitching down each side one at a time and then across the bottom of the box, folding the fabric back as you go. This stitching should land a needle's width farther from the cut edge than the facing seam, leaving the facing free, so the facing won't show at all from the outside (**H**). Press to fuse the interfacing in place, and optionally edgestitch around the opening from the outside (**I**).

Adding Buttons and Buttonholes

Most sewing machines have at least one buttonhole stitch. On some machines this might be fully automatic, using a special foot or sensor to determine what size is needed and sewing the buttonhole in a single step. In other cases, you may need to mark the buttonhole dimensions on your fabric and manually sew out the four sides of the opening. Every machine is different, so consult your manual if you're unclear on the process. To cut the buttonhole open after it is sewn, use a seam ripper (you can put a pin at each end and cut from the ends toward the center to avoid cutting too far), small scissors, or a chisel-shaped buttonhole cutter (**J**, **K**).

Hand-worked buttonholes are time-consuming and take a ton of practice to get right, but they are a good option for

Shortening a Zipper

On occasion, you may want to shorten a metal zipper. If so, you can buy metal stoppers that clamp on with pliers. Make sure you get the right size for your zipper. Use pliers to pry the teeth off for 1" (2.5 cm) or so above the desired length, and clamp the stoppers onto the zipper tape directly above the uppermost tooth on each side. Trim away the excess tape. To shorten an invisible zipper, cut any excess off the bottom end and hand stitch across the coils.

heavy fabrics that are hard to cram under the machine. They're also nice for historical costumes, if you have any sticklers for authenticity in your cosplay group. To make them, first mark and then outline your buttonhole with a running stitch or a machine stitch. Apply a fray stopper (a liquid that seals the cut fibers, like Fray Check) inside the opening, cut the buttonhole open with a seam ripper or buttonhole tool, and whipstitch the edges (see page 50) to reinforce. Then work a buttonhole stitch around the opening using heavy decorative thread, spacing the stitches about a needle's width apart. For a more prominent buttonhole, work your stitches on top of a fine gimp cord or length of embroidery thread (each available at fabric shops).

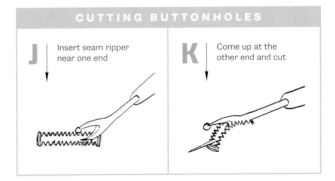

CUTTING BUTTONHOLES

J Insert seam ripper near one end

K Come up at the other end and cut

The finished buttonhole should be just a bit longer than the button width plus the button thickness. Since buttonholes can be temperamental, it's a good idea to sew a test or two on scraps and make sure your buttons fit through correctly before you move on to your final garment.

Instead of using buttonholes, you can make button loops from cord, elastic, or a tiny tube of fabric and insert them between a garment piece and its facing or lining. To do this, the loops are lined up along the seam with the loop pointing inward and the raw ends toward the fabric edge. The loops are then caught in the seam as the facing is sewn to the garment. When sewing a whole row of loops, it may be easier to sew them to a ribbon or strip of fabric before inserting them in your garment (**A**).

Sewing on buttons by hand is the most secure method of attachment; use doubled thread or special button thread. Stitch through several times (**B**), leaving a little slack in the stitches, then make a shank underneath the button by wrapping the thread around the stitching several times before knotting off. You can also attach buttons by machine (**C**). Check your machine's accessories for a button foot, or if your machine uses snap-on feet, you can remove the presser foot entirely. Place the button and fabric under the needle, and balance a pin on the button between the holes to serve as spacer. Then, set a zigzag stitch with zero stitch length (deactivate the feed dogs if your machine allows this), and fiddle the stitch width to match the holes in the button. Hand-crank the machine through the first few stitches to make sure the needle won't hit the button, then sew back and forth until the button is secure.

Adding Grommets and Eyelets

Any hole used for lacing will need some kind of reinforcement; depending on how much strain the laces will be under, you may choose to use stitched eyelets with or without extra reinforcement, metal eyelets, or two-part grommets.

Holes for lacing can be cut out with a punch or worked open with a sharp pencil or tapered awl. A punch creates a clean, perfectly round opening of pre-determined size. An awl pushes the fibers apart instead of cutting them, which makes for a stronger but less regular opening. For hand-sewn eyelets, make a line of running stitches around the opening as a guide, then work buttonhole stitches (see page 50) around the circumference in heavyweight thread. If you need a bit of reinforcement, you can incorporate a metal jump ring of the appropriate size for your opening and work the buttonhole stitches over it. Sew-in lacing tape with pre-set eyelets is another option, but make sure the eyelets are sturdy enough for functional use as opposed to just decoration. You can often find this tape in the trim section of a fabric store.

If you'd like an alternative to eyelets, you can sew metal rings into your costume or make loops from fabric or cord, add them to your garment, then thread the laces through them.

Sewing on Snaps

Sew-on snaps are a quick and easy-to-install closure. These snaps have four to six loops to sew through; use a buttonhole stitch (see page 50) to make your snaps both sturdy and attractive. As explained on page 36, there are other kinds of snaps, including magnetic snaps, some of which require a special tool to apply. If you're short on time, you can also find tapes with pre-attached snaps that you simply sew in.

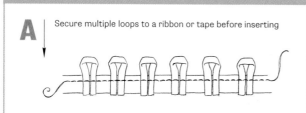

BUTTON LOOPS

A | Secure multiple loops to a ribbon or tape before inserting

SEWING ON BUTTONS

B | Hand sewn

C | Machine sewn

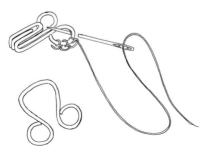

Fastening the Fasteners

The tools used to attach metal eyelets, grommets, rivets, and snaps vary. One type, sometimes included in the package with the fasteners, consists of a tiny anvil and die that are used with a hammer to pound the pieces into place. The main difficulty with this method is keeping the pieces correctly aligned; if anything is askew, the eyelet or rivet won't set correctly. A better-quality version of this tool can be purchased separately, with a larger, more stable anvil and die, and it reduces the frequency of misfires. You may also see a snap or eyelet tool shaped like a pair of pliers that clamps the fastener in place. This version can be more difficult to use for people who have small hands or relatively little grip strength. Professional-grade (i.e. very expensive) versions of these tools use a large lever-operated hand press and different dies for each type and size of fastener.

Sewing on Hooks and Eyes

As with snaps, use buttonhole stitch (see page 50) for extra security when stitching on these components. Work around the curves of the wire, and sew a few stitches across the hook end to hold it in place. Use heavyweight thread for larger sizes.

Sewing on a hook and eye

Finishing Techniques

At some point in the assembly of your costume, the edges of your garment need to be finished to control fraying and make them look neat and professional. This includes necklines, armholes or sleeves, hems, and any other edges that aren't enclosed in seams. Be sure to try on any garment that will be hemmed and mark the depth of the hem you need. Sometimes it's easiest to have a friend help you do this, especially if you're dealing with lots of fabric or complicated hemlines. Circle skirts, capes, or any other garment with a long, curved hem may need to hang up for a few days on a hanger or dress form before being hemmed, as sections hanging on the bias may droop and need trimming.

FACINGS

Bias Facing

For an unobtrusive finish around necklines, armholes, and so forth, make a narrow facing out of single-fold bias tape, which you can buy in packages or cut yourself. (To cut your own strips for bias facings or other uses, see the sidebar on page 66.) Sew the tape to the opening along the stitching line, right sides together, then trim and clip the seam allowance. Press the seam open, fold the raw edge of the tape under (**D**), then press the tape to the inside and topstitch (**E**).

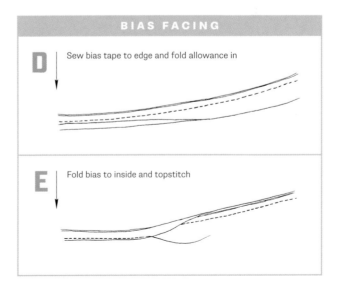

BIAS FACING

D Sew bias tape to edge and fold allowance in

E Fold bias to inside and topstitch

Cutting Bias Strips

To cut bias strips for binding, facings, or embellishment, first use an L-square or gridded cutting mat to line your fabric up exactly on the grain (see page 26). Measure equal distances along the straight and cross grain (e.g., 18"/ 46 cm] each way), mark, and use a yardstick to connect the two points. This creates a 45° angle, which is the true bias. Use a clear gridded ruler to draw additional lines parallel to the first, and cut along the lines with a rotary cutter or shears. Depending on the length of strip needed, you may need to join strips together. To do this, line them up at right angles to each other (forming an L-shape) and stitch along the straight grain, then press the seam open.

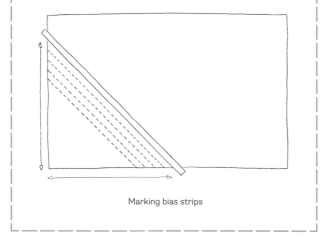

Marking bias strips

Shaped Facing

A facing is a piece of fabric that frames the opening you want to finish. You sew it to the edge with right sides together, and then flip it around to the inside so the raw edges are hidden between the garment and facing (**A-D**). This method is often used to finish necklines, especially V-necks and other shaped necklines, but it can also be used for pocket openings, decorative cutouts, hems, and more. To prevent a facing from rolling out, you should topstitch (see page 55) or understitch

it and press well. Understitching (**E**) is a line of hand or machine stitching that secures a facing or lining to the seam allowance without going through the outer fabric. This is usually enough to make a wide facing roll naturally to the inside, so no visible stitching is necessary, though usually it's a good idea to take a few stitches to tack the facing to the seam allowances inside the garment. Narrow facings will need to be topstitched to prevent them from flipping to the outside.

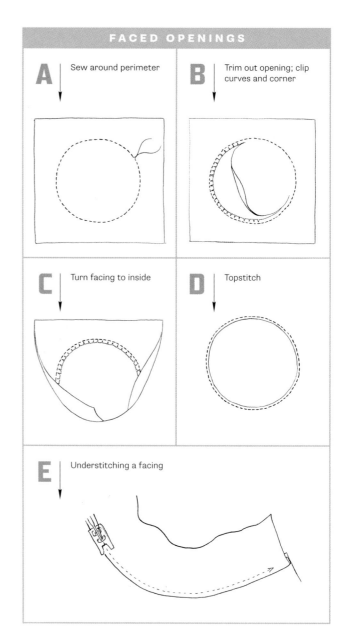

FACED OPENINGS

A Sew around perimeter

B Trim out opening; clip curves and corner

C Turn facing to inside

D Topstitch

E Understitching a facing

HEMS AND EDGES

Garments with very full hems, such as circular skirts and capes, should be hung up for at least a day before hemming. Because the hem is curved, parts of the garment will hang on the bias and may stretch out. After hanging, put the garment on yourself or a dress form and measure up from the floor to trim the hem so it's level all the way around. Narrow or faced hems are most suitable when the hem is curved.

Double-Fold Hem

This provides a very clean and basic hem finish. Fold the hem up ¼" (6 mm) and press, then fold again at the actual hemline. Secure by topstitching or with a slipstitch or catch stitch (see page 50).

Taped Hem

Sew a piece of hem lace or tape to the outside of the fabric along the raw edge of the hem, so that the tape extends slightly past the edge. Press the hem up along the marked line, then use a hand or machine stitch along the top edge of the lace to secure, concealing the raw edge of the fabric behind the lace. This makes for a very lightweight, but also decorative, finish.

Blindstitched Hem

This stitch, which you may have on your machine, can be used with a double-fold or taped hem to make it nearly invisible from the outside. After finishing the lower edge and folding up the hem, fold it back so the edge sticks out slightly from under the body fabric. Select the blindstitch and sew along the edge so that the wide zigzags just barely catch the fold (**F**).

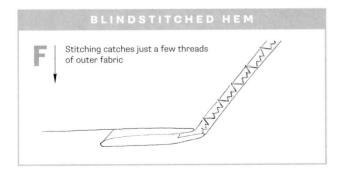

BLINDSTITCHED HEM

F Stitching catches just a few threads of outer fabric

Serged or Zigzagged Hem

This option is less bulky and more utilitarian-looking than a double-fold hem. Serge or zigzag the fabric edge to prevent fraying, then fold it up along the hemline and secure with a blind stitch, hand hem, or topstitching. Or, stitch with decorative thread and don't turn the edge up at all!

Narrow Hem (or Baby Hem)

Narrow hems are useful on delicate fabrics like silk, handkerchief linen, and fine cottons. Press the fabric up about ⅛" (3 mm) below the hemline and sew ¹⁄₁₆" (1.5 mm) from the fold. Trim the seam allowance right next to the stitching, fold along the hemline, and sew a second line of stitching on top of the first. Only the second row of stitches will be visible from the outside.

Rolled Hem

Many sergers have a rolled hem stitch that can be used to finish fine, difficult-to-control fabrics. Refer to your serger's manual for the correct settings, and adjust the differential feed to eliminate rippling or puckering. (Or, alternatively, turn the differential all the way down to create a wavy "lettuce" hem. Cosplayer's choice.)

Knit Hem

Since most knit fabrics don't fray, you can hem them without finishing the cut edge. Just turn the edge up the desired amount, hold with pins, basting, or basting tape, and topstitch with a zigzag, stretch stitch, or double needle. You can also use a serger or sewing machine blindstitch if you prefer.

Banded Edge

This method is particularly popular for knit fabrics because it can be done entirely on a serger. Cut a rectangle of fabric the length of your opening, or slightly smaller if you're using a stretch fabric. It should be twice the desired width of the finished band, plus a seam allowance on all sides. Sew the short ends of the band together and press the seam open (or flat if serging), then fold the loop in half lengthwise so the raw edges are aligned. Sew the raw edges to your garment with right sides together, finish the seam, then press the band out away from the body of the garment.

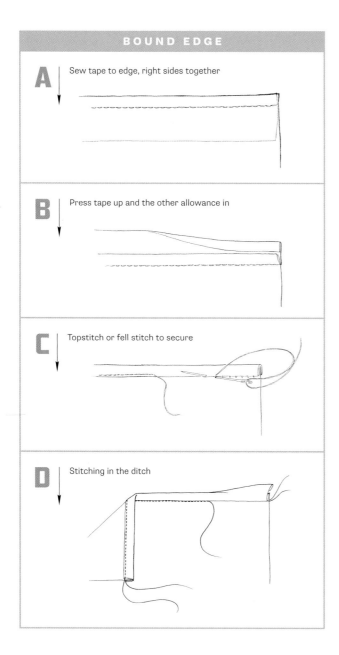

A Sew tape to edge, right sides together

B Press tape up and the other allowance in

C Topstitch or fell stitch to secure

D Stitching in the ditch

Bound Edge

Binding is a visible finish that can be made in a matching or contrasting fabric. First, trim the edge to the finished length. Take double-fold bias tape, open it flat, and sew it to your fabric with right sides together along the first fold line (**A**). Press the tape toward the edge and wrap it around to the inside (**B**). Topstitch or slipstitch the free edge along the stitching line (**C**), or arrange the folds so the free edge extends slightly beyond the line and "stitch in the ditch" (sew from the outside in the gutter of the seam between the bias and main fabric) to secure (**D**). For more color and fabric options, make your own bias tape (as suggested on page 65) instead of buying it.

Elastic Edges

Elastic helps garments stay where you want them to, so naturally it's a cosplayer's best friend. Use it to finish waistbands; arm, leg, and neck openings; and on undergarments. It's also helpful for stabilizing shoulder seams and can be used to create gathered or ruched effects (stretch it along a seam while sewing, and it'll draw up the fabric when it springs back). Always use a ballpoint or stretch needle when sewing through elastic to avoid puncturing or breaking the stretch fibers (which can weaken elastic).

There are two main ways to sew elastic into an opening: the casing method and the stitched-and-turned method. Use a casing when the elastic is gathering a large quantity of fabric, as on the waistband of a gathered skirt. The stitched-and-turned method is best for when the elastic is just a bit smaller than the opening you're sewing it to, like on the leg and arm openings of a leotard or swimsuit.

➤ **Casing method** (**E**). Make a casing about ⅛" (3 mm) wider than the elastic by attaching a separate casing piece or folding the edge over and stitching it in place. Leave an opening of 1" to 2" (2.5 to 5 cm) in a side or back seam or along the bottom edge of the casing so you can get the elastic inside. Cut the elastic to the required length with a little extra for an overlap, referring to the pattern measurements or wrapping the elastic around your body to determine what's comfortable. Safety pin one end to the garment next to the opening, and stick another pin through the free end of the elastic so you can grip it to push the elastic through the casing. When you get back to the opening, make sure the elastic isn't twisted before you sew the ends together (**F**, **G**). Sew

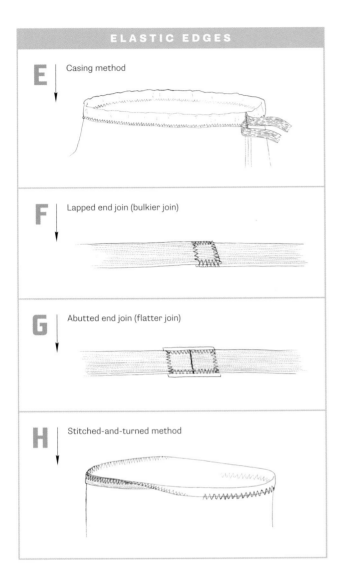

E | Casing method

F | Lapped end join (bulkier join)

G | Abutted end join (flatter join)

H | Stitched-and-turned method

the opening closed, even out the gathers, and tack the elastic and casing together at the seams to prevent it from twisting or shifting.

> **Stitched-and-turned method** (H). Sew the ends of the elastic together and mark the loop into quarters. Mark corresponding points on the garment opening (usually center front, center back, and each side) and pin the elastic into the opening on the wrong side of the fabric. Use a zigzag or overlock stitch to sew the elastic to the fabric edge, stretching as you sew so the elastic and

fabric lengths match. Fold the edge over to enclose the elastic on the inside and topstitch with a zigzag, double needle, or coverstitch to secure, stretching just enough to remove any wrinkles.

LINING

Lining your projects is a great way to cleanly finish the insides, help garments lie smoothly and neatly over other layers, and make lightweight fabrics feel more substantial. Although not all garments need to be lined, it's a good idea for most jackets and coats as well as structured, fitted dresses and skirts. The Coat on page 149 is lined, as is the Dress on page 143. Used appropriately, lining will make your costumes feel more professional.

Some patterns include separate pieces for the lining, but often you can adapt the lining from the main pattern pieces. The simplest lining method is to cut the lining pieces the same as the outer garment, assemble them separately, and join the layers around the edges of the garment. An alternative, especially if the garment is already finished with a facing, is to cut the lining so it attaches to the facing and is well hidden inside the garment. If your lining goes all the way to the edge, you'll usually need to understitch or topstitch to prevent the lining from showing outside the garment. Your pattern instructions will give you specific details about how to add a lining, as it will vary from garment to garment.

If you're sewing with a lightweight, limp, or delicate fabric and need to make it more substantial, you can do this by layering it with another fabric that has the requisite strength and/or heft. Cut the pieces out twice, once from your fabric and once from the backing fabric, then immediately baste the layers together along all seam lines, darts, and edges so that the two fabrics will behave as one while you work with them. This technique is called underlining (or "flat lining" in historical sewing) and can be used by itself or in addition to a regular lining. Silk organza is often used for underlining because it is very strong and has very little stretch, but muslin or another lightweight cotton will also work well for some fabrics.

Sewing Tricky Fabrics

Although we discussed a lot of the standard fabrics you'll encounter on pages 26 to 31, as a cosplayer, you'll find yourself working with a lot of oddball fabrics too, which have their own sets of rules. You need to have a few special tricks up your sleeve to sew them effectively, but a little preparation and the right tools can make them very manageable. Keep a supply of tissue paper on hand to help with cutting fine fabrics and feeding sticky surfaces through the machine, and stock up on a variety of needle types and sizes so you can experiment and see what the fabric likes best.

Coated Fabrics

Faux leather, metallic spandex, and the various flavors of vinyl are notoriously unforgiving. Any holes you make are permanent, so use clips, tape, and low-temperature fusible tapes instead of pins. A washable glue stick is also handy for some situations. When you're ready to sew, choose a microtex or sharp-type needle to puncture the coated surface, or go with a stretch needle if you're struggling with skipped stitches, and sew carefully to avoid having to unpick seams. These fabrics may also stick to the sewing machine, so to keep things moving smoothly, you might need to sandwich the fabric in tissue paper, or use a special foot on your machine (walking, Teflon-coated, or roller). Be careful when pressing, as these materials may also melt easily.

Faux Fur

This fabric can be very messy, so it should be cut from the back side using a razor blade or craft knife so you don't cut the pile, which will help to minimize the fluffsplosion. After you sew, use a pin or comb to liberate any fur that's caught in the seams. For some furs, you may want to do butted seams (where the two pieces are placed edge to edge and sewn over a reinforcing tape so there's no overlap) to prevent a lot of bulk in the seam allowances. The nice thing about fur is that seams will all but disappear into the pile, so it's very forgiving of shaky stitching, and you can even piece scraps together if you're short on fabric.

Heavy Denim and Canvas

These hard-working fabrics are actually pretty easy to sew, but you'll want a denim or topstitching needle to accommodate the dense fabric and heavier thread (denim or upholstery thread) that goes with it. If you have trouble sewing over bulky seams, slip a piece of cardboard under the back of the foot to boost it over the hurdle (**A**).

Leather

Use a leather needle (or glover's needle for hand sewing) and heavy thread when working with leather. As with coated fabrics, a walking, roller, or Teflon foot will help to keep the material moving through the machine (**B**). Since it won't press as well as fabric does, you'll want to flatten bulky seam allowances with topstitching or leather glue. Garment-weight leathers can be sewn on a regular home machine, but very heavy leathers will need to be sewn by hand (and you may need to pre-punch the holes).

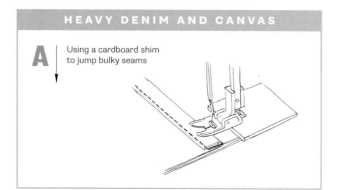

HEAVY DENIM AND CANVAS

A Using a cardboard shim to jump bulky seams

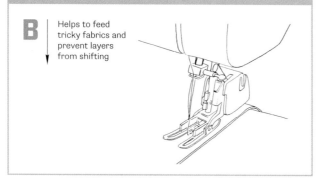

WALKING FOOT

B Helps to feed tricky fabrics and prevent layers from shifting

Slippery or Shifty Fabrics

Materials like chiffon can be difficult to cut accurately, so—if the fabric is washable—it may help to stabilize them with starch or a starch alternative. Make sure the grain is straight before you stabilize or you'll exacerbate the problem. If your fabric is not washable, you can sandwich it between two layers of tissue paper and cut both paper and fabric at the same time for a more accurate cut. Alternatively, covering your cutting surface with a sheet or length of muslin can give it a little more grip so the fabric on top stays put.

Sequined and Beaded Fabrics

These beauties can make for scratchy, bulky seams, so it's a good idea to remove beads and sequins from the seam allowances before you sew. Instead of cutting the threads, which may allow the embellishment to unravel further than you'd like, use wire cutters to remove sequins and crush beads with pliers to remove them while leaving the threads intact. If you need to go back and fill gaps after the garment is complete, you should be able to salvage the sparklies you need from leftover scraps.

Velvet

Velvet likes to creep and shed fluff as you sew it (though it's not as bad as faux fur), and it can be difficult to press without permanently crushing the pile. Cotton, polyester, and stretch velvets are pretty resilient, but if you've spent the money on silk, rayon, or acetate velvet, you should be prepared to baby it. Hand basting will help to control this wriggly fabric, and serging or zigzagging the edges is a good idea to control fraying. You can preserve the pile by pressing it very lightly with the nap face down on a fluffy towel or scraps of the velvet itself. But if you use velvet often you may want to invest in a needle board—a flat board with little needles that retains the depth of the pile when you place the fabric on it to iron. It's expensive, but unbeatable for this purpose.

Tricky Fabrics: 1. Velvet **2.** Metallic spandex **3.** Metallic mesh **4.** Faux fur **5.** Faux leather

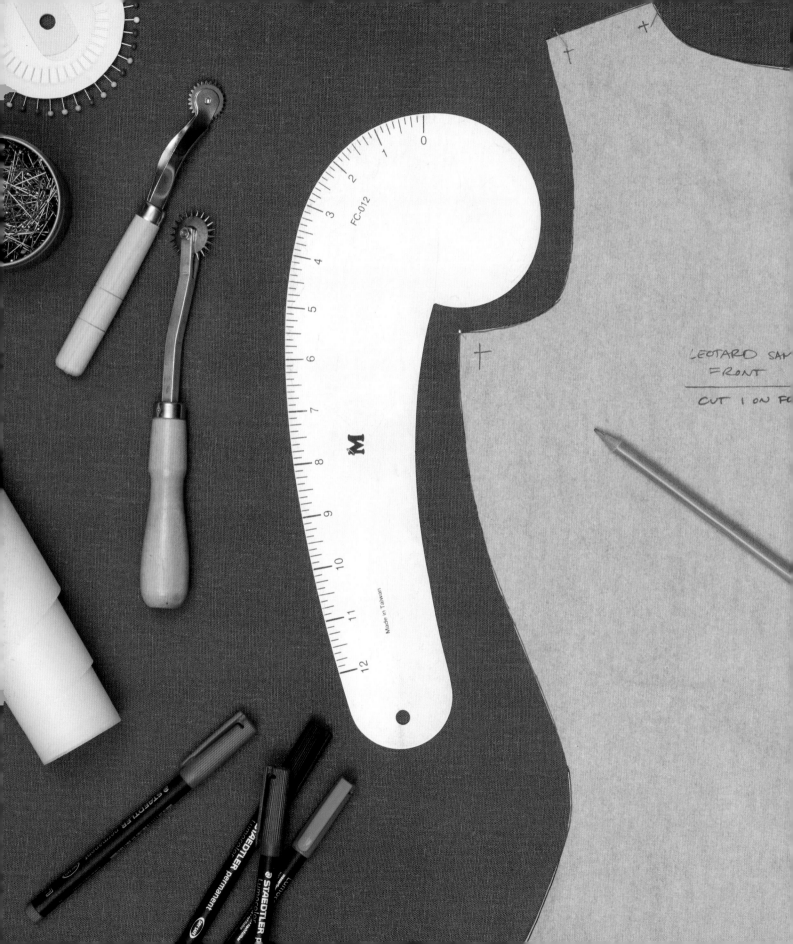

CHAPTER 4

ALTERATIONS AND MODIFICATIONS

There are a couple of important reasons why you may want to alter a pattern. The first is to make a garment fit your body better, and the second is to customize the design so it looks more like your reference image. To make sure that your costume looks great on you and is comfortable to wear, I'll begin with fit. ➔ Here's a secret about sewing patterns: they're probably not going to fit you perfectly right out of the envelope, any more than a garment you pull off the rack at a store will fit exactly how you want it to. Patterns are designed to fit an average body, in many cases based on data that was collected decades ago. Fortunately, unlike clothing off the rack, when you're sewing, you can adjust the pattern before you begin so your finished clothes will fit like they're custom made (which, uh, they will be).

Fitting Alterations

Now, it's true that fitting your hand-sewn clothing can get a little tricky because you have to do a lot of work before you get to the stage of trying things on. That's why you need to take a detailed set of measurements (see the box on page 76), and keep them up to date when your body changes size or shape. Then you can compare your measurements to the pattern's measurements and see where you might need to adjust. It's also a good idea to make a mock-up in inexpensive fabric such as muslin when you're trying something new so you don't waste a lot of costly fabric and spend hours of work time on a garment that won't fit in the end. Some common changes are very easy to do.

ALTERATION TOOLS & MATERIALS

If you plan to do a lot of altering or customizing, you may want to add some additional supplies to your Sewing Essentials toolbox (see page 44). Here are some suggestions:

1 **CURVED RULERS.** Tailoring rulers incorporate common curves for different parts of the body to help you draw smooth lines.

2 **L-SQUARE.** Use these for drawing grainlines and making sure corners are square.

3 **SPIKY TRACING WHEEL.** A needle-point tracer makes clear indentations to transfer marks between layers of paper.

4 **CHINA MARKERS.** These are good for marking up muslins, and you don't have to stop to sharpen them.

5 **CRAFT SCISSORS.** Remember never to use your good fabric scissors on paper!

6 **QUILTING RULER.** The gridded lines help with marking seam allowances, cutting bias tape, and more.

7 **TRACING PAPER.** For tracing patterns off sheets, filling gaps, and creating new pieces (like facings).

8 **TAPE.** To secure the altered pattern pieces.

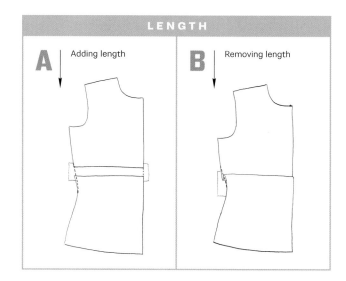

LENGTH

Length is usually the easiest thing to change, so no worries if you're tall or petite and everything in stores is too long or short. Determine how much you need to add or remove from a pattern by comparing your body measurements with the pattern. You should know your back length (from the prominent bone at the base of your neck to the narrowest point of your waist) and your outseam (from the waist to the floor along the outside of your leg) so you can compare them to the pattern measurements. For bodysuits, you should also check the torso length as shown in the box on page 76, to make sure it won't sag or ride up when you wear it. Double-check by holding the paper pattern piece up to your body and making sure that the waist and other landmarks are hitting you in the correct place.

Some commercial patterns have one or more suggested lengthen/shorten lines, indicated with a pair of closely spaced parallel lines. To lengthen, cut between the lines and spread the piece apart, making sure to keep the seam lines lined up. Tape in a strip of paper to cover the gap, then use a ruler or French curve to draw a smooth line connecting the seams above and below (**A**). To shorten, fold along the lengthen/shorten line and make a pleat (the finished depth of the pleat should be half the amount you mean to take out). Again, smooth out the seam lines (**B**).

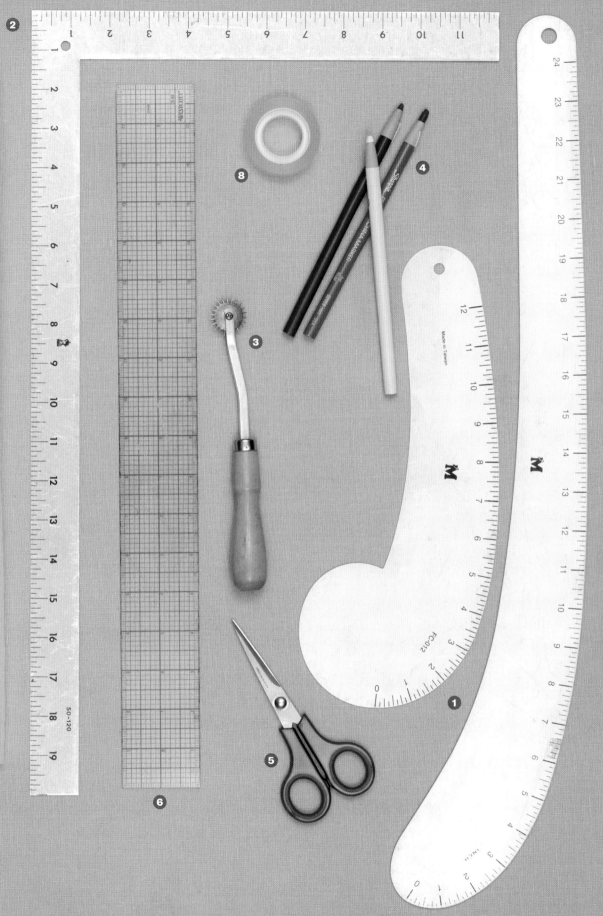

The thing you should avoid is simply adding or removing length at the hem, unless you're adjusting for style and not fit. If you're tall, you're probably long all over, so the changes need to be proportionate. If a dress is perfect in the torso but you want to show a little less leg, on the other hand, it would be perfectly reasonable to extend the hem down 1" or 2" (2.5 or 5 cm). Also, if the silhouette of the garment is tapered or flared (as with skinny pants or a full skirt), adding length at the middle will keep the finished hem circumference the same, retaining the style proportions of the garment.

Body Measurements

To do successful alterations, you need a few more measurements than are necessary to choose a pattern size. It may be easier to get accurate measurements if you have a friend help you. Unless otherwise noted, men and women should measure at the same points on the body. Here are key measurements to take:

1 BUST/CHEST. Measure around the fullest part of the chest or bustline. For men, measure around the widest part of the chest, which is usually at or slightly above the nipples.

2 UPPER CHEST. For women, measure over the breasts and under the arms.

3 WAIST. Measure at the narrowest point of the waistline.

4 HIPS. Measure at the widest point of the hips; if your thighs are more full than your hips, use that measurement instead. Also measure the distance from your waist to the fullest point in case that needs adjustment.

5 BACK LENGTH. Measure along your spine from the prominent bone at the base of your neck to your waist.

6 ARM LENGTH. Measure from your wrist bone to your elbow, and from the elbow to top of the arm, keeping your arm slightly bent. Add the two measurements together.

7 OUTSEAM. Measure from your waist to the floor along the outside of your leg.

8 INSEAM. Measure from your crotch to the floor along the inside of your leg.

9 TORSO LENGTH. Measure from the top of the shoulder in front, down through your legs, and up to the same point in back.

10 HEIGHT. Measure from top of your head to the floor.

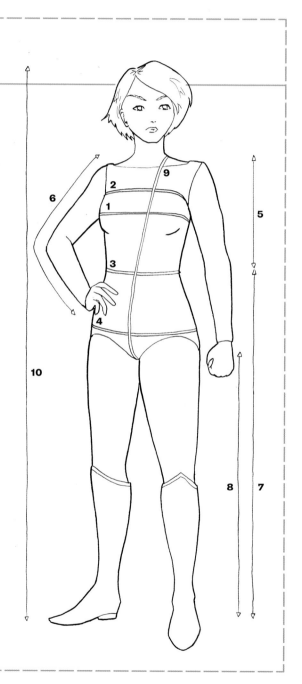

BLENDING SIZES

If you look at a size chart and your measurements fall into multiple size groups, you're in good company. Many of us, in fact, are two or three different sizes depending on the area. Patterns typically include several sizes nested together so that you can easily blend between sizes to fit different areas. First, determine which size you are in each area: bust/chest, waist, and hip. Find the corresponding points on the pattern tissue, and use a marker or highlighter to trace over the appropriate size line for 1" (2.5 cm) or so. Then, draw a smooth line connecting up the marked lines. You can do it freehand if you're confident in your drawing skills, or grab a ruler or French curve to assist (a set of curved dressmaking rulers, shown on page 75, is a great investment if you anticipate doing a lot of this) (**A**).

If you're multiple sizes and they're not all in the same commercial pattern envelope or on the same pattern piece, pick the size range based on what area will be the most complicated to fit. Often this is the shoulder and sleeve, so you'll likely want to choose the size that matches your bust/chest measurement; on the other hand, if the pattern has a lot of complicated detail around the lower torso, you may want to choose based on your hip size instead. Then, in the other areas, use the spacing of the other size lines as a guide to estimate where the line for your size should be, and adjust as needed from there.

SHOULDER ADJUSTMENTS

Any non-strapless top hangs from your shoulders. That means you can get some really wacky issues if the angle of the shoulders isn't correct—if your own shoulders are more square or more sloped than the pattern. The easiest way to check this is to pin the pattern pieces together along the shoulder seam. Line up the center front and back, pinning them to your clothes if necessary to make them hang nice and straight. Then stand naturally and take a look in the mirror.

If your shoulders are more square than the pattern, you may see the pattern straining at the tip of your shoulder or lifting up next to your neck. If so, unpin the shoulder end of the seam until it lies flat, then pin along the new seam line. Take it off, draw in the new shoulder seam, and add extra tissue if needed to maintain the seam allowance (**B**).

On sloped shoulders, you'll see the shoulder seam lifting away from your body at the end of the shoulder. Pinch out the excess tissue, then mark the new shoulder seam and seam allowance.

You may also find that your shoulder is angled forward or backward compared to the seam on the pattern. If that's the case, you'll want to add to the back and take away from the front (or vice versa) until the seam runs right along the peak of your shoulder from earlobe to tip (**C**). You may want to get a friend to check this for you, since turning your head to look can throw off the measurement.

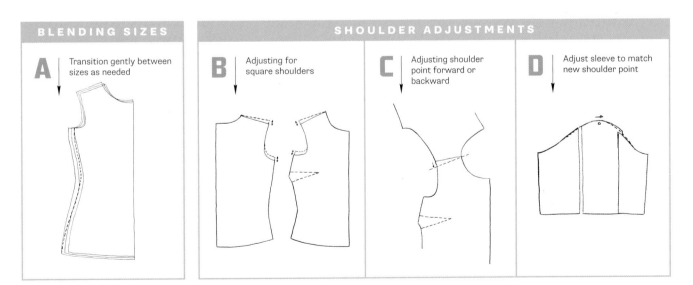

BLENDING SIZES

A | Transition gently between sizes as needed

SHOULDER ADJUSTMENTS

B | Adjusting for square shoulders

C | Adjusting shoulder point forward or backward

D | Adjust sleeve to match new shoulder point

If the shoulder seam has changed at all, you'll need to adjust the underarm and/or sleeve areas to match. If you've added to the top of the shoulder, tape in a new piece of tissue and raise the underarm by the same amount, redrawing the curve so it's the same shape as before (**B**, page 77.) If you've removed height at the top of the shoulder, you'll need to trim away the same amount under the arm so the overall size of the armhole isn't affected.

If you've moved the shoulder seam forward or backward by adding/removing tissue on the back and front, move the match point on the sleeve cap forward or backward to match (**D**, page 77).

DART CHANGES

When test-fitting a women's garment, make sure that the bust dart points toward the peak of the breast but doesn't actually touch it. The dart should end ¾" to 2" (1.9 to 5 cm) away, so the tip of the dart doesn't create an unfortunate "nipply" effect. The dart may need to move up or down, or be made shorter or longer to provide the best fit for your body. If you get wrinkles above or below the dart, especially around the armhole, you may need to make the dart deeper so it takes up more fabric. This will shorten the seam, so you'll probably need to add length elsewhere to compensate. (Often, this occurs when a full bust adjustment is needed (see page 79). If so, this will take care of both steps.) Conversely,

a dart that's too deep may result in a puffy or hollow area that floats away from your body. Sewing a shallower dart and removing length to match should remedy this.

With waist darts, you may find that they need to be made shorter or longer to provide the best fit. If the darts are too long, you might see the fabric straining at the tip. If the dart is too short, you'll see a loose "bubble" of fabric beyond the tip of the dart. You can also add waist darts in front or back to make a loose blouse more fitted—just remember that the wider you make the dart, the more difficult it will be to sew without strain lines or puckering. Start the dart 1" (2.5 cm) or so below the widest part of your chest and extend down to mid-hip. Trial the dart by basting it in, then adjust as needed. If you need to take out more than 1" (2.5 cm) or so on each side, consider spreading it out over multiple darts. The main waist dart should generally align with or point toward the bust point in front or the shoulder blade in back; additional darts are typically placed between this point and the side seam.

If you determine that a dart needs to be moved up or down, you can do this on the pattern by cutting a box around the entire dart and taping it in the correct position, then redrawing the surrounding seam (**A**). If the dart needs to be shorter or longer, first fold it in half, matching up the legs to find the center line. Place the new dart point on this line and redraw the legs to the new point, starting from the stitching line as opposed to the edge of the seam allowance (**B**).

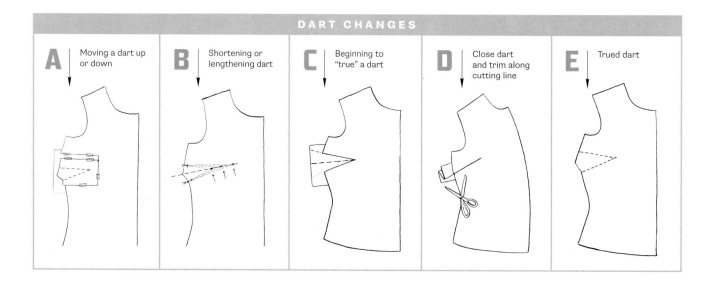

	DART CHANGES			
A Moving a dart up or down	**B** Shortening or lengthening dart	**C** Beginning to "true" a dart	**D** Close dart and trim along cutting line	**E** Trued dart

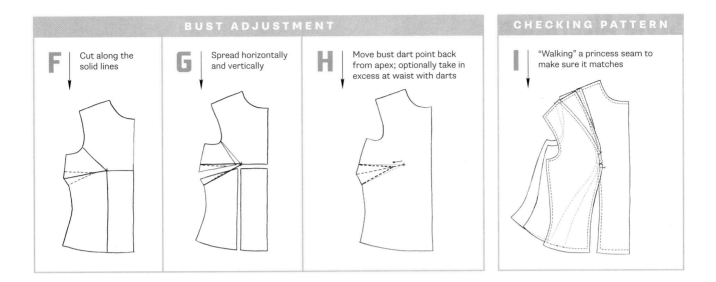

F Cut along the solid lines

G Spread horizontally and vertically

H Move bust dart point back from apex; optionally take in excess at waist with darts

I "Walking" a princess seam to make sure it matches

After altering any dart that extends to the seam allowance, fold it closed and trim along the pattern cutting line to "true" the end so it can be caught in the seam (**C-E**).

BUST ADJUSTMENTS

This one is a little more complicated, but it's worth getting right. Although I will give an overview here, for best results, consult a fitting book like the ones on page 203 for more detailed instructions. Remember those averages I explained earlier? Most women's patterns are designed for a B cup, which for the purposes of the pattern means that your full bust measurement is 2" (5 cm) larger than your chest measurement (above the breasts, under the armpits.) If your bust size is larger than that, you don't want to just increase the pattern size because then the shoulders and neckline will end up baggy. Instead, you should choose the size that matches your chest measurement and perform a full bust adjustment (FBA) to give you more room. A FBA involves slashing the pattern and spreading it at key areas to account for a fuller bust: see (**F-H**) to understand how it's done. This adds both length and width; you can get an idea of how much length is needed by measuring from the top of your shoulder (by the neck) down over the fullest part of your breast to the waist, and comparing this to the same measurement on the pattern. Make any general length or shoulder adjustments first, to avoid confusing the issue.

CHECKING THE ALTERED PATTERN

After making changes to a pattern, you should always make sure that everything still lines up the way it should. If you haven't drawn in the stitching lines on the pattern piece, you should do so now. "Walk" the seams by matching up the stitching lines for each seam in your garment, to make sure they're the same length and all the notches match (**I**). If the two sides of a seam have different curves, as with princess seams, match them up as far as they will go, stick a pin into the tissue to hold your place, and pivot the pieces to match up the next section of the seam. Continue in this way until the end of the seam. If the seam lines are mismatched or the notches don't align, you may need to add or remove length in the appropriate areas of the pattern pieces until they agree.

If one side of the seam is supposed to be gathered or eased, like sleeves, the seam lines will be different lengths by design. You can still make sure that the amount of ease makes sense for the pattern and your fabric (see page 59).

Finally, it's a good idea to make sure that the seam and edge intersections are all square. Check that the front and back pieces join smoothly at side seams and shoulders, and redraw the cutting line on both pieces to smooth out any irregularities. Check the center front and back as well, especially if pieces will be cut on the fold, to avoid any unintentional points or notches in hems and necklines.

Style Alterations

Sometimes a pattern might need a little customization to make it more like your character's costume. As long as the overall shape and fit looks right, you can make lots of relatively simple changes—alter the length of sleeves and skirts or swap them out for a completely different style, for example.

You can also reshape necklines and collars, and you can add new seams or even move the existing ones. If you like the shape of one pattern and the details of another, you can create a mash-up that combines your favorite bits of both. Some imagination and a little technique is all you need.

Making a Custom Body Pattern or Dress Form

For some projects, adjusting a pre-existing pattern to fit may be more trouble than it's worth. For extremely fitted garments that need to hug and mold your body, like corsets, evening gowns, and boned bodysuits, you can use plastic wrap and duct tape to create your own pattern directly from your body. You will definitely need a buddy for this, as moving or bending once you've started will be difficult or impossible, and may compromise the fit of the finished pattern. Also, keep a pair of safety scissors on hand so you can abort in a hurry if it gets too uncomfortable.

Wear a close-fitting t-shirt or leotard that covers the entire area you're patterning. If it's a shirt you're willing to sacrifice, you can tape directly on the fabric; otherwise tightly wrap the area with plastic wrap before you begin. Stand naturally and have your assistant start wrapping you with duct tape, using short horizontal segments to avoid wrinkles and overlapping the tape strips to make it nice and stable. If you're making a body-shaping corset, have your assistant pull the tape a bit snug so it compresses your waist the way you'd like the finished corset to do. Continue the tape a little bit past where the edges of your finished pattern will be—you'll cut off the excess later.

Grab a permanent marker and draw in the outline of your finished garment. Mark the center front and back lines, side seams, shaping seams, and any other details you want to include. When you're happy, use the safety scissors to cut along the center front line so you can get the body form off. Leave one half of the form intact for reference, and cut the other half apart along your seam lines. Each piece should lie more or less flat; if it doesn't, you'll need to add some additional darts or seam lines to get a good fit. Trace the pieces onto a piece of paper, use a curved ruler to neaten up the shapes (remembering that discrepancies as small as ⅛"/3 mm can compromise fit), and add seam allowances. It's a good idea to sew a mock-up before continuing with your good fabric, in case anything got thrown off in the translation from tape to pattern.

You can also use this same method to make a custom dress form that exactly duplicates your shape. To do this, you'll want to make sure you wrap all the way out to the end of your shoulders, and down to the widest point of your hips (or thighs, if you want a form you can use for bodysuits). Use a couple extra layers of tape to give the form some rigidity. After removing the form, tape it back together, insert a hanger to support it while you work on it, and tape across the arm and neck openings. Then you can stuff the form with newspaper or packing peanuts to maintain the shape, and close off the base with a piece of cardboard and more tape.

NECKLINES

Redrawing a neckline is one of the simplest and most obvious ways you can adapt a pattern for your own purposes. It's easiest when the pattern has a fairly high neckline to begin with, because then you can simply draw in the new shape. (On the Blouse pattern, page 131, options for both a high and V neckline are already drawn for you.) Make sure the front and back match up nicely at the shoulder seams, and hold it up to your body to check proportions. Then you can add seam allowances and cut off the excess, and you're pretty much good to go. That said, there are a few subtleties to keep in mind that will give you better results.

Very wide or deep necklines tend to be unstable. If there's a long bias edge in your neckline, as with a deep V, you'll need to stabilize it or even ease the edge slightly (see page 59) to prevent it from sagging out of shape and gaping away from your body. At the very least you should staystitch (see page 54) the seam line, but a strip of interfacing (see page 32) or organza sewn into the seam will be more secure. On stretch fabrics, elastic is often the best solution.

Also, if a neckline is deep in both front and back, you might have trouble keeping it on your shoulders. Hidden loops that snap around your bra straps are one solution for this, or you can add a tie or piece of clear elastic that connects the shoulders across the back of the neck. Alternatively, you can fill in the neckline with sheer mesh that will be invisible from a distance but keep everything nice and secure. Necklines that are low in front and high in back or vice versa are less likely to be a problem this way.

If the neckline will be finished with a facing, you'll need to create a new one to match the new shape. Do this by putting a sheet of tracing paper on top of the altered pattern piece and tracing the neck and shoulder shape, then drawing in the new facing below. Trim about ⅛" (3 mm) off the shoulder edge, tapering to nothing at the neck seam, to help it lie nice and flat when turned inside (**A**-**B**). If the garment is lined (see page 69), use the altered outer piece as a template to redraw the neck lining as well. If you're using a bias facing or band (see page 65), make sure you cut it to the appropriate length for the new neck shape.

ADDING POCKETS

Every costume needs somewhere to stash your stuff, right? Adding pockets is a really simple pattern alteration that can make your outfit much more functional. The type of pocket you add will depend on the style and fit of your costume, and some are much more challenging than others. Here are a couple of simple techniques.

SIDE SEAM POCKETS. These are unobtrusive and easy to sew. They're a great choice for looser-fitting garments like tunics and full skirts, but can be a little bulky and difficult to use on close-fitting outfits. To create a side seam pocket, first decide where you'd like it to be placed. Place a piece of tracing paper on top of the pattern piece, and trace the side seam for the length of the pocket opening. This needs to be wide enough to get your hand into, about 5" to 6" (12.7 to 15.2 cm). Draw in the rest of the pocket bag, using the shape of your hand as a rough guide (**A**, page 82). To prevent your stuff from falling out, make sure the deepest point of the pocket is below the side opening. Add seam allowances all the way around the pocket, and make sure you mark the main pattern piece for placement. To actually sew the pocket, see steps 2 and 3 of the Coat pattern (page 150).

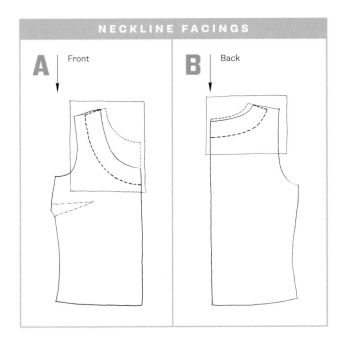

NECKLINE FACINGS

A Front

B Back

PATCH POCKETS. Although these are visible from the outside, they work well for some styles (to keep them invisible, you can add them to the lining instead). It's best to add them before the garment is assembled. Draw the shape of your

pocket on pattern paper or directly on a piece of fabric, leaving seam allowance all the way around so you can turn the edges under. Finish the top edge first (**B**), then press the edges under (**C**). If your fabric frays a lot, you can line the pockets before attaching them (**D**, **E**) or overlock the edges. Attach to your garment with topstitching or edgestitching (**F**) (see page 55).

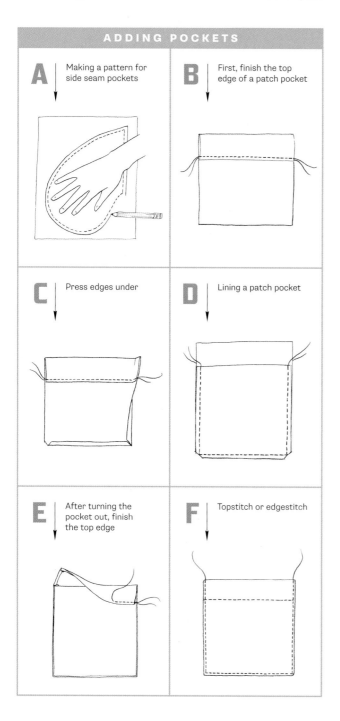

ADDING POCKETS

A | Making a pattern for side seam pockets

B | First, finish the top edge of a patch pocket

C | Press edges under

D | Lining a patch pocket

E | After turning the pocket out, finish the top edge

F | Topstitch or edgestitch

FRANKENPATTERNING

If you want to substitute a distinctive feature onto a pattern you like, you can use a method called "frankenpatterning." This involves finding a pattern that has the details you want, or something close, and copying the pieces over to the pattern you're using for the rest of the costume.

Collars and sleeves are some of the most unique features on many costumes, and while it's possible to create a new pattern piece yourself, there are a lot of pitfalls involved in getting the proportions and attachment exactly right. Frankenpatterning is a solution to this dilemma. To use a collar from a different pattern, you also need to copy the neck opening so that the pieces will match up correctly. Put the pattern you're copying down first, and your main costume pattern on top. Make sure both patterns line up at center front, center back, and the shoulders. Trace the neckline, including any marks or guidelines, onto your front and back pieces. In (**G**), the neckline from the Blouse (see page 131) is being copied to the Leotard (see page 107) so it can be used with the sailor collar. (In this example, snaps would need to be added to the crotch of the Leotard because the collar will stretch less than the original neckline.)

To substitute one sleeve for another, you repeat this process with the armhole instead of the neckline. This can be a little trickier because different patterns have different amounts of ease in the side seams, so you should try to pick patterns with roughly the same overall fit to copy from. Overlay the front and back pieces of your main costume pattern on the corresponding pieces of the pattern you're copying, matching the shoulder point on the template pattern up with the shoulder seam on your main pattern. Trace in the new armhole shape, which may start higher or lower than the old one, and make the shoulder wider or

G | Copying a neckline

H | Mark and then cut along the pleat line

I | Insert twice the finished pleat width

J | Fold and pin the pleat closed and true edges

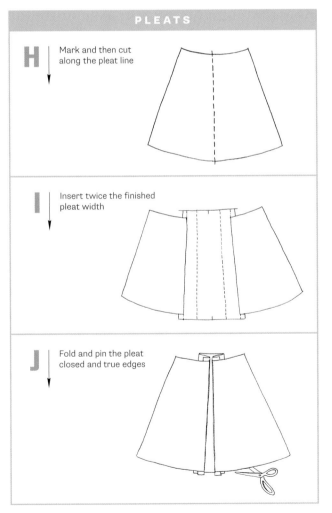

narrower. Tape in more tissue if needed, and blend the new underarm position into the original side seams. After you've copied the shapes, match up the front and back pieces at the side seams and shoulder points. Smooth out any points or jags where the pieces meet so the curve is continuous. This is an inexact method, so you may want to add a little extra seam allowance in the areas you've altered and baste the pieces in place for a trial run before sewing them permanently. For best results, practice on a mock-up first.

You can also use frankenpatterning to swap in a different skirt on a dress pattern, or to copy a detail from an untried pattern onto one that you've already fitted and perfected. It's also the easiest way to add more complicated types of pockets to your costume, including welt pockets, gusseted cargo pockets, and so forth. Look for a pattern that has the type of pocket you need; the placement doesn't matter, but try to avoid choosing one that has a seam running across the pocket location.

GATHERS AND PLEATS

To add gathers or pleats to your garment, you basically need to add extra width in the desired area. This is one way to add width to a skirt or sleeve, or you can use it as a design detail. For gathers, you want to distribute the extra width evenly across the gathered area. For pleats, you're going to pattern each pleat individually, so you can fold up the paper pattern and get an idea of what the finished garment will look like.

PLEATS. To add a pleat, first draw a line across the pattern where you would like the visible fold to appear (**H**). For a pleat that disappears or tapers to nothing, stop at the seam line on the opposite side of the pattern piece. If you're adding width overall, continue all the way through the seam line. Determine how deep you want your pleat to be, and spread the pattern pieces by twice that amount (for box pleats, page 18, you'll add this amount to both sides of the dividing line). Tape a piece of pattern paper into the gap, extending slightly beyond the base pattern at both ends of the pleat (**I**), and fold the pleat up as it will be in the finished garment. Pin the pleat closed, and cut along the original outline of the pattern to "true" the edges of the pleat (**J**).

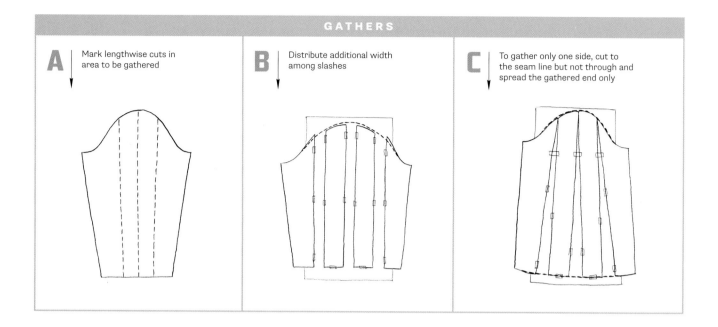

A Mark lengthwise cuts in area to be gathered

B Distribute additional width among slashes

C To gather only one side, cut to the seam line but not through and spread the gathered end only

GATHERS. To add gathers, first mark the beginning and end of the gathered area on your pattern and measure the distance between them. Draw several dividing lines across this span, spaced 1" to 2" (2.5 to 5 cm) apart (**A**). You will cut either up to the far seam line or all the way through, depending on the desired results. Above, volume is added all the way down a sleeve in (**B**), but it is gathered into the original sleeve opening, while in (**C**), volume is added at the wrist only and gathered into a cuff. Determine how full you want the gathers: the area to be gathered should be at least one and a half times the finished width to avoid looking skimpy, but can go up to three times the finished width or more if the fabric is lightweight and easy to gather. Divide the additional width evenly among your slashes and tape paper into the gaps. Draw a line that connects the segments of the original pattern edge into a smooth curve and cut out your new piece. Mark the beginning and ending points of the gathers on both the gathered piece and the piece it's sewn to, and write the finished width of the gathered area on your piece so you can remember when you sew the garment.

You can also transform a dart into gathers by marking a fixed distance above and below the dart and gathering the edge down to this measurement, or by creating several slashes that converge at the point of the dart. If you then fold the dart closed, the slashes will open up, allowing you to place the gathers in an entirely different seam (**E**, **F**).

ADDING SEAMS

Creating new seam details is another way to customize a pattern. You can use seams to incorporate blocks of a different color or texture, to insert piping (see page 92), or just break up the lines of a garment. You don't necessarily have to mess with the shape of the garment to do this, and although it makes the assembly a little more complicated, it can really make a difference in the verisimilitude of a costume.

The trick when adding new seams to a pattern is getting the proportions correct. If you're comfortable working with flat patterns and can picture how the pieces will go together, then you can simply draw the new seam lines on the tissue, cut them apart, and add seam allowances to each side. Make sure you copy the grain line onto each piece, and add notches to help you match up the pieces (**G**, **H**). If you have a good reference available, you can measure

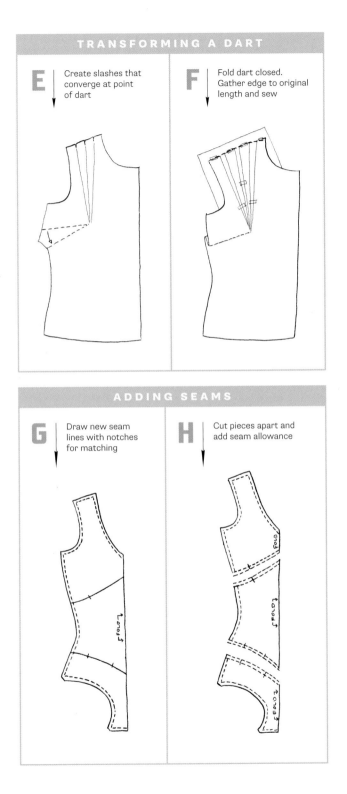

TRANSFORMING A DART

E Create slashes that converge at point of dart

F Fold dart closed. Gather edge to original length and sew

ADDING SEAMS

G Draw new seam lines with notches for matching

H Cut pieces apart and add seam allowance

it and scale the proportions to your own body to help you place the lines correctly (see page 14).

If you prefer a more hands-on approach, start by sewing a mock-up of the garment in inexpensive fabric. Put it on a dress form or similarly sized friend, and draw in your seam lines with marker or mark them with narrow strips of tape. (If you have a buddy you trust to draw the seams while *you* wear the costume, then so much the better.) Take a couple photos for reference later when putting the pieces back together, label each piece, and make sure you add notches for matching. Then, cut the pieces apart and either use the mock-up as a pattern or transfer everything to pattern paper so you can use it over and over. This method is especially good for creating detailed bodysuits, since it can be difficult to predict what a flat pattern will look like when stretched for wear. Just make sure your mock-up fabric has the same amount of stretch as the material you'll be using for your final version.

To assemble a garment after you've added seams, the simplest approach is to sew the new seams first, re-assembling the original pattern pieces, and then continue with the original construction method. For more complicated piecing, you may need to plan out the order of construction more carefully to avoid having to sew a lot of tricky corners. Remember that sewing straight lines will nearly always have less potential for error than trying to pivot mid-seam, although sometimes the latter is unavoidable. For extremely complex designs, you may find that appliqué is a better method than piecing (see page 89).

COMPLEX STYLE MODIFICATIONS

If your sewing skills allow, you can also make more complicated style changes to customize a pattern. Although not covered in this book, you can add many of the features mentioned in Chapter 1, Step 4: Identify Design Elements (see page 14), as well as in the style glossary on page 198, such as gussets, godets, flounces, and different types of sleeves and collars. Refer to the Resources on page 203 for suggestions on advanced sewing and tailoring references.

CHAPTER 5

TRIMS AND EMBELLISHMENTS

You've planned out the broad strokes of your costume, with fabric and pattern and construction techniques. Now it's time to nail the details, whether that means appliqué or embroidery or picking out exactly the right lace.

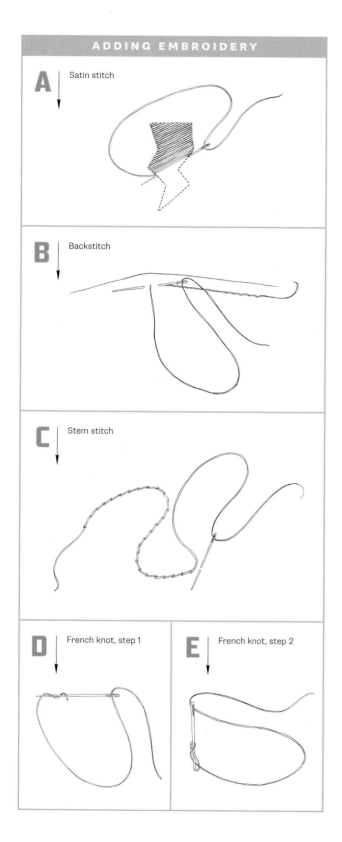

A Satin stitch

B Backstitch

C Stem stitch

D French knot, step 1

E French knot, step 2

When to Embellish

It's natural to think of trims as a last finishing touch, but on many projects, the embellishment might actually be the first thing you do. For instance, if you're doing a lot of embroidery, it may be easier to work on an uncut piece of fabric so that you can stretch it evenly on a frame or hoop. If you plan to sew trims on by machine, attaching them before you assemble the garment makes the pieces much easier to maneuver and allows you to catch the ends in the seams for a clean finish. If nothing else, you want to attach them before the garment is lined (see page 69), so the stitching is neatly hidden inside. If you're attaching trims by hand, you can do it at any stage, but you may still find it easier to work with smaller components instead of a full garment.

When you're putting a lot of effort into embellishing a garment, it's a good idea to do a trial run of the pattern first so that you can check the fit and work out any construction issues. You don't want to pour your heart into the embellishment only to discover that the finished product is unwearable. Many types of embellishment make the fabric stiffer, so you should allow a bit more ease than you usually would. A mock-up is also a good opportunity to check the placement and proportions of your embellishments; you can do this by pinning trims in place or drawing in embroidery and appliqué designs with a marker.

Adding Embroidery

Time-consuming it may be, but embroidery is a beautiful and durable way to add detailing to your projects. It's especially common on historical styles and on anything intended to look rich and luxurious.

While there's no reason to limit yourself to basic rayon embroidery floss, it's cheap, easy to work with, and available in a plethora of colors. The most common type comes as a thick yarn composed of six smaller strands, which should be separated before you start stitching. Two or three strands makes a good thickness for many projects, but plan on experimenting and doing a few samples to find the look that works best for your fabric and project. Cotton, silk, wool, fine ribbon, and many other types of decorative thread and yarn can also be used to produce different embroidered effects.

There's a whole world of hand embroidery stitches and techniques out there, and if it's something that interests you, there are lots of books that will fill in the details. But if you're just getting started, and especially if your references aren't specific about the technique that's being used, you can get by with just a few basics.

> **Satin stitch**, which consists of parallel lines of stitching, is good for filling large areas (**A**).
> **Backstitch** is good for outlining (**B**).
> **Stem stitch**—a backstitch on a slant with a slight overlap—makes a slightly bolder outline and works well on curves (**C**).
> **French knots** can be used for individual dots or adding texture. To make a French knot, hold the thread as it emerges from the fabric and wrap it over the needle at least twice (**D**), then stick the needle back into the fabric very close to the spot where it emerged (**E**). Hold the knot tight and close to the fabric as you pull the thread through to prevent loops.

If machine sewing is more your thing, even low-end mechanical machines usually have a decorative stitch or two, and you can get some interesting fill effects by zigzagging or straight stitching back and forth over an area in different directions. There are quite a few decorative threads designed for machine sewing, so experiment a bit and see what works for your project. Later on, if you get inspired, you may want to look into a machine with computerized embroidery features, but there's a lot you can do with a basic model in the meantime.

When embroidering on fine or lightweight fabrics, you'll need to stretch your fabric over a hoop or frame to keep it taut as you stitch. If this doesn't do the trick, or if you're doing your embroidery by machine, you may need to add a stabilizer. This can mean a liquid starch or starch alternative if your fabric is washable, a layer of interfacing on the back side, or a stabilizer product intended to be cut, torn, or dissolved away after the stitching is complete. Plastic-coated freezer paper works well as a tear-away—you can adhere it to the fabric with a warm (not hot!) iron, and it should peel away cleanly afterward. When you remove it, try to tear the paper without

tugging on your stitches. Dissolving, wash-out, or permanent stabilizers are better if the stitching will be very dense.

Doing Appliqué

Appliqué is the term for sewing one piece of fabric to another piece for decorative effect. Use this method for patches, insignias, and surface details that are too large for embroidery. In the standard version, the decorative piece is placed on top of the base fabric and stitched down around the edges. For reverse appliqué, the decorative patch is placed underneath, and the base fabric is cut away to reveal it after stitching. See this method in action on the Superhero 2 costume (see page 162).

After cutting out your appliqué, you'll need to secure it so that it doesn't shift or wrinkle while you sew it in place. Pins are sufficient if your materials are fairly stable and if the pins are small enough that they don't distort the fabric too much. In other cases, you might be better off with fusible web (see page 38), dissolvable tape, or a temporary spray adhesive. In a pinch, a washable glue stick will often work just fine. Hand basting also works well but can be time-consuming.

You should always sew your appliqués to make them permanent. Even if the glue or fusible web seems secure, it most likely won't hold up to wear and washing, and you don't want your cosplay to be ruined after just one time out. You can work by hand or by machine. If the appliqué fabric doesn't fray, you can sew it down with an ordinary straight stitch. More often, you'll need to cover or finish the edges somehow—with a satin stitch, which is like a very dense zigzag sewn all the way around the fabric edge, or by turning the edges under before you sew. If you're turning the edges under, sew a line of basting stitches just outside the fold line as a guide for folding and pressing (**A**, page 90). You may need to clip corners or cut wedges out around curves to avoid a lot of bulk under the appliqué, and the basting shows you where to stop.

Appliqué is also a useful technique for stretch fabrics, but you may need to stabilize the layers of fabric to prevent them from shifting or rippling as you work. A fusible or adhesive stabilizer is best because it prevents the fabric from stretching out of shape, but make sure your choice can

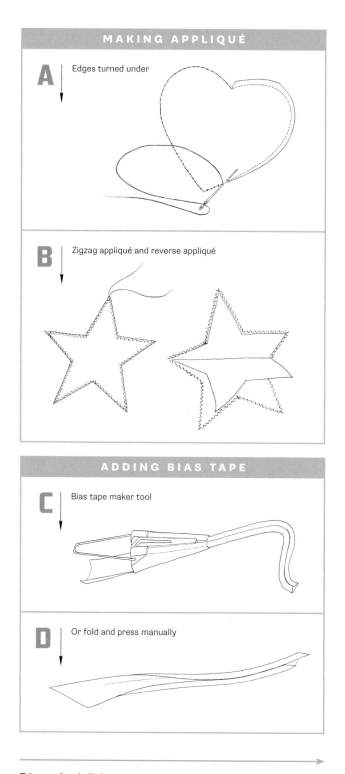

A Edges turned under

B Zigzag appliqué and reverse appliqué

C Bias tape maker tool

D Or fold and press manually

Trims and embellishments: 1. Iron-on embroidered trim **2.** Grosgrain ribbon **3.** Embroidered ribbon **4.** Velvet ribbon **5.** Lace trim **6.** Metallic ribbon **7.** Metallic braid **8.** Satin ribbon **9.** Soutache **10.** Stretch piping **11.** Middy braid

be fully removed when you're finished sewing—don't place it where it can get stuck between fabric layers unless it can be dissolved for removal. Sew with a medium zigzag stitch (about 3 mm width and 1.5 to 2.5 mm length) that just over-hangs the edge of the appliqué, or use a stretch stitch. Don't make the stitching too dense or it will ripple the fabric and make it difficult to fully remove any stabilizers. Use a walking foot if you have it to keep the layers perfectly aligned. In (**B**), regular applique is shown on the left, and reverse applique is shown on the right.

Adding Bias Tape

Trimming your costume doesn't have to mean anything fancy. Often, all you need is a line or stripe of bias tape in a contrasting color to add some pizzazz. Bias tape is great for embellishments because the flexibility allows you to shape it around curves without wrinkles and puckers, so it's a little easier to handle than a ribbon or twill tape. Many costumes use a contrast binding at the edges, so it does double duty as a decoration and functional finish.

If you're buying prepackaged bias tape, you want the double-fold type for binding edges and the single-fold type for flat surface embellishment. But don't limit yourself to the commercial stuff—for many costumes you'll need (or prefer) to make your own, so you can get the color and width exactly right. Use a see-through gridded ruler to mark your strips, and a rotary cutter and mat for quick, accurate cutting (see Cutting Bias Strips on page 66). The strips should be twice as wide as your finished tape for flat applications so you can turn the edges under, and four times as wide for binding. A bias tape maker tool is handy for making perfectly even folds (**C**), but you can also measure and fold by hand if you don't have one or need a different size (**D**).

I've already covered binding with bias tape (see page 68), and it works the same whether you're using a match-ing or decorative fabric. Flat tape can be stitched along both edges by machine, or with a hand fell stitch (see page 50) if you want the stitching to be invisible. For very compli-cated designs, you may want to use adhesive basting tape to secure the bias before you sew.

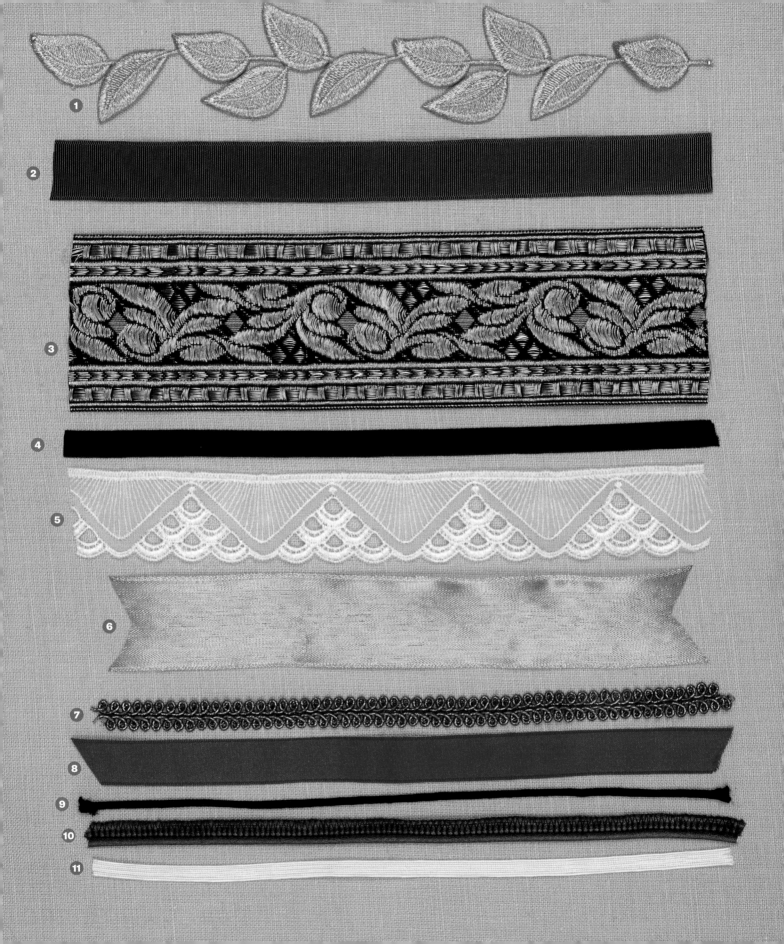

Inserting Piping

Piping is a fabric-wrapped cord that's inserted in seams to add dimension or contrast. You can find a limited range of colors in packages at the fabric store, but you can easily make custom piping to match your other materials. Choose a lightweight fabric, and cut bias strips (as described on page 66) that are twice the width of your seam allowance plus enough to wrap around the cord. Wrap the strips around a cord or string of the appropriate size (use 2 to 3 mm elastic cord if you need stretch piping) and baste it in place.

When you sew the seam, baste the piping to one or both seam allowances first, so the piping extends beyond the seam allowance (**A**), and use a zipper foot or piping foot to stitch as close to the cord as possible (**B**). Afterward, you may need to trim some bulk out of the seam allowances to make them sit smoothly. In places where piped seams intersect, work the cord out of the casing and trim away the portion that crosses into the seam allowance so you won't have a lump in the seam.

If you want the look of piping with less bulk, you can make flat piping from a folded strip of fabric with no cord. This can be a little trickier to sew accurately, since you don't have the cord as a guide for your stitching, so you'll have to be extra careful about measuring and basting.

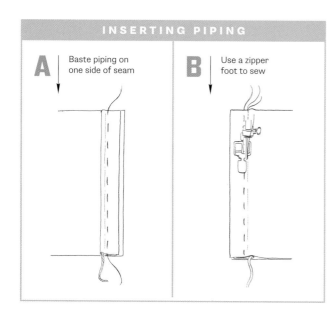

INSERTING PIPING

A Baste piping on one side of seam

B Use a zipper foot to sew

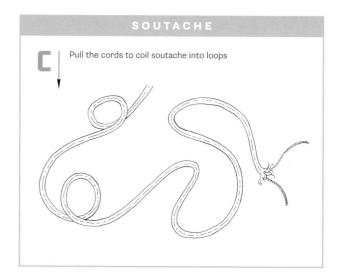

SOUTACHE

C Pull the cords to coil soutache into loops

Adding Braids and Cords

A word of advice when selecting these kinds of trim: if it looks like it belongs on a lampshade or couch, think hard before putting it on your body. That said, home decorating suppliers can be a great source for interesting cords and braids as long as you're selective. Stick with finer, more flexible trims to be safe.

GIMP. This is a decorative cord made by wrapping shiny rayon or silk fibers around a sturdy core. You can find it in plain form, or as the base material for a variety of braids. Some are very bulky, so be careful how you place them and make sure the underlying fabric is substantial enough to take it. Always finish the ends to prevent fraying, whether that means tucking them under, catching them in an intersecting seam, or binding them with thread or fabric.

SOUTACHE. This trim is similar to gimp, but it has two parallel threads at the core. This lends itself to a neat trick: by pulling on just one of the cords, you can draw the braid up into sharp curves for convoluted embellishments. If you see a jacket or uniform trimmed with intricate loops and whorls, you're probably looking at soutache. To create soutache embellishments, you'll want to shape the soutache first, holding it in place with pins as you pull the curves into position (**C**). Once you have it shaped and arranged the way you want, you can stitch along the channel between the cords to permanently secure it.

Hand stitching is the most unobtrusive way to attach braids and cords, because you can use an invisible fell stitch (see page 50) or tuck your threads into the pattern of the braid. If you need something quicker and aren't worried about a little of the thread showing, you can machine sew with a straight or zigzag stitch—whichever works better with the pattern of your trim. Narrow braids and cords can also be secured by sewing across them with decorative thread, a technique called couching: sew the trim with a wide zig-zag stitch right over the top, or wrap it with a whipstitch by hand. See couching used to sew on beads on page 94.

Using Ribbon

Ribbons may be satin, velvet, grosgrain (ribbed), metallic, embroidered, printed, or novelty weaves. You can find them single or double-sided, and some have wired edges that help them hold their shape in loops and bows. When attaching ribbons to garments, note that some of them aren't as flexible as braids and cords. Stick with straight line applications, or sew tucks or darts to shape them around corners and curves. (One exception is rayon Petersham ribbon, which looks like grosgrain with a tiny scalloped edge—though sometimes tricky to find, this stuff takes well to shaping with steam, so with a little finesse, you can give it a nice curve.)

Attach ribbons with a straight stitch along each edge, thread them through slits or eyelets, or try making ruffles or pleats with them (a bonus—they don't need to be hemmed). If you want long dangling ribbons, choose a two-sided type for the prettiest effect. If you're sewing the ribbon down, though, a one-sided type is fine.

Applying Lace

Depending on the type and placement, lace can look sweet, sexy, or simply luxurious. It also makes a great substitute for large-scale embroidery like you find on some historical-style garments. However, lace can be tricky to get right, because

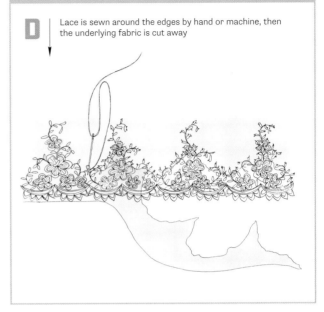

SCALLOPED LACE EDGE

D | Lace is sewn around the edges by hand or machine, then the underlying fabric is cut away

it can take some hunting to find the perfect type and quality, and cheap lace can look very cheap indeed (which might work for some characters, but not where royalty is concerned). It's difficult to generalize given the variety of laces available, but keep in mind that good lace should *feel* good—not scratchy or stiff—and while it may be lustrous, it shouldn't look plasticky or shiny. Lace usually isn't available in many colors, but white is almost always one of them, so you can dye it yourself if you get the appropriate dye for the fiber type. Lace is available as a trim in varying widths and as yardage.

The nice thing about sewing with lace is that the busy designs are great at hiding seams, so you can piece together motifs from different parts of a lace fabric for a custom pattern. Since many laces don't fray, you don't have to worry about turning the edges under—just trim around the edge of the motif, overlap the pieces, and join them with a small zig-zag stitch or hand whipstitch. You can cut away the lower layer afterward if you don't want it to show through; just use a sharp pair of trimming scissors and cut close to the stitching. Create lacy cutouts by sewing a lace appliqué and then cutting away the backing, or trim around the contours of a lace border design and apply it to an edge or hem for a fancy scalloped effect (**D**).

Adding Sparkly Stuff

Beads, sequins, paillettes (similar to a sequin, but larger), and rhinestones definitely amp up the drama on your costume. Depending on the type and quantity of embellishments, it may make sense to sew, glue, or even buy pre-embellished fabric.

Beads are best attached by sewing. You can sew them individually, or if your design calls for unbroken rows, you can use a couching stitch to attach a pre-strung strand (**A**), making a stitch every few beads or so. If you're working with loose beads, pour them out onto a piece of felt or a velvet-lined tray to make them easier to pick up. For the small openings on seed and bugle beads, you'll probably need a beading needle, but in other cases any small fine needle will do. Use a strong thread like silk or nylon beading thread for small beads, and heavyweight thread or even dental floss for large beads. If the beads are over ¼" (6 mm) in diameter or heavy, you should sew through each one at least twice for a secure hold. Knot the thread often, so that your work doesn't all unravel if a stitch breaks somewhere.

Beads, especially metal or glass beads, can add a lot of weight to a garment. Make sure your base fabric can take it, and add reinforcement if necessary. If your fabric is opaque, consider a layer of fusible or sew-in interfacing behind the beaded area. For sheers, an underlining of silk organza is a great way to support dense embellishment without losing the delicate effect.

Sequined fabrics and trims are widely available and may be the most efficient option if you want to cover a large area (see page 71 for working with such specialty fabrics). If you're sewing loose sequins in rows, you can use an overlapping pattern to hide the threads (**B**). To attach individual scattered sequins, bring your needle up through the hole, pick up a seed bead in a matching color, and go back down through the same hole. The bead anchors the sequin so the thread isn't visible (**C**).

Larger rhinestones sometimes come with holes for sewing or with metal claw settings, but most smaller types are designed to be glued. A good quality glue is important unless you like shedding sparkles wherever you go—look for heavy-duty adhesives or glues specifically designed for attaching jewels to fabric, if possible. To avoid smearing a lot

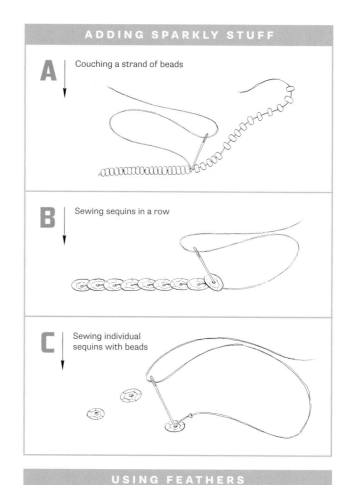

ADDING SPARKLY STUFF

A Couching a strand of beads

B Sewing sequins in a row

C Sewing individual sequins with beads

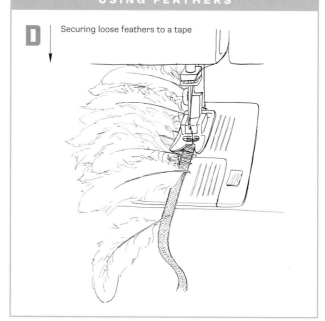

USING FEATHERS

D Securing loose feathers to a tape

of glue where you don't want it, use a toothpick or syringe-style nozzle to apply it and a pair of tweezers to pick up and place your stones. Alternatively, look for "hot fix" stones that come with a pre-applied heat-activated adhesive. These are a popular option for athletic and performance costumes, so they should hold up to cosplay abuse just fine. Just note that you'll also need a heat tool to attach them, and not all materials can tolerate the temperatures required, so you should test first.

Using Feathers, Flowers, and Other Delicacies

Feathers add a touch of fantasy to any outfit, for effects both angelic and villainous. Working with feathers is a lot easier if you buy them pre-assembled into a ribbon trim, which you can apply in rows to cover large areas. If you get them loose, consider attaching them to a strip of ribbon or twill tape before sewing them to your costume. Use a straight or zigzag stitch with a short stitch length, pile the feathers in front of your machine, and line them up on top of the ribbon as you feed it through (**D**). This should secure the feathers firmly enough for easy handling, but you can also run a line of glue or fray blocker on top of the stitching for extra security. Then you can attach the feathers by basting along the ribbon edge. You can also glue your feathers, especially if you don't anticipate cleaning the piece after it's finished, but be judicious with your adhesives to avoid matting and stiffening the downy fluff.

If your costume calls for feathers, flowers, antique trims, painted items, or delicate handmade accessories, you may need to take a little bit of extra care in how you incorporate them. Often these details require special cleaning or can't be cleaned at all, so you should think about making them detachable so the rest of the costume can be washed normally. Snaps and hook-and-loop tape are good for some situations, or you can attach the fragile elements with a loose basting stitch that can be removed as needed. For accessories that you want to attach and remove at will, magnets are another option. You can often find them in stores that offer bag-making supplies.

Weathering and Distressing

Most characters lead eventful lives. Many of them are pretty hard on their clothes. Painful as it may be to think of intentionally damaging the costume you've labored over, a little artful weathering can make a huge difference in the realism of your look. This can be done in innumerable ways, and the technique you choose will depend on the materials involved. Natural fibers tend to take to distressing the best—they soften and fray beautifully when you beat on them, and they absorb stains and other treatments more readily. Synthetic fibers are mostly tougher, so they don't break down as easily or naturally, and some materials (like faux leather) tend to lose their realism when damaged. In those cases, you'll want to pick non-destructive weathering methods like painting. Always test distressing techniques on scraps before proceeding to your actual garment—in most cases, they are *not* reversible.

To create authentically frayed fabric, think abrasion: rub it with sandpaper, drag it over concrete, or attack it with a cheese grater. Think about where your character's clothes would wear out the fastest—at hems and edges, elbows and knees. Machine washing the garment afterward can help to loosen the threads and fluff them up so the damage looks like it occurred gradually, and abusing the fabric by washing on hot and drying on high can help to give it a "lived-in" look. If you want clean cuts and slashes, for example on a character who fights with blades, you can make them with a razor blade or craft knife and cutting mat.

Also, think about how age and wear will affect the colors of your fabrics. Tea, coffee, and unsweetened cocoa powder can be used to create a variety of muddy, stained, or yellowed effects. If you want the fabric to look faded, this can be done in some cases by spraying with diluted bleach. Use gloves and protect your work surface with plastic if you try this method, and make sure you're working in a well-ventilated area. Don't use bleach on materials like silk or wool as it will destroy the fibers. Alternatively, you can try your hand at painting the fabric with fabric paint and a dry brush (which helps to create uneven textured effects). You can use white or gray paint to simulate fading, or darker colors to imitate dirt and grime.

PART TWO

PATTERNS

Now that you've learned the basics about sewing and embellishing, here are eleven basic patterns that you can use as a starting point for your own costumes. Use the charts on page 188 to decide what size you need. Each pattern is written in either men's sizes, women's sizes, or is unisex, and the sizing type is noted on each pattern. This is not to say that you can't make a man's pattern for a woman or vice versa, but be aware that you may need to adjust the length and other proportions if you do. To make other fit adjustments, refer Chapter 4, Adjustments and Alterations, on page 73. All of the patterns assume the use of a sewing machine, but feel free to substitute a serger or hand sewing where appropriate.

CAPE

Capes may have their naysayers, but is there anything more fun to wear than the most iconic of superhero accoutrements? This luxuriously swishy rendition is a generous half circle, with stacked box pleats at the shoulders. It's also kept on with snaps, so you can swiftly detach in the event of an emergency. Because you figure out your own fabric requirements for the cape based on some simple math, this pattern is good practice for the Pleated Skirt (page 125), for the Dress (page 143), and even for designing your own patterns further down the line.

TOOLS AND MATERIALS

▶ Sewing Essentials (see page 44)
▶ Lightweight fabric with a soft drape, such as blouse-weight cotton, silk/cotton blends, silky polyester, charmeuse, crepe de chine, or even lining fabric— amount based on step 1 (I used 3½ yds/3.2 m of 54"/137 cm wide gray plain-woven cotton shirting.)
▶ 10" (25.4 cm) of twill tape, ½" to 1" (1.3 to 2.5 cm) wide (Anything in this size range will work.)
▶ 1 yd (.9 m) of bias tape, ½" (1.3 cm) single-fold (optional)
▶ 6 large sew-on snaps
▶ Large safety pins
▶ All-purpose thread in a matching color
▶ Trim or decorative medallions for the shoulders (optional)

PATTERN PIECES

Pattern piece on sheet 4; see cutting layout on page 189
▶ **Cape:** fold the fabric widthwise and cut 1 on the fold; see steps 2 and 3 for details

NOTE

▶ Choose stable fabrics that don't stretch or fray much, and make sure that both the garment you're attaching the cape to and your chosen fastening method can stand up to the weight of the cape. If you want to use a heavy, bulky fabric like velvet, you may need to reinforce the attachment point with interfacing or a piece of twill tape behind the snap area. If you're attaching the cape to a stretch garment, stick with very lightweight fabrics for the cape to avoid straining the fabric.

INSTRUCTIONS

⅜" (1 cm) seam allowances are used for this pattern.

1 Begin by determining how much yardage you need to buy for your cape. The amount of fabric required will be twice your finished length + your shoulder width (measured across your back) + 16" (40.6 cm) for shoulder extensions and hem allowance. Excess width will fall into draped folds down your back, so if you like that look, feel free to exaggerate it by adding even more width to your shoulder width measurement. (Because the pattern is cut on the fold, any adjustment in the measurement should be halved when placing the template.) The maximum cape length will be the width of the fabric minus 9" (22.9 cm) unless you want to add a seam; for a long cape, make sure you're buying a sufficiently wide fabric. For this cape, 3½ yds (3.2 m) of 54"- (137 cm-) wide fabric was used, based on a finished length of 45" (114 cm) and a shoulder width of 16" (40.6 cm).

2 Fold the fabric along the cross grain, aligning the selvages. Place the cape template at the top of the folded edge, making sure to place the half-shoulder width mark at the appropriate distance from the fold. (Compare your shoulder width to the bar on the cape template to determine where to place the template on your fabric.) Use the pleat lines as a guide to extend the cape to the desired length, adding the same amount onto the end of each pleat line and at the center back (**A**).

3 Connect the marks into a smooth curve to create the hemline of your cape. Cut along the hem curve, around the top edge of the cape template, and parallel to the selvages for the straight front edge (it's best to trim the selvages off as they're more tightly woven than the rest of the cape and may pull or ripple). If there is a gap at the center back neckline, simply cut straight across to the fold. Mark the pleat positions with small snips in the seam allowance.

4 Sew a narrow or double-fold hem (see page 67) on the two straight front edges of the cape. Finish the curved neckline edge with a narrow bias facing, as shown on page 65 (**B**). The facing used here is a bias strip (see page 66) cut out of leftover cape fabric that is 1" (2.5 cm) wide and stitched on with a ⅜" (1 cm) seam allowance.

5 Use the snips you made in step 3 and the center notch as a general guide to form the pleats on each shoulder. Arrange the pleats to your liking and pin in place (**C**). For example, you may want to make the pleats shallower or deeper to adjust the amount of shoulder coverage. Make sure both sides match.

6 Place a 5" (12.7 cm) strip of twill tape on top of the end of the pleats on the right side of the fabric as shown in (**D**). Sew in place along the upper edge of the tape.

7 Wrap the ends of the twill tape around the edges and fold to the underside. Stitch around the edges of the tape through all layers. Attach the male side of the snaps to the twill tape (**E**) and the female side to the garment. Repeat steps 6 and 7 for the second shoulder.

8 Clip the shoulder pieces to a hanger and let the cape hang for a day or two so the fabric can relax. Pin the cape on a dress form or safety pin it to a helpful friend and check the length. Trim if necessary to make it nice and even and sew a narrow double-fold hem around the long curved edge (**F**). If you like, attach trim or decorative medallions to hide the shoulder ends.

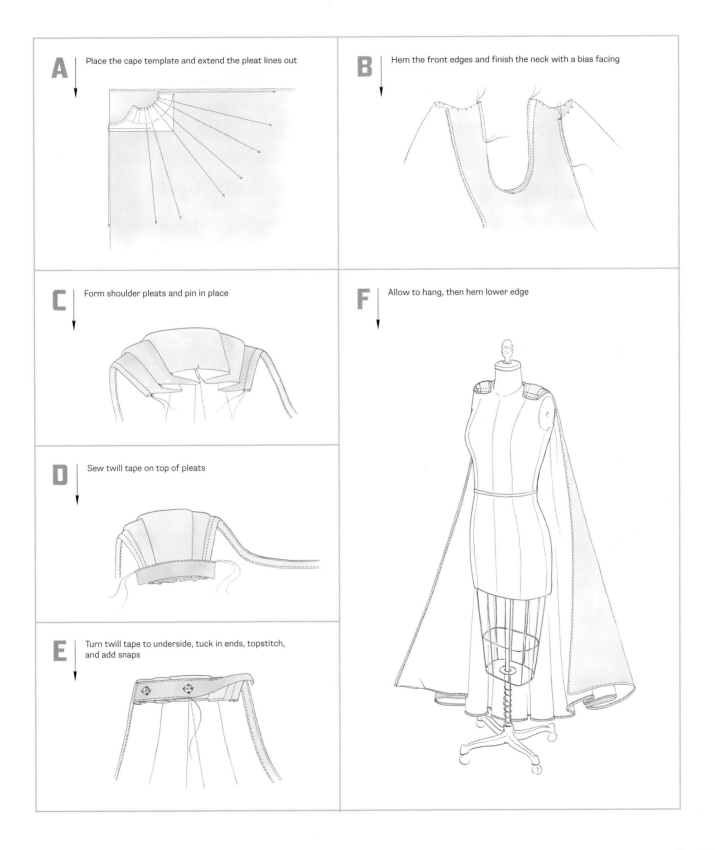

A Place the cape template and extend the pleat lines out

B Hem the front edges and finish the neck with a bias facing

C Form shoulder pleats and pin in place

D Sew twill tape on top of pleats

E Turn twill tape to underside, tuck in ends, topstitch, and add snaps

F Allow to hang, then hem lower edge

LEGGINGS

If you've never sewn four-way stretch fabrics before, leggings are a great place to start. Wear them for superheroing, with a tunic or doublet for fantasy/historical looks, as a base for armor pieces, or to supplement body paint when cosplaying characters with unusual skin colors. They're good for layering during chilly outdoor photo shoots, too. Or make them in a geeky print and wear them for your workout!

TOOLS AND MATERIALS

▶ Sewing Essentials (see page 44)
▶ 1⅓ yds (1.2 m) of 60" (152 cm) wide four-way stretch fabric, such as nylon/spandex or polyester/spandex tricot knits, cotton/spandex jersey, or stretch mesh (I used a brown brushed-finish poly/spandex knit with 100% stretch in both directions.)
▶ 1¼ yds (1.1 m) of 1" (2.5 cm) wide elastic for the waistband
▶ 100% polyester all-purpose thread in a matching color
▶ Stretch sewing machine needles (size 11/75)

PATTERN PIECES

Pattern pieces on sheet 1; see cutting layout on page 189
▶ **Leggings Front/Back:** cut 2 on the straight grain

NOTES

▶ This pattern is designed for four-way stretch fabric. If the leggings will be worn on their own, choose a substantial fabric that won't turn see-through when stretched.
▶ Use a serger, stretch, or zigzag stitch for assembly and a stretch, zigzag, or double-needle stitch for topstitching.

INSTRUCTIONS

⅜" (1 cm) seam allowances are used for this pattern.

1 With right sides together, sew the inseams (inner leg seams) of each legging piece to turn each leg into a tube (**A**).

2 Turn one leg right side out and slip it inside the other so the right sides face each other. Match up the inseams and center front and back edges and sew the U-shaped crotch seam (**B**).

3 Try the leggings on and wrap the elastic around your waist to determine a comfortable length. (You can also make any fit tweaks at this stage.) After cutting the elastic, stitch the ends of the elastic to join (see page 69).

4 Install the elastic with the stitched-and-turned method presented on page 69: Fold the loop in half to mark the center front and back, then match those marks up and fold the other way to mark the sides, dividing the loop into quarters. Pin the elastic inside the leggings waist, matching the quarter marks to the dots at the center front, center back, and halfway between on each side. Join with a zigzag (4 mm width/2 mm length) or serger stitch around the upper edge, stretching the elastic to match the waist opening (**C**). Do this by holding the fabric and elastic before and behind the presser foot, pulling evenly from both sides and allowing the feed dogs to move the fabric through. Takes a bit of practice, but you'll get it!

5 Roll the elastic to the inside and topstitch it in place with the same zigzag stitch, stretching just enough to get rid of any puckers in the fabric. Fold the hem allowance on each leg to the inside (since this is a knit, there's no need to finish the edge first) and topstitch with a zigzag to finish (**D**).

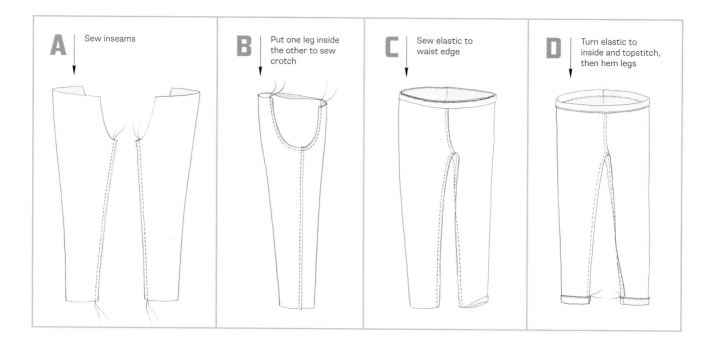

A Sew inseams

B Put one leg inside the other to sew crotch

C Sew elastic to waist edge

D Turn elastic to inside and topstitch, then hem legs

LEOTARD

Here's your superhero staple! This long-sleeved leotard is quick to sew, and it's designed with a high, wide neckline and a lower leg cut to stay put while you save the world (but you can easily redraw either to suit your preference). Appliqué your superhero crest on the front, or use it as a foundation under armor or other costume pieces. Once you're comfortable with the basic construction, you can think about adding decorative seaming or other details. It doesn't require a lot of fabric, so take the opportunity to experiment!

TOOLS AND MATERIALS

▶ Sewing Essentials (see page 44)
▶ 1¼ yds (1.1 m) of 60" (152 cm) wide four-way stretch spandex fabric, such as nylon/spandex or polyester/spandex tricot knits, cotton/spandex jersey, stretch velvet, or stretch mesh (I used blue nylon/spandex milliskin with 110% stretch in both directions.)
▶ 2½ yds (2.3 m) of ¼" (6 mm) elastic to finish the neckline and leg openings
▶ 100% polyester all-purpose thread in a matching color
▶ Stretch sewing machine needles (size 11/75)

PATTERN PIECES

Pattern pieces on sheet 1 ; see cutting layout on page 189
▶ **Leotard Front:** cut 1 on fold
▶ **Leotard Back:** cut 2 on straight grain
▶ **Leotard Sleeve:** cut 2 on straight grain

NOTES

▶ Either serge the seams or use a stretch or narrow zigzag stitch on your sewing machine.
▶ A zigzag or double-needle stitch is best for topstitching.

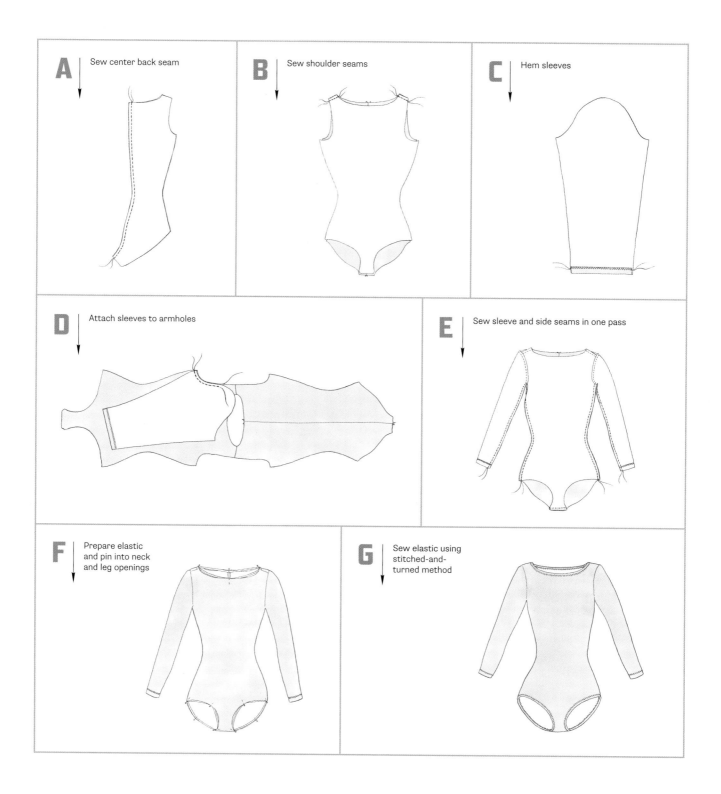

A Sew center back seam

B Sew shoulder seams

C Hem sleeves

D Attach sleeves to armholes

E Sew sleeve and side seams in one pass

F Prepare elastic and pin into neck and leg openings

G Sew elastic using stitched-and-turned method

INSTRUCTIONS

⅜" (1 cm) seam allowances are used for this pattern.

1 Place the back pieces with right sides together and sew the center back seam using a stretch or serger stitch as described on page 57 (**A**).

2 Stitch the front and back pieces together at the shoulder seams, right sides together (**B**).

3 Hem the sleeves with a zigzag, stretch, or double-needle stitch (**C**).

4 Pin the sleeves into the armholes, right sides together, matching the notch in the sleeve cap to the shoulder seam, and the others to the notches in the front and back armholes (**D**). Sew the entire seam, stretching the armhole slightly to match the curve of the sleeve. Make sure you remove the pins as you sew and don't stitch over them, especially if you're using a serger.

5 With right sides together, sew the crotch seam. Align the front and back along the side seam, making sure the armhole seam matches up at the underarm, and sew continuously from the wrist down to the leg opening on each side (**E**).

6 Cut three pieces of elastic to finish the openings at the neck and legs. The elastic should be about ½" (1.3 cm) shorter than each opening, stitched together at the ends to form a loop. Divide the elastic and opening into quarters and pin at each quarter, then sew the elastic to the inside of the opening, ⅛" (3 mm) inside the cut edge, with a zigzag or serger stitch, stretching the elastic to match the opening (**F**).

7 Roll the elastic to the inside to make a clean edge and secure with a zigzag or double-needle stitch to finish (**G**). This is the stitched-and-turned method of applying elastic (see page 69).

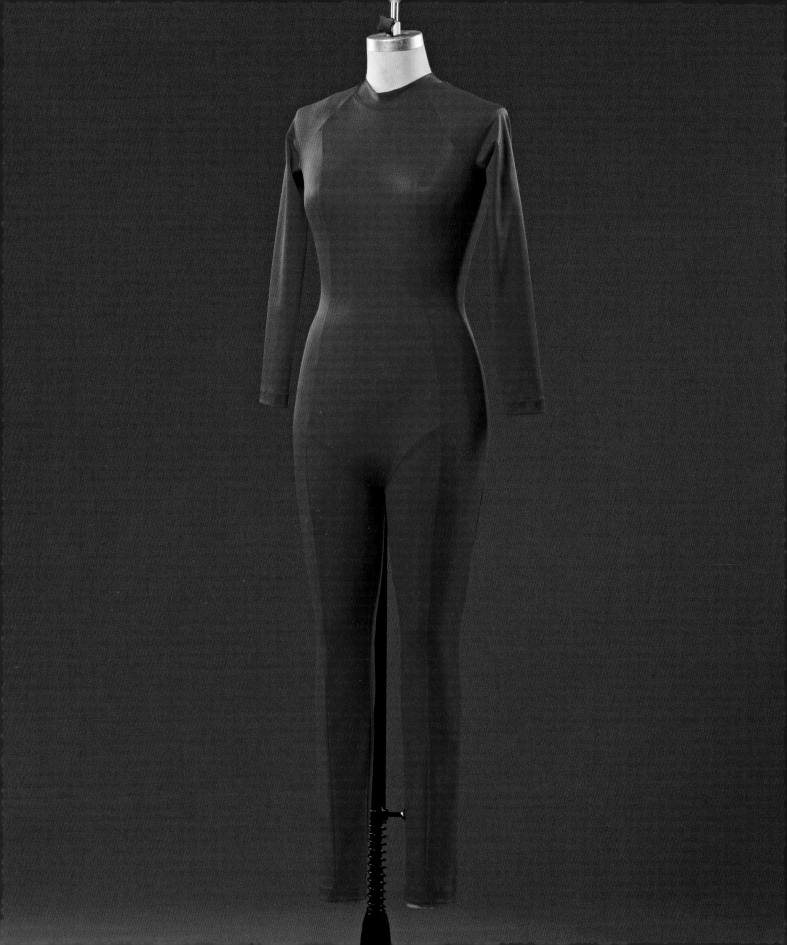

SEAMED JUMPSUIT

If you want to make one of the intricate, textured jumpsuits that are common in science fiction movies and games, or a bodysuit fit for a cinematic version of a superhero, you'll want to venture beyond basic spandex. This jumpsuit is designed with a little more shape than a simple leotard, and has seams that allow for more precise fit adjustments. I've also included a few fun variations to the basic pattern, so you can easily customize the design. Use this piece as an opportunity to experiment with mixing fabrics, seaming details like piping and topstitching, or other decorative techniques to take your project up a notch. If you're really ambitious, a structured jumpsuit makes a great foundation for more elaborate costumes with lights, armor, and more.

TOOLS AND MATERIALS

▶ Sewing Essentials (see page 44)
▶ 2½ yds (2.3 m) of 60" (152 cm) wide medium to heavyweight four-way stretch knit, such as milliskin, moleskin spandex, scuba knit, rayon/nylon/spandex Ponte knit, or stretch pleather (I used red matte-finish nylon/spandex tricot with 80% horizontal/60% vertical stretch.)
▶ 20" to 22" (51 to 56 cm) invisible zipper
▶ 3" (7.6 cm) or so of ⅛" (3 mm) wide flat elastic for the button loops
▶ Two ½" (1.3 cm) ball-type buttons, in a matching color
▶ 100% polyester all-purpose thread in a matching color
▶ Stretch sewing machine needles (size 11/75 or 12/80)

PATTERN PIECES

Pattern pieces on sheet 2; see cutting layout on page 189
▶ **Seamed Jumpsuit Front:** cut 1 on fold
▶ **Seamed Jumpsuit Side Front:** cut 2 on straight grain
▶ **Seamed Jumpsuit Back:** cut 2 on straight grain
▶ **Seamed Jumpsuit Side Back:** cut 2 on straight grain
▶ **Seamed Jumpsuit Front Inner Leg:** cut 2 on straight grain
▶ **Seamed Jumpsuit Back Inner Leg:** cut 2 on straight grain
▶ **Seamed Jumpsuit Sleeve:** cut 2 on straight grain
▶ **Seamed Jumpsuit Back-Opening Collar:** cut 1 on fold
For variations only:
▶ **Seamed Jumpsuit Halter Collar:** cut 1 on fold (for halter jumpsuit variation)
▶ **Seamed Jumpsuit Front-Opening Collar:** cut 2 on fold (for zip-front jumpsuit variation)

NOTES

▶ Choose heavyweight spandex or any knit with good recovery and at least some stretch in both directions for comfort and mobility. Depending on your specific fabric, you may need to adjust the size, so leave a little extra seam allowance in the side seams in case you want to let them out.
▶ If you make the halter variation of this pattern, you will only need 2 yards (1.8 m) of fabric.
▶ Check the torso measurements (see page 76) and lengthen or shorten before cutting. The body-suit torso should be the same as your body measurements or up to 2" (5 cm) shorter, depending on your fabric, but not longer.
▶ The jumpsuit can be assembled on a sewing machine or serger. Use stretch stitches for four-way stretch fabrics, but if you're using a beefy, stable material like spacer fabric, you can sometimes use a regular straight stitch for seaming and topstitching. Just test first!

INSTRUCTIONS

⅜" (1 cm) seam allowances are used for all variations of this pattern.

1 Insert an invisible zipper in the center back seam following the instructions on page 61 to connect the back pieces (**A**).

2 Sew the front to the back at the crotch seam, right sides together (**B**). Press open or toward the front.

3 With right sides together, stitch the front and back inner leg pieces at the inseam (**C**).

4 Sew the inner leg assembly to the leg curve on the front and back pieces, right sides together, matching the inseam to the crotch seam (**D**).

5 With right sides together, sew the side fronts to the front assembly along the princess seams. On stretch fabrics I find it easiest to sew curved seams with the straighter edge underneath, where it is firmly gripped by the feed dogs, and stretch it slightly to match the curved edge. Press seam allowances toward the side seam; topstitch with a stretch stitch if desired. Repeat for the side backs (**E**).

6 Sew the front body and sleeves together along the angled raglan seams, right sides together. Repeat for the back sleeve seams (**F**).

7 Align the front and back at the sides, matching the seams at the underarm, right sides together. Sew from the wrist all the way down the side to the ankle (**G**).

8 Make two loops for the button closures as follows: cut 2 pieces of the ⅛" (3 mm) flat elastic, each approximately 1½" (3.8cm) long. Fold each in half and baste to one end of the collar piece, spaced about ¾" (1.9 cm) and 1¼" (3.2 cm) from the long edge, as shown in (**H**).

9 Fold the collar in half and stitch across both ends, right sides together. Turn right side out. Edgestitch if desired. Match the ends of the collar to the zipper at center back and the dots to the front raglan seams. Sew or serge through

all three layers (**H**), stretching the collar slightly to match the neckline at the stitching line. Press the seam allowance down and edgestitch (see page 55) around the neckline to keep it in place. Sew buttons on the collar end opposite the elastic loops.

10 Hem the ankles and sleeves with a zigzag or double-needle stitch (**I**). Or, if the fabric does not roll, you can tie off the thread ends and leave the edges raw for less bulk when tucking them into boots and gloves.

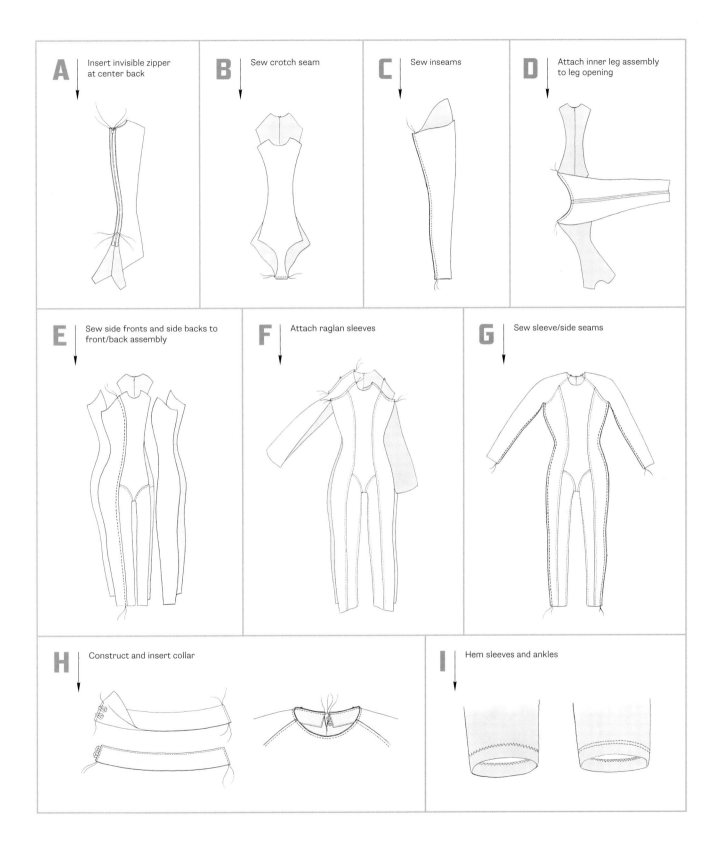

A | Insert invisible zipper at center back

B | Sew crotch seam

C | Sew inseams

D | Attach inner leg assembly to leg opening

E | Sew side fronts and side backs to front/back assembly

F | Attach raglan sleeves

G | Sew sleeve/side seams

H | Construct and insert collar

I | Hem sleeves and ankles

Princess-Seamed Leotard

To make any version of the jumpsuit into a leotard, cut the side front and side back pattern pieces off along the dotted line and do not cut out the inner leg pieces. Assemble as described on page 112, omitting steps 3 and 4. Finish the leg openings with elastic as described in the Leotard, steps 6 and 7 (see page 109).

Front-Opening Collar

ADDITIONAL SUPPLIES

▶ 16" to 20" (41 to 51 cm) decorative zipper (instead of the invisible zipper used in the example garment)
▶ 3" (7.6 cm) wide strip of woven or weft-insertion fusible interfacing that is 2" (5 cm) longer than your zipper for the zipper facing

To make a front-opening jumpsuit, sew the center back seam completely in step 1 and follow the directions on page 63 to insert an exposed zipper along the center front line. Assemble the front-opening collar by sewing the two layers, right sides together, along the front and top edges. Shorten the stitch length to accurately sew the rounded corners. Trim the seam allowances to ⅛" (3mm) around the curves, turn right side out and edgestitch. Align so the collar edges meet the zipper front. Attach as described in step 9 on page 112.

Halter Jumpsuit

ADDITIONAL SUPPLIES

▶ 1¼ yds (1.1 m) of ⅜" (1 cm) elastic
▶ 1" (2.5 cm) swimsuit hook

To make the backless version of the seamed bodysuit used for the Superhero 3 costume on page 167 (shown opposite), cut the side front, back, and side back pieces off along the dotted lines and use the back-opening halter collar pattern. Do not cut out any sleeves. A zipper is not necessary if you choose fabrics with four-way stretch, but can be included for decorative reasons or if you prefer to wear the jumpsuit unzipped (see below). If you do use a zipper, you won't need the swimsuit hook for the collar closure.

1 Stitch the back pieces together, right sides together.

2 Assemble the jumpsuit as in steps 2 through 7 on page 112, but omit step 6 and sew up the side seams only in step 7, as there are no sleeves in this version.

3 Measure the top edge of the bodysuit, from the front neckline down under the arms and around the back to the other side of the front neckline, and cut a piece of ⅜" (1 cm) elastic 1" (2.5 cm) shorter than this length. Find the center point of the elastic and pin it inside the upper edge at center back. Pin the ends at the sides of the front neckline, aligning the edge of the elastic with the cut edge of the fabric.

4 Zigzag stitch using a stitch length of 2 to 2.5 mm and a width of 3mm, stretching the elastic to match the fabric. Turn the elastic toward the inside to enclose and topstitch.

5 Sew one long edge of the collar to the front neckline, right sides together and matching the center point at center front and the dots to the neckline edges. Fold in half with right sides together and sew from the dot to the end on both sides. Turn right side out and fell stitch (see page 50) the collar to the inside neckline and itself, enclosing the seam allowances.

6 Fold the left end of the collar band under ¾" (1.9 cm) and topstitch to secure, forming a loop. Loop the right end through a swimsuit hook and topstitch.

7 Finish the leg openings with your preferred hem method.

Halter—Decorative Zipper Version

If including a decorative zipper, use the size indicated in the Tools and Materials list, insert it in the front using the exposed zipper method on page 63, and use the front-opening collar. After inserting the zipper, follow the Halter Jumpsuit variation instructions above through step 4. You will need to attach the collar by sewing just the outer layer to the neckline, aligning the collar edges with the zipper at center front, then tucking the seam allowances inside the collar and hand sewing or edgestitching (see page 55) to close.

SEAMLESS SUPER-SUIT

MEN'S

Superhero outfits tend to fit like a second skin—often without any visible seams or means of entry. We cosplayers, on the other hand, are bound by the realities of fabric and physics. This bodysuit is about as close as you can get to that seamless look with real-world materials. It uses the magic of four-way stretch to eliminate the front and side seams, so you can cut the entire body of the suit in a single piece and use a bold print or embellishment without interruption. A built-in crotch gusset helps to make the inseam even less visible, while allowing a little extra mobility in the legs.

TOOLS AND MATERIALS

▶ Sewing Essentials (see page 44)
▶ 2¾ yds (2.5 m) of 60" (152 cm) wide four-way stretch knit, such as nylon/spandex or polyester/spandex knits like milliskin and moleskin, printed spandex, foiled knit, or stretch pleather (I used gold "mystique" spandex, a polyester/spandex knit with mini foil dots and 100% horizontal/80% vertical stretch.)
▶ 22" to 24" (56 to 60 cm) invisible zipper
▶ 1 yd (.9 m) of ¼" (6 mm) elastic to finish the neckline
▶ Small scraps of fusible tricot (knit) interfacing
▶ 100% polyester all-purpose thread in a matching color
▶ Stretch sewing machine needles (size 11/75)

PATTERN PIECES

Pattern pieces on sheet 2; see cutting layout on page 190
▶ **Seamless Super-Suit Front/ Back**: cut 1 on fold
▶ **Seamless Super-Suit Sleeve**: cut 2 on straight grain

NOTES

▶ The minimal seaming on this bodysuit means it sews up fast, but accurate sewing is very important for a smooth fit around the inset corners of the gusset area. If you're a beginner and don't feel up to this yet, you can substitute the leggings pattern for the leg portion of the bodysuit and add a seam at the center front for a version that's somewhat easier to sew.

▶ When checking the torso length (see page 76), measure the front length to the dot at the top of the gusset. The gusset itself is included in the back length.
▶ Use a straight stretch stitch if your machine has it. Otherwise you may want to experiment with stretch threads like woolly nylon to get more stretch out of a narrow zigzag.
▶ If you plan on using a serger, you may want to baste the gusset section with a straight stitch on a standard sewing machine first for better accuracy. Don't try to pivot the serger around the sharp corners; instead serge off the edge and start again for the next length of seam.

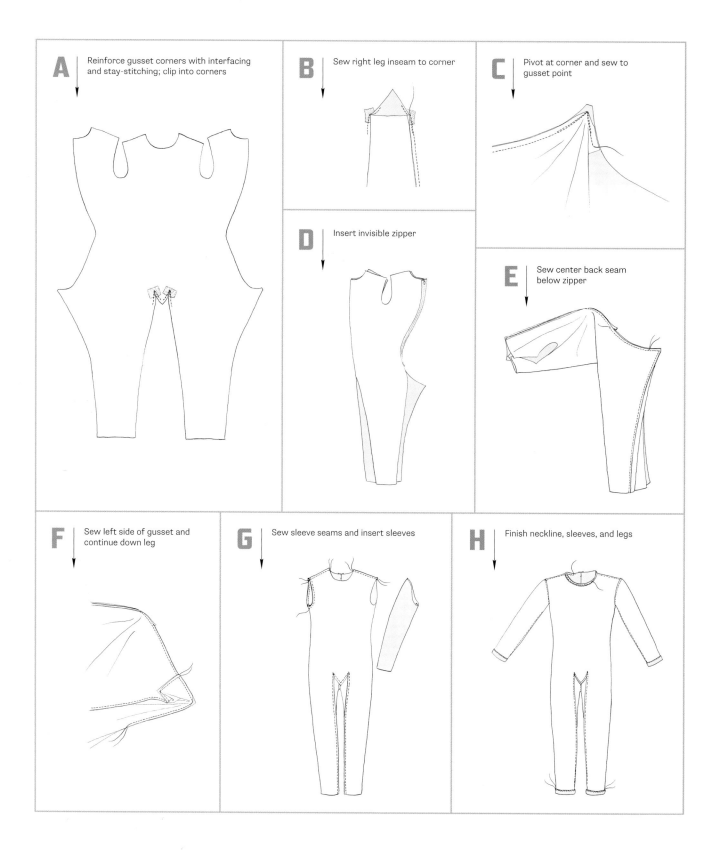

A | Reinforce gusset corners with interfacing and stay-stitching; clip into corners

B | Sew right leg inseam to corner

C | Pivot at corner and sew to gusset point

D | Insert invisible zipper

E | Sew center back seam below zipper

F | Sew left side of gusset and continue down leg

G | Sew sleeve seams and insert sleeves

H | Finish neckline, sleeves, and legs

INSTRUCTIONS

⅜" (1 cm) seam allowances are used for this pattern.

1 First, reinforce the corners at the top of the crotch gusset with scraps of fusible tricot interfacing placed on the wrong side of the fabric. Lightly pencil the stitching line onto the interfacing so you know exactly where it is. Using a straight stitch and stitch length of 2 mm, sew a needle width outside the stitching line (within the seam allowance) for 2" (5 cm) on each side of the corner, pivoting at the dot with the needle down. Use a sharp pair of scissors to clip all the way into the corner, being careful not to cut the reinforcement stitching (**A**).

2 Pin the front and back inseams together with right sides together. With the front side on top, sew the right leg from the ankle to the gusset corner, staying just inside the reinforcement stitching so it doesn't show on the outside (**B**). Stop with the needle down, exactly at the dot. Note: if you don't get within a thread or two of the corner you'll get bunching in the seam, so precision is key here.

3 The sides of the gusset are sewn to the center back/crotch seam. Pivot the pieces so they align, right sides together, then drop the foot and continue stitching down to the center point of the gusset (**C**). Stop at the center line (don't continue to the cut edge), backstitch, and cut your thread.

4 Insert an invisible zipper in the center back seam—see page 61 for directions (**D**). Because the seam is curved, you may want to stabilize it with a strip of fusible knit interfacing and baste the zipper by hand to prevent stretching when you stitch.

5 Starting at the base of the zipper, and using a zipper foot to stitch ¹⁄₁₆" (1.5 mm) from the zipper stitching, sew the center back seam below the zipper (**E**). Make sure that the notches align, and stop and backtack when you meet the previous line of stitching at the point of the gusset.

6 Lift the needle and foot to fold the gusset seam allowance up out of the way, then drop them on the other side to continue stitching past the gusset point, up to the inside corner of the gusset. Pivot at the corner and continue down the left inseam to the ankle (**F**).

7 Sew front to back at the shoulder seams, right sides together, and stitch the underarm seams on the sleeves,

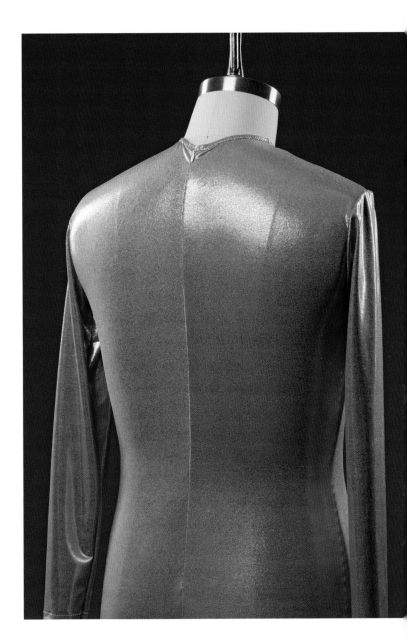

right sides together. Match the sleeve head notch with the shoulder seam and the sleeve seam with the underarm notch, right sides facing. Sew in the sleeves, stretching the armhole slightly to fit, matching notches (**G**).

8 Finish the neckline with elastic: measure around the neckline from one side of the zipper teeth to the other side along the seam line and cut the elastic to this measurement. Use the stitched-and-turned method (see page 69) to apply the elastic. Hem the leg openings and sleeves (**H**).

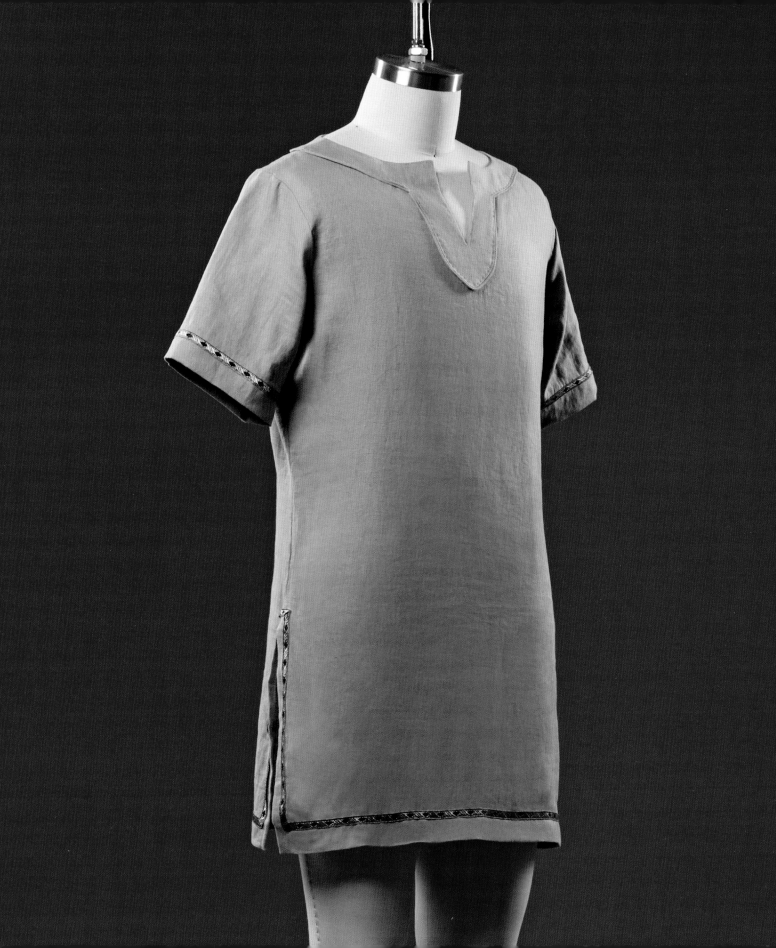

TUNIC

When you're adventuring to far-off lands and searching for magical treasure, you need a simple, rugged tunic that won't get in your way. This one has a split hem and a piped external facing. The basic version is simple to sew, but it has opportunities for further embellishment if you're ready to take the next step; for example, you could add lacing to the front. The piping around the collar can be corded or uncorded, depending on your preference, though the corded type is slightly easier to sew. You can also skip it entirely if you prefer: just staystitch around the outer edge of the facing, roll the edge under, clipping as needed, and topstitch in place.

TOOLS AND MATERIALS

▶ Sewing Essentials (see page 44)
▶ 1¾ yds (1.6 m) of 60" (152 cm) wide medium-weight woven fabric such as linen, cotton twill, or suiting (I used light gray 5.5 oz-weight linen.)
▶ ½ yd (46 cm) knit or woven interfacing, slightly lighter in weight than your fabric
▶ 1½ yds (1.4 m) of purchased piping or trim
▶ 4 yds (3.7 m) of ½" (1.3 cm) wide flat trim (I chose a metallic band trim with a woven-in design.)
▶ All-purpose thread in a matching color

PATTERN PIECES

Pattern pieces on sheet 4; see cutting layout on page 190
▶ **Tunic Front:** cut 1 on fold
▶ **Tunic Back:** cut 1 on fold
▶ **Tunic Front Facing:** cut 1 on fold, cut 1 interfacing on fold
▶ **Tunic Back Facing:** cut 1 on fold, cut 1 interfacing on fold
▶ **Tunic Sleeve:** cut 2 on straight grain

NOTES

▶ Linen makes a nice basic tunic, but for a fancier look, you can use jacquard or brocade. The facing can be made in the same fabric as the rest of the tunic or in a contrasting fabric.
▶ Remember to finish your seam allowances to prevent fraying. A simple zigzag or serger stitch will do the trick for this tunic, or see page 54 for more options.
▶ If you want the piping to match your main fabric, make your own as described on page 92. Buy at least ½ yd (45.7 cm) of extra fabric to cut the bias strips.

INSTRUCTIONS

This pattern uses ⅝" (1.5 cm) seam allowances for the side, shoulder, and sleeve seams, and a ⅜" (1 cm) seam allowance around the neckline.

① With right sides together, stitch the front to the back at the shoulder seams (**A**). Press the seams open.

② Interface (see page 32) the front and back facing pieces. With right sides together, stitch the front facing to the back facing at the shoulder seams; press the seams open. Pin the piping on the right side of the facing, aligned just inside the stitching line with the flange sticking out into the seam allowance, beginning at the center back outside edge. When you reach the center back again, trim the piping to fit, leaving about ½" (1.3 cm) to fold under and overlap the other end. (If using corded piping, pull the last ¼"/6 mm of cord out from each end and trim it away so you can overlap the piping without bulk.) Clip into the flange as needed to maneuver around corners, stopping just short of the cord. Baste the piping to the facing (**B**).

③ Place the facing right side down on the wrong side of the tunic. Sew around the neck opening with a short stitch length of 2 to 2.5 mm, taking one horizontal stitch across the bottom of the center front notch at the dot (**C**). Cut down the center of the notch, ending right at the point but being careful not to cut any stitches. Clip the corners at the top of the notch and grade the seam allowances to about ⅛" (3 mm) or a little more if the fabric is prone to fraying, leaving the facing side of the seam a hair longer. Flip the facing to the outside and press well.

④ Edgestitch around the neckline and notch. Clip the inside and outside corners and flip the outer edge of the facing to the underside, press, and use a zipper foot to topstitch right next to the piping (**D**).

⑤ With right sides together, stitch the sleeves to the flat tunic, matching the sleeve head notch to the shoulder seam and aligning the front/back side and underarm edges, matching remaining notches (**E**).

⑥ Sew the underarm and side seam, right sides together, stopping at the marked dot (**F**). Zigzag, serge, or pink the seam allowances and press them open.

⑦ Topstitch up, across, and down the side seam vent. Hem the sleeves and lower edge of the tunic (**G**) as desired.

⑧ Stitch the trim to the sleeves and to the hem, placing it over the existing stitching lines. Fold a little triangular pleat in the trim (a miter) to neatly turn the corners. When you reach your starting point, fold the end under and overlap the trim to cover the raw edge.

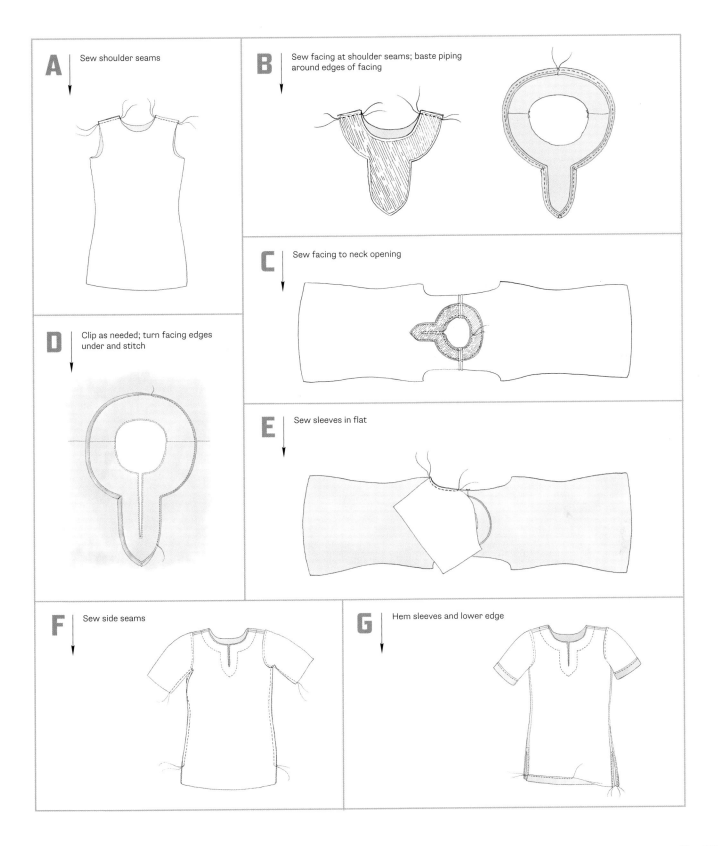

A | Sew shoulder seams

B | Sew facing at shoulder seams; baste piping around edges of facing

C | Sew facing to neck opening

D | Clip as needed; turn facing edges under and stitch

E | Sew sleeves in flat

F | Sew side seams

G | Hem sleeves and lower edge

PLEATED SKIRT

Pleated skirts come up so often in manga and anime cosplays that you may quickly find yourself with a closet full. Fortunately, they're straightforward to make and require basically no fitting, as long as you're careful and accurate about measuring and pleating. Although you have to do a little math for this skirt, the result will be a custom design constructed to your exact specifications! To make a pleated skirt look good, one of the most important things you can do is choose an appropriate fabric. This is one situation where synthetics and synthetic blends have a clear advantage, because it's possible to create permanent creases. Since many of these fabrics are also fairly wrinkle-resistant in everyday wear, the result is a crisp, tidy skirt that holds its shape. Wool and sturdy cottons like twill and sateen are also appropriate.

TOOLS AND MATERIALS

▶ Sewing Essentials (see page 44)
▶ Light- to medium-weight suiting fabric, twill, or gabardine, amount based on Measuring and Template instructions, step 2 (I used 1⅞ yds/1.7 m of 57"/145 cm wide gray rayon/polyester blend suiting.)
▶ 7" or 9" (18 or 23 cm) standard zipper (see Notes)
▶ ¼ yd (23 cm) woven or weft-insertion interfacing
▶ Hook-and-bar trouser closure or button
▶ Hem lace or seam binding equal to quantity [d] in the calculations on page 127, plus a little extra for overlap
▶ All-purpose thread in a matching color

PATTERN PIECES

None. Instead of using a pattern, this skirt is based on your desired pleat width and your body measurements. See cutting layout on page 190.

NOTES

▶ A 7" (18 cm) zipper is a good length for straighter figures; if you have a dramatic waist-to-hip ratio, you may prefer a 9" (23 cm) zipper.
▶ Hem the skirt with hem lace or seam binding to prevent bulk that could interfere with the pleats.
▶ Press carefully and use a press cloth to avoid marring your fabric with the iron. A wooden clapper (see page 47) is useful to achieve the sharpest creases. Do not pick fabrics containing spandex because they will not crease well and may be damaged by the heat of the iron.

INSTRUCTIONS

⅝" (1.5 cm) seam allowances are used for this pattern.

Measuring and Template

1 Refer to the sample figures in the box on page 127 throughout this section as needed. Have a pencil and paper handy to write down your calculations. An important note: accurate measurements are critical, because small errors will be multiplied over lots of pleats. Even if you normally measure in inches, work in metric here; it will give you a little more precision in this instance. Decide how wide you would like your pleats to be at hip level [a]. (If your fabric has a print or plaid, factor the pattern repeat into the width of the pleats; for example, you may want to make the pleat one-third of the width of the repeat so each pleat hits at the same place in the pattern. Try folding your fabric at various widths to see what you like best.) Measure around your hips at the widest point, add 5 cm for ease, divide by [a], and round up to the next even number of pleats [b]. Multiply [a] x [b] to yield the skirt's hip circumference [c].

2 Multiply the hip circumference [c] by 3 to yield figure [d], the total width of fabric for the skirt. Divide [d] by 2 and add two additional pleat widths [a] to allow some overlap for join-ing the panels at each side. This will determine how much fabric you need [e]. (Note: this assumes a knee-length or shorter skirt, cut in two panels stacked on top of each other across the width of the fabric. If the skirt including waist-band, two seams, and hem allowance is longer than half your fabric width, you will need to use the full width [d] instead of half.) If you're using a plaid or print, get an extra ¼ yard (22.9 cm) or two pattern repeats, whichever is larger, to make sure you have enough to match up the design. You may also want to allow a little extra in case of shrinkage or uneven cutting.

3 Tie a piece of string or elastic around your waist at the point where you would like the skirt to sit. Measure and add 2.5 cm for ease for the skirt waist [f]. Divide by the number of pleats [b] to get the waist pleat width [g]. Measure the verti-cal distance between your waist string and the fullest part of your hip (the hip depth) and jot down this measurement [h].

4 Refer to the illustration above right to make a pleating template, which will allow you to create perfectly consistent tapered pleats without measuring individually. To make the

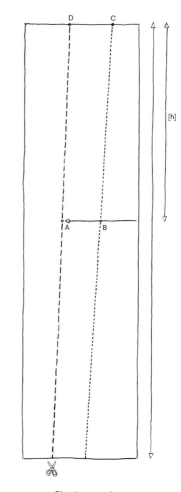

Pleating template

template, cut a strip of cardboard about 7.5 cm longer than your finished skirt will be and three times the pleat width at the hip ([a] from step 1). Draw lines across the template for the waist and hem edges (remembering to include seam and hem allowance). Draw in the hip depth line [h] based on the vertical distance measurement you wrote down in step 3. Divide the hip line into equal thirds and mark points A and B as shown.

5 On the waist line, measure the waist pleat width [g] from the right edge and mark it point C. Find the point halfway between point C and the left edge and mark it point D. Draw straight lines connecting point C to B and D to A, continuing each down to the hem. Cut along the D-A line. When you form your pleats, this edge will form the valley of the pleat, and the peak will align along the C-B line.

Sample Skirt Calculations

To help you plan and construct your custom pleated skirt, here is an example of the math used in steps 1 through 4 and step 13. I'm using metric measurements for better precision. This sample is based on a desired pleat width at hip level of 4.5 cm, hip measurement of 97 cm, and a waist measurement of 69 cm. These measurements equate to a size small pattern, the same as the sample in the photo. Use the blank column to record your own calculations. To be on the safe side, buy a little more fabric than your calculations yield—perhaps ¼ yard (22.9 cm) more.

Measurement	Sample Calculation	Sample Result	Your Results
[a] pleat width	(Your choice)	4.5 cm	
[b] # of pleats	97 cm (your hip measure) + 5 cm (ease) = 102 cm 102 cm ÷ 4.5 cm (pleat width) = 22.6 Round up to an even number	24	
[c] skirt circumference at hip	4.5 cm x 24	108 cm	
[d] fabric width	108 cm x 3	324 cm	
[e] yardage needed	(324 cm ÷ 2) + 9 cm (2 extra pleats for joining panels)	171 cm (67.3″) of fabric, or 1⅞ yds)	
[f] skirt waist	69 cm (your waist measure) + 2.5 cm (ease)	71.5 cm	
[g] waist pleat width	71.5 cm ÷ 24 (# of pleats) = 2.97 cm Round to nearest mm	3.0 cm	
[h] hip depth	(Distance from your waist to your hip)	21.5 cm	
[i] waistband length (see step 13)	71.5 cm + 3 cm (C-D length on template) + 3 cm (seam allowance)	77.5 cm	

Cutting and Sewing

⑥ Measure enough fabric to create half the required number of pleats [b], with one extra pleat width [a] on each end. With the fabric spread flat (not folded), cut two identical equal-size pieces to create the skirt front and back (don't fold the fabric to cut them at the same time, or you'll get mirror images and the pleats will run in opposite directions). The height of each panel is the length of the skirt + 1.5 cm waist seam allowance + 4 cm hem allowance. Mark every three pleat widths across the entire fabric span of each panel to guide your pleating. Chalk, a basted line, or just a snip in the seam allowance on the upper edge will do the trick.

⑦ Line the template up so that point A is one pleat width from the left edge of the fabric and the right edge of the template is perpendicular to the top and bottom fabric edges. Use the left side of the template to draw in the first fold line. Add a 1.5 cm seam allowance and cut off the excess. Do the same thing on the right edge of the fabric, again placing point A one pleat width from the edge. This time, remove the template and draw the seam allowance on the right side of the fold line (**A**). Repeat for the other piece of fabric.

⑧ Sew the front and back together along one end, right sides together, making sure they're both oriented the same way (top to top and hem to hem). Note that the seam is on a slight angle, so that it fits into the valley of a pleat and is invisible from the outside. Press the seam open. Hem the lower edge with lace or tape to avoid bulk (see page 67), starting and stopping about 7.5 cm from each end (**B**).

⑨ To use the template, slip it into each pleat and align the folded edge with the marked line while you press. To begin, work on the right side of the fabric, placing the template one pleat width beyond the first marked line (three pleat widths from the end) and pulling the fabric up to the mark to form the first pleat (**C**). Traditionally the pleats overlap from right to left, so you can conceal the zipper behind a pleat on the left side.

⑩ Pin the pleats closed as you go to make them easier to handle. The final pleat should end in a mountain fold (a single outward fold), with a full pleat width plus seam allowance on the back side. If you choose, you can edgestitch the pleats closed for a short distance down from the waist to keep them neat; if so, pull the threads through to the inside and knot them off instead of backtacking. When you've pleated the full skirt, baste the pleats closed along the top and bottom edges to make them easier to handle. Leave the final pleat free so you can insert the zipper (**D**).

⑪ Place the zipper face down on the underlap (back) side of the skirt panel, positioned so the outermost edge of the zipper is 2 cm from the cut edge. Sew 3 mm from the teeth on the outer side of the tape, stopping and backtacking right next to the zipper stop (**E**). Clip the seam allowance at an angle down to the end of the stitching, cutting the fabric but not the zipper tape.

⑫ Flip the zipper outward and press, tucking the triangular corner down under the seam allowance. Line the overlap side up on top of the zipper so the pleats appear uninterrupted from the outside, and sew from the raw hem edge up over the zipper to the waistline (**F**).

⑬ Press the seam open below the zipper and finish stitching the hem in place. Take the waist measurement calculated in step 3 and add the pleat overlap, which you can get by measuring the C-D width on the pleating template; then add 3 cm to yield the waistband length [i]. Cut a rectangle of fabric for the waistband with length [i] and width 9.5 cm. Interface (see page 32) the waistband rectangle and sew it to the skirt, right sides together, leaving room for seam allowance on each end (**G**).

⑭ Press the waistband up and fold the inside seam allowance toward the wrong side, then fold the waistband in half with right sides together. Stitch across the ends (**H**).

⑮ Turn the waistband right side out, and fell stitch (see page 50) or stitch in the ditch (see page 68) to close up the inside of the waistband. Close with a trouser hook and bar, or button and buttonhole if you prefer (**I**).

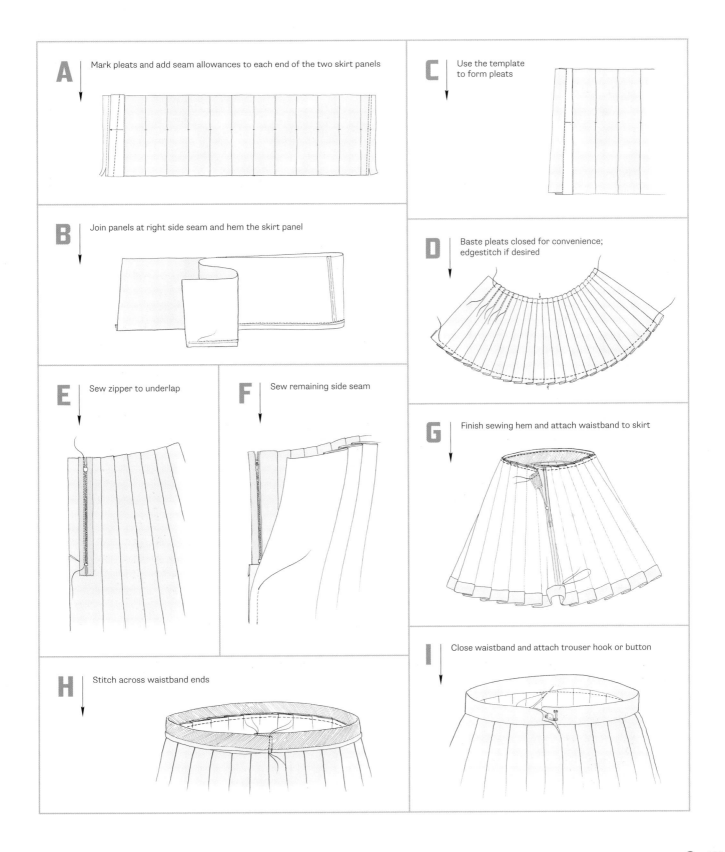

A Mark pleats and add seam allowances to each end of the two skirt panels

B Join panels at right side seam and hem the skirt panel

C Use the template to form pleats

D Baste pleats closed for convenience; edgestitch if desired

E Sew zipper to underlap

F Sew remaining side seam

G Finish sewing hem and attach waistband to skirt

H Stitch across waistband ends

I Close waistband and attach trouser hook or button

BLOUSE

Is it fair to say that almost every anime cosplayer will end up making a school uniform at some time or another? The sailor fuku in particular is both iconic and versatile, adaptable for dozens of characters across every genre with slight changes in color, styling, and trim details. The long-sleeved version shown here is suitable for a winter uniform, but you can easily choose a lighter fabric and/or chop the sleeves off short for a summer version.

TOOLS AND MATERIALS

- Sewing Essentials (see page 44)
- 2¼ yds (2.1 m) of 45" (114 cm) wide light- to medium-weight suiting fabric, twill, or gabardine; also cotton or blended blouse fabrics (I used 57" (145 cm) wide gray rayon/polyester blend suiting to match the pleated skirt.)
- 2 yds (1.8 m) of ¼" (6 mm) purchased flat braid or trim (this is enough for one row each on the collar and cuffs)
- ½ yd (45.7 cm) of fusible tricot (knit) interfacing
- 12" (30 cm) invisible zipper
- Seven ⁵⁄₁₆" (8 mm) sew-in snaps
- All-purpose thread in a matching color

PATTERN PIECES

Pattern pieces on sheet 4; see cutting layout on page 190

- **Blouse Front**: cut 1 on fold
- **Blouse Back**: cut 1 on fold
- **Blouse Front Facing**: cut 1 on fold, cut 1 interfacing on fold
- **Blouse Back Facing**: cut 1 on fold, cut 1 interfacing on fold
- **Sailor Collar**: cut 2 on fold
- **Blouse Sleeve**: cut 2 on straight grain
- **Blouse Sleeve Cuff**: cut 2 on straight grain, cut 2 interfacing
- **Blouse Neckline Insert**: cut 2 on straight grain (revise the top edge of the piece to suit your character if desired), cut 2 interfacing

For High-Collar Blouse variation only:
- **Stand Collar**: cut 2 on straight grain, cut 2 interfacing on straight grain

NOTES

- Blouse fabrics are often semi-sheer. If your fabric is white, make sure your interfacing and zipper are, too.
- If making the collar and cuffs in a contrasting color, you will need 2 yds (1.9 m) of the blouse fabric for the body and sleeves and ¾ yd (69 cm) of the contrast fabric for the collar, cuffs, insert, and facings.
- When choosing trim, look for flat ribbons and braids that will fold nicely around the square corners of the collar. Soutache is also an option, and can be twisted into decorative loops at the corners.
- Finish seam allowances by serging or zigzagging unless otherwise indicated. French seams (see page 54) are also a great choice if you're working with lighter-weight blouse fabrics.

INSTRUCTIONS

This pattern uses ⅝" (1.5 cm) seam allowances for the side, shoulder, sleeve, and outside of collar seams, and ⅜" (1 cm) seam allowances for the cuff, stand collar, and neckline seams.

1 Fuse interfacing to the back side of the facing and sleeve cuff pieces. You may also wish to interface the collar, especially if your fabric is drapey and you plan on using a heavy trim. Stitch the facing pieces together at the shoulder seams, right sides together (**A**).

2 Pin your trim in place on the upper collar piece. Remember to account for the seam allowance when determining how far from the edge to place it. Sew the trim down, using a single line of stitching for narrow trims or stitching along both edges if the trim is wide. You can also hand sew the trim if you prefer less noticeable stitching (**B**). Miter the corners of the trim as in the Tunic pattern (step 8, page 122).

3 Put the two layers of the collar together with right sides facing. Sew around the outer edge, leaving the curved neckline edge open. Grade the seam allowances (see page 55), trimming the bottom layer slightly narrower, and clip across the corners. Turn the collar right side out and press; edgestitch if you like to keep the layers together (**C**).

4 Sew the front darts (see page 57). Stitch the front piece to the back piece at the shoulder seams, right sides together. Fuse a small scrap of interfacing behind the center point of the neckline to stabilize it (**D**).

5 Pin the collar into the neckline, trim side up, on the right side of the blouse. Baste just outside the stitching line, within the seam allowance. Make sure the front points of the collar meet exactly on the stitching line at center front and do not cross (**E**).

6 Sew the facing on top of the collar with right sides together (**F**). Clip to the stitching line at the center point of the neckline and grade the seam.

7 Understitch (see page 66) the neckline facing. Flip the facing to the inside and tack it in place at the shoulder seams with a couple of hand stitches (**G**).

8 Insert an invisible zipper (see page 61) in the left side seam, positioned so it opens at the hem. Shorten if necessary so the zipper ends just below the stitching line at the armhole. Sew the remaining side seam of the blouse (**H**).

TIP

If you prefer a more fitted style, you can pin out excess around the waist in front or back and sew it as a dart (see page 78 for more on altering darts). Add a pocket or embroidered school insignia if that's what your character calls for, and don't be afraid to reshape the collar as needed. There's a variation for a blouse with a high collar, too, that is used in the Magical Girl Costume (page 183). You can always trial different shapes in paper or muslin to nail down the proportions before you cut out the real deal.

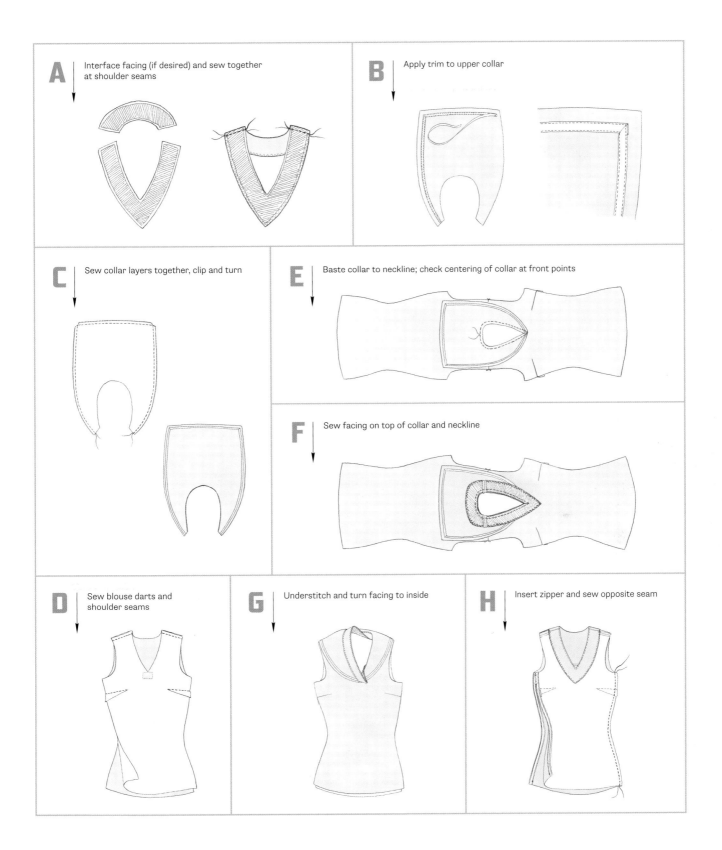

A Interface facing (if desired) and sew together at shoulder seams

B Apply trim to upper collar

C Sew collar layers together, clip and turn

E Baste collar to neckline; check centering of collar at front points

F Sew facing on top of collar and neckline

D Sew blouse darts and shoulder seams

G Understitch and turn facing to inside

H Insert zipper and sew opposite seam

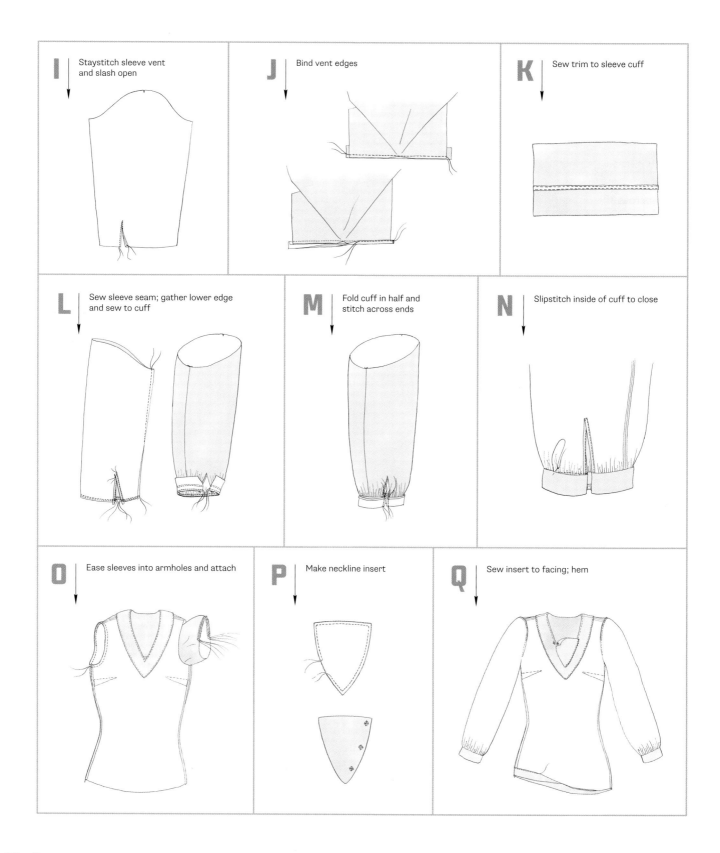

I Staystitch sleeve vent and slash open

J Bind vent edges

K Sew trim to sleeve cuff

L Sew sleeve seam; gather lower edge and sew to cuff

M Fold cuff in half and stitch across ends

N Slipstitch inside of cuff to close

O Ease sleeves into armholes and attach

P Make neckline insert

Q Sew insert to facing; hem

9 Stitch ⅛" (3 mm) from the line on each side of the sleeve vent, tapering to a point at the dot. Cut down the center (**I**). Open the vent out flat. Cut a 1" x 10" (2.5 x 25.4 cm) bias strip (see page 66) of the blouse fabric and sew it in place, right sides together; double fold to enclose the edge. Fell stitch or topstitch (see page 68) in place and trim the excess (**J**).

10 Sew trim to one side of the cuff, remembering that the fold line marks the lower edge of the finished sleeve (**K**). Stitch across the fold of the vent binding. With right sides together, sew and press the sleeve seam. Gather the sleeve end (see page 58) and sew it to the cuff edge that's closer to the trim, right sides together, adjusting the gathers to leave ⅜" (1 cm) seam allowance on either end (**L**).

11 Fold the remaining edge under ⅜" (1 cm), then fold the cuff in half with right sides together. Stitch across the cuff ends right next to the edge of the sleeve (**M**). Turn the cuff right side out and slipstitch the inside to close it up (**N**). Attach two small snaps to each side of the cuff opening.

12 Set the sleeves into the armholes, right sides together, matching the notches; stitch. Finish the armhole seam by serging, zigzagging, or binding the edge with lining fabric (**O**).

13 Trim the neckline insert interfacing slightly smaller so it doesn't add a lot of bulk to the seams. If appropriate, sew trim to the outer layer of the insert to match the collar or add an embroidered monogram to the right side. Align the two pieces with right sides together and stitch around the outside edge, leaving a gap of about 1" (2.5 cm) on one side. Grade the seam (leaving the unsewn portion intact) and turn right side out. Fold the seam allowances to the inside and sew the female side of three snaps to the edge of the insert as shown (**P**).

14 Position the insert behind the neckline and sew it to the right side of the neckline facing, closing up the opening at the same time. Mark the snap positions and sew the male side of the snaps to the left side of the facing. Hem the blouse by folding the edge up ¼" (6 mm), then again at a width of 2" (5 cm). Topstitch or blindstitch (see page 67) to secure (**Q**).

VARIATION High-Collar Blouse

This version of the blouse pairs nicely with the dress, as you'll see in the Magical Girl costume (see page 183).

1 Cut the higher-neck version of the Blouse pattern, and use the stand collar instead of the sailor collar. You will not need facings if using this collar. Cut the sleeves off 4½" (11.4 cm) below the underarm, and cut two cuffs, each about 3" (7.6 cm) wide (twice the finished width plus seam allowance) and 2" to 3" (5 to 7.6 cm) longer than your biceps measurement. Cut a 1⅛" x 10" (2.8 x 25.4 cm) strip of fabric to bind the keyhole neckline.

2 Staystitch (see page 54) a ¼" (6 mm) wide slot in the center front, tapering to a point 5" (12.7 cm) below the neckline. Cut down the center to the point. Bind the opening as shown for the sleeve vent in steps 9 and 10 above.

3 Sew the front darts and shoulder seams as shown in step 4 on page 132.

4 Construct the stand collar as in step 11 for the Coat (see page 152). Sew the outside layer to the neckline, right sides together, matching dots to the shoulder seams, aligning the seam at center front with the edge of the keyhole opening. Clip the neckline curve as needed, press the collar up, and tuck the seam allowances inside. Close with a fell stitch or by stitching in the ditch (see page 68). If you wish, hand sew a ¼" (6 mm) ribbon or a bias tube (see page 60) of contrasting fabric around the base of the collar and tie in a bow to hold the keyhole closed.

5 Sew the sleeve seams, right sides together. Stitch one cuff piece together along the short ends, right sides together, and press the seam open. Gather the sleeve to fit the cuff and sew the sleeve to one edge of the cuff with right sides together, aligning the cuff seam with the underarm seam. Fold the remaining cuff edge under ⅝" (1.5 cm), fold the cuff to the inside, and fell stitch or stitch in the ditch to close up the cuff. Repeat for the remaining cuff.

6 Sew the zipper and side seam as shown in step 8 on page 132, and set in the sleeves as shown in step 12 above. Hem the lower edge.

PANTS

Pants can be as simple or as complicated as you want them to be. On the difficult end of the scale, you have close-fitting historical breeches with all kinds of buttons and flaps, intricately seamed and strapped gothwear, and other styles that need tons of work on fitting, construction, or both. On the easier end, a plain pair of drawstring or elastic-waist pants works perfectly well for any number of costumes. With a tunic or jacket to cover the waistband, who could tell? These pants fall somewhere in the middle, with an adjustable structured waistband that doesn't slide down and loose, billowy legs that accommodate a variety of body shapes. Once you've worked out the fit to your satisfaction, you have a lot of options for playing with the style. Use them for pirates, historical or steampunk looks, fantasy, ouji style, and more.

TOOLS AND MATERIALS

- ▶ Sewing Essentials (see page 44)
- ▶ 2¼ yds (2.1 m) of 54" (137 cm) wide bottom-weight woven fabric, such as cotton twill, wool or blended suiting, brocade, velvet, or pinwale corduroy (I used brown fine-cotton twill.)
- ▶ 1¼ yds (1.1 m) of ribbon or suede cord for the back waistband lacing
- ▶ 1½ yds (1.4 m) of lightweight woven or weft-insertion interfacing
- ▶ 6 metal eyelets, or heavy topstitching thread for hand-sewn eyelets
- ▶ Ten ⅝" (1.5 cm) fabric-covered buttons for the center front fly and knee cuffs
- ▶ All-purpose thread in a matching color

PATTERN PIECES

Pattern pieces on sheet 1; see cutting layout on page 191

- ▶ **Pants Front**: cut 2 on straight grain
- ▶ **Pants Fly Facing**: cut 1 on straight grain, cut 2 interfacing
- ▶ **Pants Back**: cut 2 on straight grain
- ▶ **Pants Front Waistband**: cut 4 on straight grain, cut 4 interfacing
- ▶ **Pants Back Waistband**: cut 2 on fold, cut 2 interfacing on fold
- ▶ **Pants Cuff**: cut 2 on straight grain, cut 2 interfacing
- ▶ **Pants Waistband Tab**: cut 2 on straight grain, cut 2 interfacing

PATTERN PIECES

- ▶ Because of their volume and dense gathering, these pants are best in a relatively lightweight or fluid fabric.
- ▶ Since the buttons will be visible, take a swatch of fabric when shopping to ensure a good match; you could also get a kit to make fabric-covered buttons.
- ▶ If you want to create variations in style, you can size up or down in the leg pieces to make slimmer or poufier pants, and adjust the gathers to fit the waistband you've already fitted to your body. You can also skip the buttons and sew the cuffs closed, swap the cuffs out for drawstrings, or lengthen the pants so you can tuck them into boots.
- ▶ Finish all seam allowances with an over-edge zigzag or serger stitch, except those that will be completely enclosed in the finished garment.

INSTRUCTIONS

This pattern uses ⅝" (1.5 cm) seam allowances for the crotch, outseam, inseam, waist, and waistband seams, and ⅜" (1 cm) seam allowances for the knee cuffs, fly extension, and fly facing seams.

1 If desired, make fit adjustments before you begin sewing. Cut a sample waistband out of paper and wrap it around yourself to decide if it needs any adjustments. Add or remove length as necessary so the pants will sit where you want them. Then, measure from the bottom of the waistband in back to the bottom of the waistband in front, and compare to the crotch length on the pattern pieces to decide if you need to add or remove any length from the rise (the distance from the crotch to the waistband). Add or remove length at hip level, above the sharpest part of the crotch curve.

To adjust the overall length, lengthen the leg pieces by extending the outseam and inseam straight down, perpendicular to the lower edge. To shorten, pleat out the excess length a hand's width or so above the lower edge and redraw the seams to make them smooth again. Make sure your length adjustments are the same in front and back so everything matches up correctly.

2 On the left front, interface the fly extension from the fold line to the edge, trimming the interfacing as needed. Staystitch (see page 54) the crotch curve at the bottom corner of the extension. Clip into the corner of the extension to the large dot. Fold the extension edges in ⅜" (1 cm) and fold the extension back along the center front line (**A**).

3 Staystitch the right front the same as the left, as in step 2. Interface (see page 32) the fly facing. Fold the inner edge in ⅜" (1 cm). Place the facing on top of the right extension, right sides together, and stitch down the outside edge and across the bottom, stopping at the dot. Clip the seam allowance to the dot, and trim the corner of the extension and facing. Turn the facing to the inside and press (**B**).

4 Edgestitch the right facing and left extension to the small dot. Sew buttonholes (see page 63) in the extension (**C**).

5 Sew the front crotch seam below the fly. Use two lines of straight stitching ⅛" (3 mm) apart, trim close to the second line of stitching (**D**), and zigzag over the seam to help prevent fraying.

6 Press the front crotch seam toward the left front and stitch across the bottom of the fly. Sew two lines of gathering stitches between the notches on the top edge of each side (**E**), one at ½" (1.3 cm) and one at ¾" (1.9 cm).

7 Sew the back crotch seam. Press open, then stitch a second time for security and trim to ¼" (6 mm). Zigzag or serge the seam allowances and press to one side (**F**).

8 Sew two lines of gathering stitches across the back waistline. With right sides facing, line up the inseams, making sure the front and back crotch seams match, and sew. Sew the outseams, stopping 2" (5 cm) above the hem, and press open. Serge, zigzag, or bind the seam allowances as you prefer (**G**).

9 There are two sets of waistband pieces; one set will become the facing. Interface each of the waistband pieces (see page 32). With right sides together, sew the front waistband to the back waistband at the side seams on both sets (**H**).

10 Sew the two waistband pieces together along the top edge, grade the seams, and understitch (see page 66) as in (**I**).

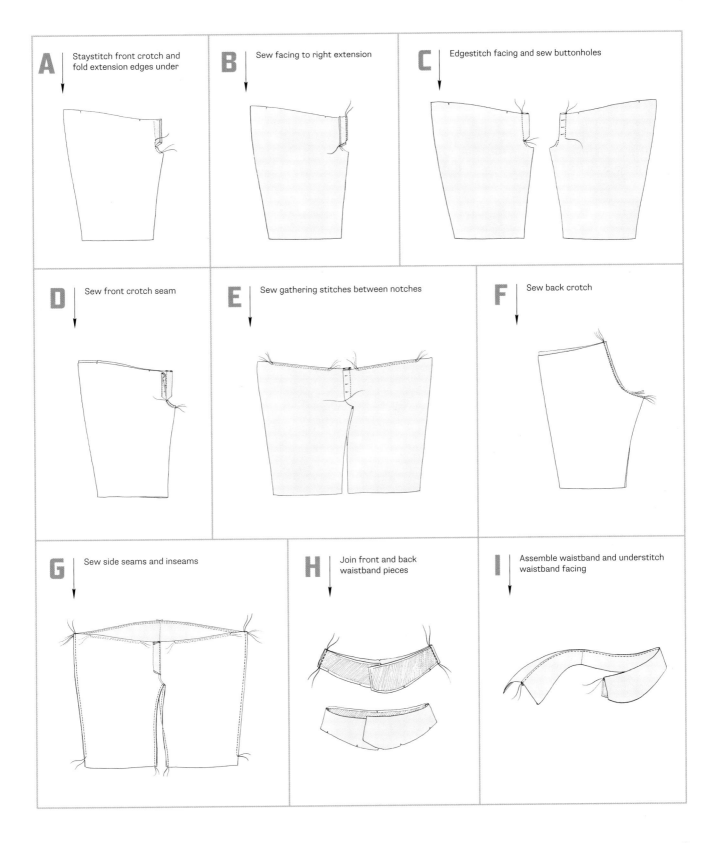

A | Staystitch front crotch and fold extension edges under

B | Sew facing to right extension

C | Edgestitch facing and sew buttonholes

D | Sew front crotch seam

E | Sew gathering stitches between notches

F | Sew back crotch

G | Sew side seams and inseams

H | Join front and back waistband pieces

I | Assemble waistband and understitch waistband facing

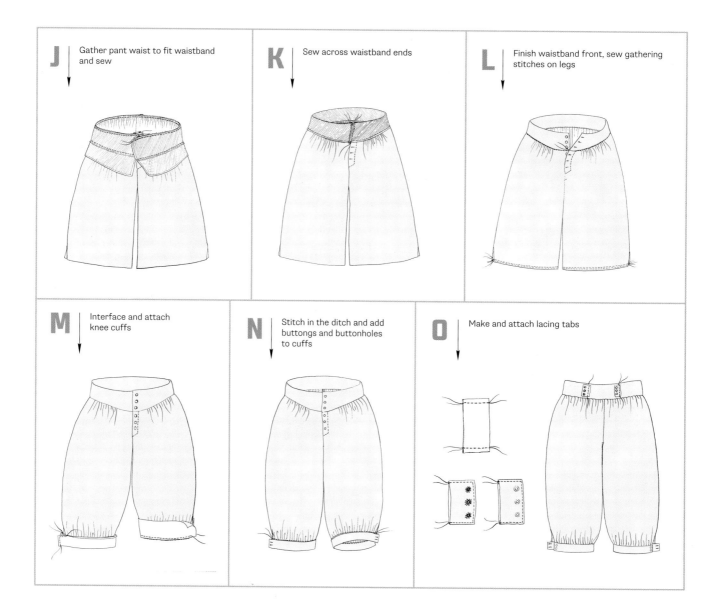

J | Gather pant waist to fit waistband and sew

K | Sew across waistband ends

L | Finish waistband front, sew gathering stitches on legs

M | Interface and attach knee cuffs

N | Stitch in the ditch and add buttongs and buttonholes to cuffs

O | Make and attach lacing tabs

11 Pin the outside layer of the waistband to the gathered pants waist, right sides facing and notches matching. Adjust the gathers so they're even (see page 58) and sew (**J**). After stitching the waistband to the pants, remove any visible gathering stitches.

12 Press the inside lower edge of the waistband up ½" (1.3 cm). Fold the waistband layers together so the right sides face each other and sew across the waistband ends (**K**). Turn the waistband right side out.

13 Stitch in the ditch (see page 68) of the waistband, making sure you catch the inner layer on the underside. Sew buttonholes in the left waistband. Mark and sew buttons (see page 64) on the right front. Sew two lines of gathering stitches around the leg openings (**L**).

14 Interface each of the cuffs. Gather the leg openings to fit the pants cuffs, and stitch with right sides together, leaving

the seam allowances free on both ends of the cuff and aligning the front edge with the dot to leave an extra 1" (2.5 cm) of cuff free for overlap. Turn the cuff down, and fold the inside edge of the cuff under ⅜" (1 cm). Fold the cuff in half with right sides together. Stitch across the top edge of the front cuff extension and across both ends of the cuff with a ⅜" (1 cm) seam allowance (**M**).

15 Clip the corner of the extension and turn the cuff right side out. Stitch in the ditch from the right side, catching the inside edge of the cuff on the underside. Sew buttonholes in the cuff overlap, and mark and sew buttons to close the cuff (**N**).

16 Interface the tab pieces. Fold each tab in half along the dotted line, right sides together, and stitch along the top and bottom edges. Turn right side out. Edgestitch (see page 55), then insert eyelets or make hand-sewn eyelets (see page 64). Sew the tabs to the back waistband at the marks, pointing outward, then fold them toward the center and topstitch (**O**).

DRESS

In addition to making you feel amazing, a dress is a unique medium to show off your craftsmanship and share your fandom. (And yes, a dress can consist of separate bodice and skirt pieces, as this one does.) In addition to all the memorable dresses and gowns our favorite characters have worn, cosplayers the world over create dresses inspired by robots, architecture, spaceships, animal characters, and everything else in the multiverse. ➔ This dress is a jumping off point, ready to be transformed into your heart's desire. The princess seams are easy to adjust for a perfect fit, and the silhouette is fitted through the chest and waist, with a little flare at the hips to accommodate a full skirt and a fluffy petticoat. Instead of using a pattern piece for the skirt, the voluminous double circle is drafted directly from your measurements.

TOOLS AND MATERIALS

▶ Sewing Essentials (see page 44)
▶ 1 yd (.9 m) of 45" (114 cm) wide medium-weight fabric such as twill, brocade, or duchess satin for the bodice (I used purple cotton sateen that came pre-interfaced with tricot knit)
▶ Lightweight fabric with some body for the skirt, such as cotton shirting, sateen, lightweight satin, or organza—amount based on Cutting the Skirt instructions on page 144 (I used 45"/114 cm wide cream and fuchsia cotton shirting.)
▶ 1 yd (.9 m) of 45" (114 cm) wide cotton muslin or twill for lining
▶ 1 yd (.9 m) of ½" (1.3 cm) twill tape or sturdy ribbon for boning channels at side seams
▶ 18" (45.7 cm) separating zipper for the bodice, in a matching color
▶ 3 yds (2.7 m) of plastic boning
▶ 1 yd (.9 m) of 1" (2.5 cm) or wider elastic

PATTERN PIECES

Pattern pieces on sheet 3; see cutting layout on page 191
▶ **Dress Front**: cut 1 on fold, cut 1 on fold of lining
▶ **Dress Side Front**: cut 2 on straight grain, cut 2 lining on straight grain
▶ **Dress Side Back**: cut 2 on straight grain, cut 2 lining on straight grain
▶ **Dress Back**: cut 2 on straight grain, cut 2 lining on straight grain
▶ **Dress Strap**: None. Cut 2 rectangles on straight grain, 3¼" (8 cm) wide by 21" (53 cm) long

NOTES

▶ French seams are a good choice for lightweight skirt fabrics; if using heavier satins, a pinked edge is great to avoid show-through when the seams are pressed. Otherwise, use whatever finishing method you like.
▶ For the more advanced sewist with some alteration skills, the two pieces can be combined into a single piece at the waist or high hip; the bodice pattern includes an alternative cutting line for a different shape, too.
▶ For an extra-bouncy skirt, incorporate horsehair braid (see page 35) in the hem. Use the hem circumference calculated on page 144 to determine how much you need.
▶ Boning should be cut ½" (1.3 cm) shorter than the channel where it will be inserted.

INSTRUCTIONS

⅝" (1.5 cm) seam allowances are used for this pattern.

Cutting the Skirt

To make the skirt pattern, you'll need to do a little math. You'll be cutting one full circle for the front (on the fold) and two halves for the back for each layer of the skirt. (The skirt in the photo consists of two layers; the upper is 16"/40.6 cm long and the lower is 10"/25.4 cm long with an 8" /20.3 cm ruffle.) Refer to the illustration below and the Cutting Layouts on page 191 for this section of the instructions.

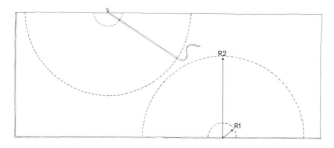

Marking a double circle skirt (one layer)

1 Measure around the widest part of your hips, add 3¾" (9.5 cm) for six seam allowances, then divide the measurement by 12.5. (This is 2 x pi x 2 [for two circles]—trust me.) This gives you the radius for the circle for the waist opening, R1. R2 is the total radius of the skirt, which is equal to the finished length + 1¼" (3.2 cm) for seam and hem allowance + R1.

You will need an amount of fabric for each skirt layer equal to 4 x R2, up to a maximum R2 of half your fabric width. (So if your fabric is 44"/111.8 cm wide, your R2 cannot exceed 22"/55.9 cm). For a longer skirt, you will not be able to cut the front piece as an unbroken circle, and the fabric requirements will increase. Note that this is a rough calculation and will give you slightly more than you need if you use the most efficient possible layout. If you're using expensive fabric and don't want a lot of leftovers, make a paper pattern and lay it out on the floor to determine the exact yardage you need.

The hem circumference is equal to 4 x 3.14 x R2, and the ruffle circumference should be one and a half to three times

that length. To avoid having to purchase a huge amount of yardage, cut strips across the width of the fabric and seam them together to create the necessary length. For an 8" (20.3 cm) finished ruffle as shown here, cut 9¼" (23.5 cm) strips to allow for seaming and hemming. As shown, in size small, the upper skirt layer requires 2¼ yards (2.1 m) of fabric, and the lower skirt needs 3¼ yards (3 m) of fabric—this includes about 1½ yards/1.4 m of fabric for the ruffle, which is one and a half times the length of the hem circumference. You will need more if you want longer or fuller ruffles for your skirt.

2 To cut your fabric, start by marking the lengths R1 and R2 on a piece of string or ribbon. Stick a pushpin through the ribbon at the center point of the waist circle, then pivot around this point and chalk mark each length at intervals along the arc. Cut along the marked lines.

3 Measure around your waist at the spot where you would like the skirt to sit and cut elastic to this length, plus a little overlap. Cut the skirt waistband twice as wide as your elastic plus 1¼" (3.2 cm) for seam allowances; the length should be 2" (5 cm) longer than your hip measurement so you can pull the skirt on. Do not interface, as you want the band to gather nicely over the elastic. If your waistband length is greater than the width of the fabric, make sure you get enough fabric to cut two side-by-side pieces.

TIP

> Take the time to really fit the bodice to your shape. If possible, make a mock-up and have a friend help you adjust it. Then, you can tweak the fit to suit the specific costume. If the dress will be worn with a blouse underneath, you may want to allow 2" to 3" (5 to 7.6 cm) of wearing ease; less ease is needed if the dress is worn alone or made of stretch woven fabric. If it's strapless, reduce the ease to nothing at the waist and add extra boning (see step 3) to help it stay up.

Sewing the Dress

1 Mark the bottom seam allowance on the back pieces. Insert a separating zipper in the center back seam (see page 60), setting the lower stop about ⅛" (3mm) above the seam allowance mark (**A**). Shorten the zipper at the top as needed.

2 Sew the front and back princess seams, and join the front and back at the side seams. If you wish, insert piping in the front and back princess seams (see page 92). Press all the seams flat and then open. Fold each strap in half lengthwise, right sides together, and sew with a ⅜" (1 cm) seam allowance. Stick a dowel inside the strap so you can press the seam open. Turn the strap inside out using your favorite method (see page 59, for options). Pin the straps to the upper edge of the bodice just outside the princess seam, right sides together, and tack in place within the seam allowance (**B**).

3 Assemble the lining in the same manner as the bodice, leaving the center back seam open. Press all the princess seams toward the front, clipping if necessary to make them lie flat. Topstitch the seam allowances ⅜" (1 cm) from the original stitching line to make a channel for boning (see page 34). The side seams are very curved, so they have to be clipped to make them lie flat. Press the seams open, then toward the back. Edgestitch both sides of a strip of ½" (1.3 cm) ribbon or twill tape over the top of the seam allowance to create an additional boning channel on each side seam, ending the tape ⅛" (3 mm) before the stitching line at the top and bottom edges to avoid creating lumps (**C**). Sew on additional channels as desired; for example, you may want boning to add support at the center front.

4 Match the bodice and lining along the top edge, right sides together, making sure that they align at all the seams. Sew, clip, and grade the seam as needed to make the curves turn out neatly, and understitch. Insert boning in all channels and sew across the ends of any channels that will not be caught in the seams (**D**).

5 Align the outer fabric and lining along the lower edge, right sides together, and sew. Clip outside and inside corners and grade the seam allowances. Also sew the lining to the bodice on the side of the zipper without the slider, leaving the other side open (**E**).

6 Turn the bodice right side out. Use a chopstick or point turner to make sure the corners turn out neatly. Fell stitch (see page 50) the lining closed next to the zipper on the slider side. Edgestitch (see page 55) the lower edge or understitch (see page 66) by hand if you don't want the stitching to be visible. Try the bodice on and adjust the straps to fit, then trim off the excess length, tuck the raw edges inside the straps, and hand sew in place (**F**). (For security, stitch the ends of the straps to the lining and also stitch through the seam allowances at the top edge of the bodice).

7 Each layer of the skirt is cut as one full circle and two half circles, with the center cut out for a waist opening. For each layer, sew the two corresponding half circles together along one straight edge to form a complete circle. Cut the full circle open along the straight grain and stitch a half circle to each side of the opening. Note: Because circle skirts have portions that hang on the bias, they can end up uneven in length once gravity takes hold. To avoid this, allow your skirt pieces to hang for a few days and trim the hem to even it out before continuing (**G**).

8 Hem the upper layer of the skirt, incorporating horsehair braid (see page 35) if you want to give it more bounce. Sew the strips for the skirt ruffle together into a single continuous loop, making sure not to sew in any twists, and zigzag or serge the seam allowances if necessary to prevent fraying. Hem, using horsehair if desired (**H**). Make eight equally spaced marks to help match the ruffle up to the skirt, then gather using your preferred technique (see page 58).

9 Sew the ruffle to the circle skirt, ensuring the marks are equally spaced around the hem. Sew the short ends of the waistband together (**I**). Slip the upper layer of the skirt over the bottom layer, right sides out. Sew two rows of gathering stitches, ⅜" (1 cm) and ⅝" (1.5 cm) from the edge of the waist opening; this will keep the layers together without basting. Ease the skirt waist slightly to match the length of the waistband, and sew the band to the skirt with right sides together.

10 Fold the remaining waistband edge to the inside and fold it down to form a channel, covering the seam. Stitch in the ditch (see page 68) to secure the inside of the waistband, leaving an opening to insert the elastic (**J**). Thread the elastic through and join the ends; close the opening by hand or by machine. (See page 68 for a refresher on applying elastic.)

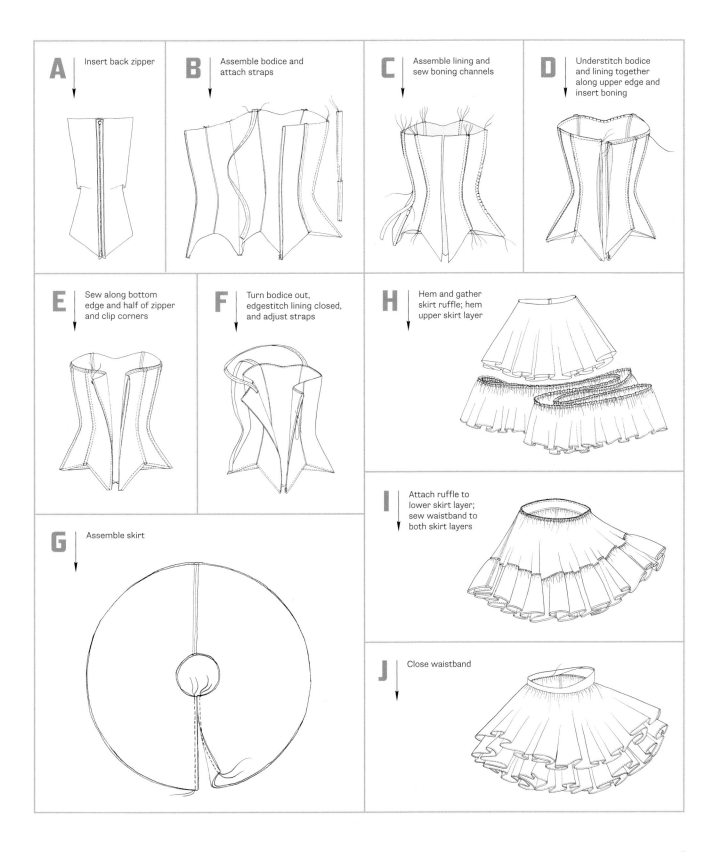

A | Insert back zipper

B | Assemble bodice and attach straps

C | Assemble lining and sew boning channels

D | Understitch bodice and lining together along upper edge and insert boning

E | Sew along bottom edge and half of zipper and clip corners

F | Turn bodice out, edgestitch lining closed, and adjust straps

H | Hem and gather skirt ruffle; hem upper skirt layer

I | Attach ruffle to lower skirt layer; sew waistband to both skirt layers

G | Assemble skirt

J | Close waistband

COAT

Coats are a cosplayer's delight and nemesis. Few costume components are more spectacular, but a fantastic coat or jacket doesn't come cheap. A coat is an investment in materials, time, and skill, and when you've created a few of your own, you'll probably agree the price is justified—making them yourself is *so* worth it! Even one simple coat pattern has so many possibilities, from regal court dress to military uniforms to tattered adventurer gear, depending on your fabric choices, detailing, trims, and weathering. This pattern offers multiple lengths for even more options like a regal floor-length robe, a cropped jacket, and everything in between.

TOOLS AND MATERIALS

- Sewing Essentials (see page 44)
- 5½ yds (5 m) of 60" (152 cm) wide medium-weight fabric with some body, such as twill, gabardine, faux leather or suede, velvet, brocade, or duchess satin (I used a sage-and-cream brocade with a small vine motif.)
- 5¾ yds (5.3 m) of 45" (114 cm) wide lining fabric
- 1½ yds (1.4 m) of weft insertion or woven interfacing
- 12 fabric-covered buttons, ⅝" (1.5 cm) wide
- 8 yds (7.3 m) of lace or novelty trim (I used an iron-on metallic embroidered leaf trim.)
- All-purpose thread in a matching color

PATTERN PIECES

Pattern pieces on sheet 3; see cutting layout on page 192
- **Coat Front:** cut 2 on straight grain, cut 2 lining on straight grain, cut 2 facings on straight grain
- **Coat Back:** cut 2 on straight grain, cut 2 of lining on straight grain
- **Coat Side:** cut 2 on straight grain, cut 2 lining on straight grain
- **Coat Top Sleeve:** cut 2 on straight grain, cut 2 lining on straight grain
- **Coat Under Sleeve:** cut 2 on straight grain, cut 2 lining on straight grain
- **Coat Collar:** cut 2 on straight grain, cut 2 interfacing
- **Coat Side Pocket:** cut 4 on straight grain

NOTES

- The coat has three main pattern pieces, along with a two-piece sleeve. The single-breasted closure buttons all the way up to the neckline, with the option of a two-piece collar or simple stand. The longer versions of the coat include side pockets so you have somewhere to stash necessities, or you can design your own patch pocket (see page 82) for a more casual option.
- As designed, the back vent extends up to just below hip height. If you want to make a shorter coat but keep the vent, continue the extension upward. Don't bring it up higher than the hipbone, though, as that will most likely cause it to gape when worn.
- On the pattern sheet the front lining and front facing are included in the front piece, each with a different cut-off line (seam allowance is included). Trace each one as a separate piece.
- The pattern is marked at the waist, hip, and knee to help guide you in cutting the coat off at your desired length. The yardages on page 149 are sufficient for a floor-length coat, in the largest size. If making a small size or a shorter coat you will probably need less fabric, so you may want to lay your pattern pieces out on the floor and measure them to determine the actual yardage before going shopping.

INSTRUCTIONS

⅝" (1.5 cm) seams are used everywhere except the collar. For the collar and neckline seams, a ⅜" (1 cm) allowance is used.

1 Sew the back pieces together from the neckline to the dot at the top of the vent, right sides together. Press the seam open. On the right coat back, clip the seam allowance at the top inside corner of the vent so that when you press the seam open, the vent extension can stay folded over on top of the left vent extension. Sew the front and back sleeve seams for both coat and lining, right sides together (**A**).

2 Align the pocket pieces between the dots on the front and side panels, right sides together. Stitch ½" (1.3 cm) from the edge, then press the pockets outward (**B**).

3 Sew the front and back pieces to the side panels, right sides together. When sewing the side front seams, stop with the needle down on the mark and pivot to stitch around the outside edge of the pocket. After sewing the seam, clip into the corners above and below the pocket opening so the rest of the seam can be pressed open. Sew the shoulder seams with right sides together, ease the sleeve caps (see page 59), and sew in the sleeves, right sides together and matching notches on shoulder seams and side panels (**C**).

4 On the overlap side of the vent, the vent extension folds back to create a facing. Sew a mitered corner: Mark a point 1¾" (4.4 cm) in from the hem and vent edges, then fold diagonally to bring the hem and vent edges together, right side facing in, as shown in (**D**). Sew across the corner perpendicular to the raw edge, beginning at the mark and stopping ¾" (1.9 cm) before the edge.

5 Interface the front facing and assemble the lining, sewing front to side to back and the center back seam, right sides together. Leave the shoulder seams open for now, and don't sew the lining and facing together yet (**E**). Set lining aside.

6 Stick your finger in the mitered corner of the vent overlap of the coat and hold it while you turn the corner right side out, then press it flat. If you will be applying trim to the hem, as in this example coat, topstitch it in place. (If you don't plan

TIP

When cutting out the lining, trim off the hem and sleeve hem allowances so the lining is slightly shorter than the outer layer of the coat. Also trim the vent extension away from the left back lining along the marked line. (The left back lining is the piece that will be on the left side of your body when the coat is worn.) Leave the vent extension intact on the right lining and both outer pieces.

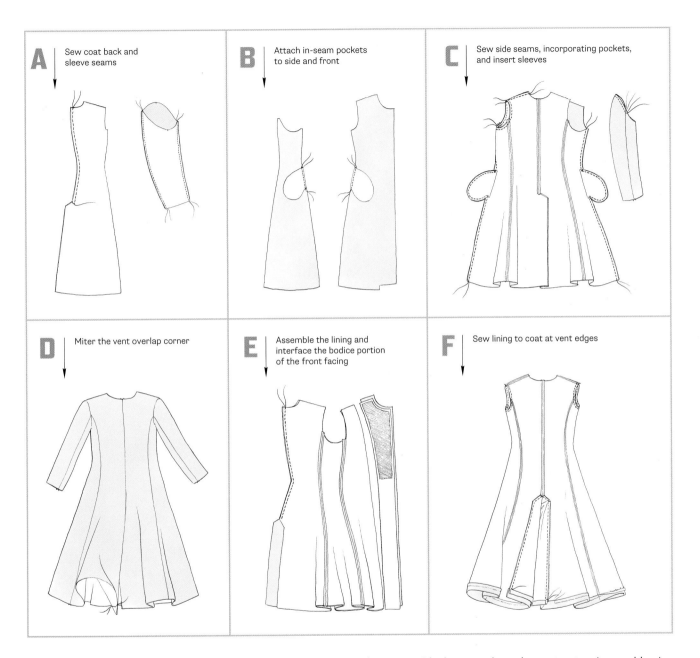

A Sew coat back and sleeve seams

B Attach in-seam pockets to side and front

C Sew side seams, incorporating pockets, and insert sleeves

D Miter the vent overlap corner

E Assemble the lining and interface the bodice portion of the front facing

F Sew lining to coat at vent edges

to use trim, use a hand or machine blindstitch to sew the hem in place ¾"/1.9 cm below the raw edge, making sure to catch just a few threads on the outer fabric so that the stitching will not be visible.) Stop about 10" (25.4 cm) short of the front edge on each side. Match the right (underlap) side of the back

lining up with the coat along the vent extension, and beginning ⅞" (2.2 cm) above the bottom of the lining, stitch up the vent, continuing around the corner until you meet the center back seam. Trim the corner. Repeat on the left, clipping into the corner so that it can pivot. Fold the bottom ⅞" (2.2 cm) of the lining up and press in place (**F**).

7 Refer to (**G**) for steps 7 and 8. Match the coat and lining up with right sides together and stitch the lower edge of the lining to the edge of the hem allowance (folding the rest of the hem back out of the way), sewing from the vent around to the front. Stop and backtack on the stitching line where the lining will join the facing. Match the facing up with the front edge of the coat. Keeping the lining seam allowance out of the way, stitch from the dot at the bottom corner of the facing (on the stitching line where the lining and facing will join) across the lower edge of the facing, up the front, and around the corner to the neck. Stop at the small dot on the center front line and backtack, leaving the rest of the neckline open, and clip into the seam allowance at the point where the stitching ends.

8 When you match the coat and lining up, you'll find a little extra length in the lining that forms a ¼" (6 mm) pleat at the lower edge. This is called a "jump pleat," and it's there because the lining is usually less flexible than the outer fabric so it needs a little extra room to prevent it from pulling. Sew the front lining/facing seam from the shoulder down, catching the jump pleat at the lower edge of the lining, and stop as close to the hem as you can get (**H**). Sew the lining shoulder seams and set the lining sleeves into the lining, as shown on the right side in (**G**), being careful to keep the rest of the coat out of the way.

9 Turn the coat right side out through the neckline. Press the sleeve hems up 1⅜" (3.5 cm) and baste them ½" (1.3 cm) from the fold. Pull the lining down into the sleeves, then reach through the neckline between the coat and lining layers. Grab the sleeve hem and lining together and pull them out where you can see them. The end of the lining sleeve goes over the end of the inside-out coat sleeve like a sock, with the right side of the lining facing the folded-back sleeve hem. Match up the front and back sleeve seams, making sure neither sleeve nor lining is twisted, use lots of pins to secure the edges, and sew the lining edge to the sleeve hem allowance (**I**).

10 Pull the sleeves right side out again and press the whole coat thoroughly. Stitch in the ditch (see page 68) for 1" (2.5 cm) at the bottom of each sleeve seam to secure the sleeve

hem and lining. Machine baste the layers together at the neck, stitching slightly inside the seam allowance (**J**).

11 Interface (see page 32) the collar pieces and align the two pieces with right sides together. Stitch around the outer edges, leaving the bottom free. Clip the corners and turn right side out (**K**).

12 Clip the neckline seam allowances to open up the curve and match the outer layer of the collar up with the neckline. The collar ends at the marked center front line; it does not extend all the way to the front edge. Sew the collar to the neck opening, right sides together, matching notches to shoulder seams (**L**).

13 Press the inner collar band seam allowance up inside the collar and stitch in the ditch, making sure the inner layer of the collar is secure. Edgestitch or topstitch (see page 55) along the front and top edges of the collar to give it structure. Sew buttonholes (see page 63) on the left front of the coat, starting ¾" (1.9 cm) below the neckline and spacing the buttons 2½" (6.4 cm) apart. Mark and sew the buttons on the right front (**M**).

14 Apply iron-on or hand-sewn trim as desired. On this coat, trim is applied at the hem, on the sleeve hem, around the wrists, and across the shoulders.

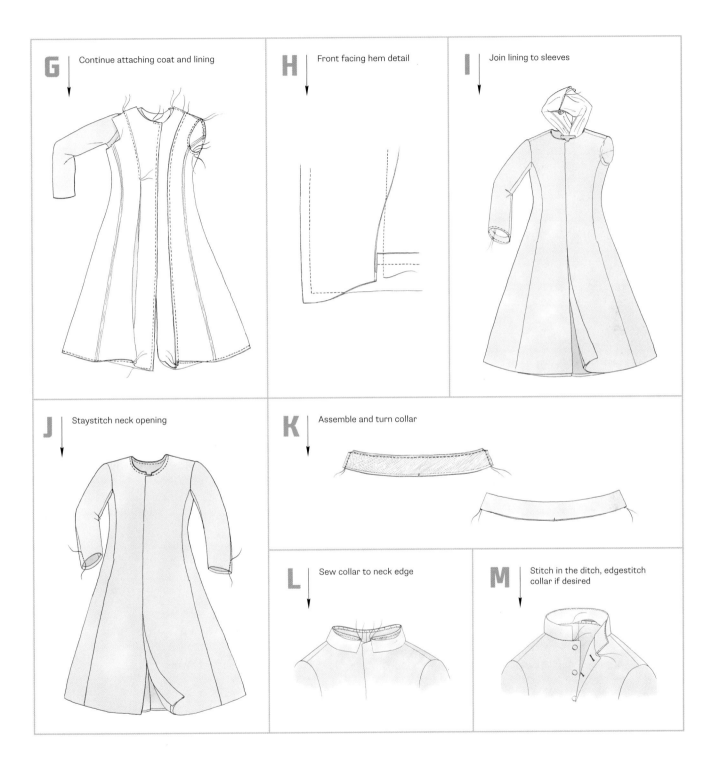

G Continue attaching coat and lining

H Front facing hem detail

I Join lining to sleeves

J Staystitch neck opening

K Assemble and turn collar

L Sew collar to neck edge

M Stitch in the ditch, edgestitch collar if desired

PART THREE

COSTUMES

To help get you thinking about building your own costumes, these projects show how you can combine the patterns and techniques from the previous chapters into a variety of costumes across all different genres and styles. Some of the patterns have several variations, so you can see how they adapt to different projects. I've also listed the accessories that complete a costume. I hope this section jump-starts your imagination and sparks your creativity!

COSTUME WARM-UP

Here's a simple appliqué exercise that will let you practice hand and machine sewing while showing off your geek pride. It starts with an existing shirt, so you don't need to worry about assembling or finishing anything just yet, and it doesn't need a ton of materials or supplies. Revisit the appliqué section on page 89 as needed. If this is your first time sewing, try to pick a relatively simple design. I'll talk about appliqué for fabrics that need to retain their stretch in the Superhero 1 Costume (see page 159).

TOOLS AND MATERIALS

▶ Sewing Essentials (see page 44)
▶ A plain, stable cotton T-shirt or sweatshirt
▶ A worn-out T-shirt or other small piece of contrasting stable knit fabric for the appliqué
▶ All-purpose thread to match the appliqué fabric
▶ Lightweight fusible web
▶ Appliqué template (pattern sheet 1)

NOTE

▶ Instead of overlapping your machine stitches or backtacking, leave long thread tails at the beginning and end. When you've finished stitching, use a hand needle to pull these threads through to the underside of the fabric and tie them together. A dab of fray stop will prevent the knots from unraveling.

INSTRUCTIONS

1 Cut a piece of fusible web slightly larger than your design. Peel the paper backing away from one side of the web, leaving the other side intact. Lay the web on the back side of your appliqué fabric and fuse it in place, using the iron temperature recommended on the web's packaging.

2 Trace or draw your design on the remaining paper backing. Remember that the finished appliqué will be reversed, so your drawing should be a mirror image of the desired shape. Try to orient the design so the grain of the fabric runs from top to bottom. Cut out the appliqué and peel away the paper backing.

3 Lay the T-shirt out on your ironing board, making sure it's nice and smooth. Arrange the appliqué on top, fusible side down. Make sure it's centered and oriented correctly. Press with the iron to fuse the appliqué in place, using a press-and-lift motion, instead of sliding from side, to side, so you don't distort the fabric.

4 Stitch around the edges of the appliqué. If sewing by hand, use a whipstitch (see page 50) that wraps around the cut edges. A zigzag stitch is the most common choice for machine appliqué, but feel free to experiment with straight or decorative stitches. If your machine has a speed control knob, you may want to turn the speed down for more control. Sew close to the edge of the appliqué, or slightly overlapping it if you use a zigzag stitch. If you come to a sharp corner, stop with the needle down and lift the foot so you can pivot the fabric. Remember to lower the foot again before you continue stitching. Continue all the way around the appliqué, until all the raw edges are secured.

SUPERHERO 1

A long-sleeved leotard and cape add up to a super-classic superhero look that's a snap to sew and can be customized for a huge variety of characters. For this version, I added a layer of flannel to the cape shoulder pleats, which helped to bulk them up and give them a little extra definition. I also added a big, splashy crest to the front of the leotard, which can obviously be switched out for whatever motif your character requires.

PATTERNS

▶ Leotard, page 107
▶ Cape, page 99
▶ Appliqué template (pattern sheet 1)

ACCESSORIES

▶ Booties

*This costume is composed of two new garments, one from the **Cape** pattern and one from the **Leotard** pattern.*

TOOLS AND MATERIALS

▶ Sewing Essentials (see page 44)

For the Leotard:

▶ 1¼ yds (1.1 m) of 60" (152 cm) wide four-way stretch spandex (I used a crimson Supplex athleticwear knit.)
▶ ¼ yd (23 cm) or a sizeable scrap of four-way stretch spandex in a contrasting color for the appliqué (I used a gold nylon/spandex metallic knit.)
▶ 2½ yds (2.3 m) of ¼" (6 mm) elastic to finish the neckline and leg openings
▶ 2 spools of 100% polyester all-purpose thread—one to match the leotard fabric and one to match the appliqué fabric
▶ Tear-away or dissolvable stabilizer (see page 89)
▶ Temporary fabric adhesive (if the stabilizer does not have its own adhesive)
▶ Stretch sewing machine needles (size 11/75)

For the Cape:

▶ Lightweight drapey fabric, 56" (142 cm) wide, amount based on step 1 of the Cape Pattern (see page 100) (I used a silky blue synthetic with a matte satin finish.)
▶ ¼ yd (23 cm) of cotton flannel in a matching color
▶ 10" (25.4 cm) of twill tape, ½" to 1" (1.3 to 2.5 cm) wide (Anything in this size range will work.)
▶ 6 large sew-on snaps
▶ Large safety pins
▶ All-purpose thread in a matching color

INSTRUCTIONS

1 Stabilize the base fabric with a removable (tear-away or dissolving) material on the back side of the front piece, extending about 1" (2.5 cm) beyond the appliqué area on all sides. Freezer paper is the most economical option but may be more difficult to remove afterward than a specialty product.

2 Apply another piece of stabilizer on the right side of your appliqué and place it on top of the leotard front so the fabrics are sandwiched together between the stabilizers. You can

either stabilize the appliqué before cutting and draw your design directly on the stabilizer (not reversed since you're working on the right side), allowing for more accurate cutting, or you can do it after cutting and placing the appliqué so the stabilizer extends over the appliqué edges and helps to hold it in place. Note: If using a metallic or other coated fabric for your appliqué, test the stabilizer on scraps first to make sure the adhesive will not damage the coating. If it does, use a temporary adhesive between the fabric layers instead of putting stabilizer on top.

3 Pin or baste through all layers of the sandwich. Use the finest, sharpest pins you can find to reduce distortion in the fabric. For large or complicated appliqués that need extra help, use a wash-away fabric spray adhesive (often available in quilt shops) or dissolvable fabric tape to temporarily hold the layers together.

4 Stitch around all edges of the appliqué, using a small zigzag (try 3 mm width and 1.5 to 2 mm length), stretch, or decorative stitch. Remove any pins before they touch the foot, as trying to sew over them will stretch the fabric and make your stitching uneven. Backstitch or whipstitch (see page 50) is suitable if you prefer to attach the appliqué by hand. If sewing by hand, you will have more control and may be able to forgo one or both layers of stabilizer.

5 Wash out or tear away all stabilizers and adhesives. Finish assembling the leotard as described in the basic pattern, page 109. When making the cape, cut two pieces of flannel to the shape of the pleated area in the cape template. Baste the flannel and cape together along the valley folds (the evenly dashed lines) before forming the pleats. Make the cape as described on page 100, making sure to catch the edges of the flannel padding in the front hem and bias facing. Add snaps to the leotard and the cape as in step 7. If your leotard fabric is lightweight, consider appliquéing reinforcement patches to the shoulders first to give the snaps a little extra support.

NOTES

→ So the finished appliqué is just as supple and stretchable as the original fabrics, this project uses a different method from the one in the Costume Warm-Up (see page 156). Here the fabric layers are temporarily stabilized with a material that can be torn or dissolved away after the stitching is complete. Sometimes you can dispense with stabilizers entirely if your fabric holds its shape well and you pin or baste carefully, but use a stabilizer if the appliqué shifts or the stitching ripples.

→ The basic rule when adding details to a costume is that detail work should be done as early as the garment construction permits. This makes your life easier for a few reasons: it's easier to maneuver smaller pieces of fabric; it's easiest to get a smooth result if your base fabric is perfectly flat; and if something goes badly wrong and you need to recut the piece—which happens to beginners and pros alike—you won't have to repeat a lot of work. The only exception is if your appliqué or other detail continues across a seam, in which case the seam should be sewn first. The steps on this page should be completed after the leotard is cut out, but before beginning assembly.

SUPERHERO 2

The Seamless Super-Suit is a great canvas for big wrap-around designs. You can lay out the entire design while the fabric is still flat, so it's easier to handle, and you only have to match up the design at the center back and sleeve seams (or plan your design to avoid them, if you so choose). In reverse appliqué, the contrast fabric is applied behind the main fabric, and then the top layer is cut away after stitching around all the outlines. It can be used in pretty much any way a standard appliqué would be and is slightly better for small details, narrow lines, and tight corners because you do all the sewing before cutting, so it's more stable to work with. The layers of fabric also lend themselves to some interesting dimensional effects, as in this costume where the design suggests cracking lava or a flare of energy from within.

*This costume is a new garment from the **Seamless Super-Suit** pattern combined with the example garment from the **Cape** pattern.*

PATTERNS

▶ Seamless Super-Suit, page 117
▶ Cape, page 99

ACCESSORIES

▶ Boots with Boot Covers (see instructions on page 170)

TOOLS AND MATERIALS

For the suit:

▶ Sewing Essentials (see page 44)
▶ 2¾ yds (2.5 m) of 60" (152 cm) wide stable light- to medium-weight four-way stretch fabric for the base fabric (I used navy nylon/spandex milliskin, which is ideal for this design.)
▶ 2¾ yds (2.5 m) of 60" (152 cm) wide stable light- to medium-weight four-way stretch fabric for the reverse appliqué (I used greenish-gold nylon/spandex activewear knit.)
▶ 18" to 20" (46 to 51 cm) invisible zipper
▶ 1 yd (.9 m) of ¼" (6 mm) elastic to finish the neckline
▶ Small scraps of fusible tricot (knit) interfacing
▶ 100% polyester all-purpose thread in a color to match your base fabric
▶ Stretch sewing machine needles (size 11/75)

INSTRUCTIONS

1 After sketching to plan your ideas, cut out the main fabric for your super-suit and for the reverse appliqué, referencing (**A**) at right. (Remember that the final design will be reversed.) The appliqué should be large enough to cover the entire design area, but doesn't need to be cut exactly to the finished size, and in fact should have a margin of 1" (2.5 cm) or more all the way around to allow for any inaccuracy in the stitching. If you prefer, you can cut the entire suit double and trim away the excess later.

2 Pin the appliqué in place all the way around, with the right side facing the wrong side of the base fabric, and sketch your appliqué design on the back side of the appliqué fabric using chalk or a white gel pen. If your design crosses any seams, you will need to plan carefully to ensure the lines match up when sewn.

3 As in the Superhero 1 costume (see page 159), the layers need to be prevented from shifting and creating puckers while you sew. Because the appliqué in this case is very large, freezer paper or more specialized stabilizers may be impractical and difficult to maneuver through the machine. This leaves you with a few options. You can lay the pieces out on a flat surface and baste them by hand inside the stitching line, or you can use a temporary fabric adhesive or basting spray. If using adhesives, test on a scrap of your actual fabric first to make sure it holds well and washes out completely. Then, transfer your design to the top side by machine basting ¼" (6 mm) inside the stitching lines using a walking foot, within the area that will be cut away.

4 It's best to sew from the visible side of the fabric as much as possible, as the top side of the stitching is usually a little more attractive. Follow your basted lines to stitch out the design with a zigzag or stretch stitch, leaving long tails at the beginning and end of each line of stitching so you can pull them to the underside and knot. After all the appliqué is sewn, remove all basting and cut away the top layer just inside the stitching. Rounded-point or lace scissors may help to avoid snagging the lower layer while you trim. Appliqué scissors, designed to cut very close to a line of stitching, are another option. Trim most of the excess from the underside as well, though you may want to leave some in place for reinforcement in the area where the cape snaps will be sewn.

5 To sew the suit, follow steps 1 through 8 on page 119. Add snaps to the suit and cape as described in the Cape pattern, step 7 (see page 100).

NOTES

→ Choose fabrics with similar weight and stretch properties so the suit fits evenly all the way around.

→ Depending on how much of the bodysuit your design will cover, you may not need as much of the reverse appliqué fabric as you do of the main fabric. You may want to plan out your design before shopping to avoid getting more fabric than you need.

→ If the fabric creeps as you sew, use more pins or hand-baste the layers in place. If you have one, this is a great time to take out the walking or even-feed foot to prevent the seams from shifting or puckering.

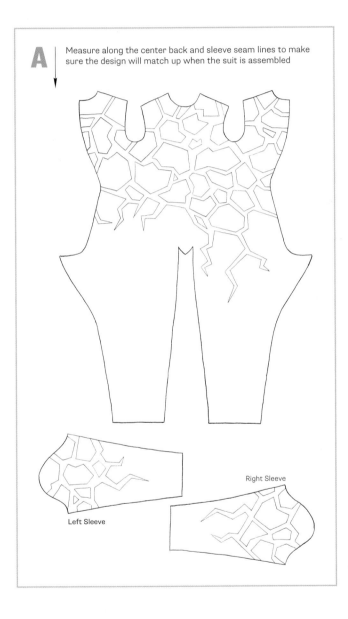

A Measure along the center back and sleeve seam lines to make sure the design will match up when the suit is assembled

Left Sleeve

Right Sleeve

SUPERHERO 3

A full-coverage jumpsuit is a great starting point for many costumes, even those that ultimately cover quite a bit less. This costume uses the Halter Jumpsuit variation of the Seamed Jumpsuit, and includes faux leather details and a sheer mesh panel. Faux leather can be a little difficult to sew, so follow the instructions on page 70 to ensure success. Although incredibly popular in designs for superheroes, game characters, and others, cutout details in bodysuits can be trickier than you might think. Usually, the stretch of a bodysuit is evenly balanced around your body. If you cut away part of that, the remaining fabric loses tension. This can make it difficult to predict what the final shape will look like, but with a little planning, you can account for and counteract that. A sheer panel is one way to do this, and this project will show you how.

PATTERNS

- ▶ Seamed Jumpsuit, page 111
- ▶ Superhero 3 Optional Details, pattern sheet 4

ACCESSORIES

- ▶ Mask
- ▶ Elbow-length gloves
- ▶ Boots with Boot Covers, page 170

*This costume is a new garment from the **Seamed Jumpsuit** pattern, **Halter Jumpsuit** variation.*

TOOLS AND MATERIALS

- ▶ Sewing Essentials (see page 44)
- ▶ 2 yds (1.8 m) of 60" (152 cm) wide four-way stretch fabric for the jumpsuit (I used a plum-colored heavyweight nylon/spandex knit.)
- ▶ ¼ yd (23 cm) of 60" (152 cm) wide powernet or four-way stretch nylon mesh fabric for the inset panel (I used purple powernet.)
- ▶ ½ yd (46 cm) of 60" (152 cm) wide stretch faux leather for leg accents, collar, and facing (I used navy.)

- ▶ 1 yd (.9 m) of ⅜" (1 cm) plush-back elastic
- ▶ 1" (2.5 cm) swimsuit hook
- ▶ 100% polyester all-purpose thread in a matching color
- ▶ Roller or non-stick foot for your sewing machine (if using faux leather or similar fabric)
- ▶ Stretch needle (size 11/75 or 12/80, depending on fabric weight)

INSTRUCTIONS

1 The sheer area in this costume is an inset panel. The inset is created by cutting the pattern pieces apart and adding seam allowances; see Adding Seams in Chapter 4 (see page 84). Sew the panel to the rest of the front piece before proceeding with the construction.

2 For this version I sewed the side seams before the princess seams, so I could sew the stretch faux leather leg accents across the side seam. The four side accents are chevron shapes; in this costume, the upper shapes are 1¼" (3.2 cm) wide and the lower shapes are 1¾" (4.4 cm) wide, spaced about 1¼" (3.2 cm) apart; cut them long enough to catch in the princess seams, based on your size. The accents were stitched in place along each folded-under edge, a simple appliqué technique (see page 89).

Stretch faux leather requires its own set of tricks for the best results. Use a stretch needle to prevent skipped stitches, and hold the layers together with binder clips or temporary adhesives to avoid marring the coated surface. Double-sided dissolvable tape is especially handy for securing stretch appliqués. Also, use a roller or non-stick/Teflon foot anytime you're stitching on the surface of the faux leather to prevent it from sticking to the foot. If it sticks to the machine bed, slip a piece of tissue paper underneath and tear it away after the stitching is complete.

3 After attaching the inset, stitching the side seams, and applying the appliqués to the legs, construct the costume as for the Seamed Jumpsuit, Halter Jumpsuit variation (see page 116), steps 1 and 2. The faux leather border around the halter edge is constructed as follows: Measure and cut the elastic as in step 3 on page 114. The pattern pieces for the faux leather border and leg appliqués are given on pattern sheet 4, or create your own by drawing the outline onto the pattern pieces, then tracing off each segment and joining them at the seams to form one continuous length (**A**). Remember to add allowances for seams and to turn under at the edge. Because faux leather edges aren't very nice against skin, I covered them with plush-back elastic. To apply the elastic, baste the bodysuit and border together along the top edge of the bodysuit, wrong side of border to the right side of the bodysuit, using a ¼" (6 mm) seam allowance. Instead of doing the stitched-and-turned elastic application as described in the Halter Jumpsuit variation, place the elastic over the seam allowance on the right side of the border, plush side facing out, so that it just covers the basting. Zigzag stitch in place along the top edge, then fold to the inside and pin so the top of the elastic is about ⅛" (3 mm) below the fold, covering the seam. Secure the lower edge with a zigzag stitch, holding the faux leather border up and out of the way so you're just sewing through the spandex layer. Finally, fold the border back into place, turn the edge under ⅜" (1 cm), and edgestitch from the right side with a stretch stitch.

4 Complete the costume by following steps 5 through 7 of the Seamed Jumpsuit, Halter Jumpsuit variation.

VARIATIONS

As you get comfortable working with stretch fabrics, you can create cutouts or sheer insets in several different ways in addition to the method described in step 1. You can do a mesh appliqué or reverse appliqué with the opaque fabric trimmed away after stitching, as was done in the Superhero 2 costume (see page 163). Matching the mesh to your fabric will give a subtle sheer effect, or you can match the mesh to your skin tone so it disappears when viewed from a distance. For a true skin-exposing cutout, one option is to sew elastic around the edges of the opening, similar to how the elastic is applied to the leg openings of the Long-Sleeved Leotard (see page 107), and another is to create a faced opening as

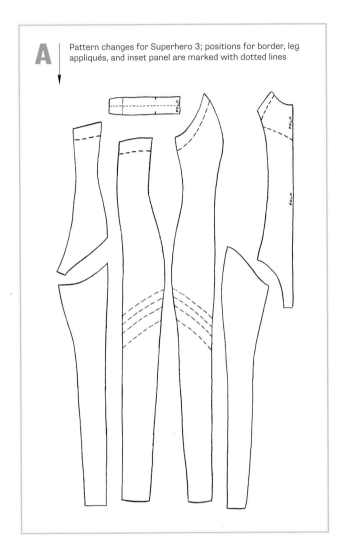

A | Pattern changes for Superhero 3; positions for border, leg appliqués, and inset panel are marked with dotted lines

described in Chapter 3 on page 66, using a fusible knit interfacing to support the opening and preserve its shape. You may need to cut the bodysuit in a slightly larger size so that the cutout isn't stretched out of shape when you wear it.

BOOT COVERS

Shoes are the cause of many a cosplay headache. Buying a new pair of shoes for every costume is expensive, and you can't count on finding the exact color and style you need. But in many cases, you can get around all this by making decorative covers to wear over an existing pair of shoes or boots. The instructions below show how to make boot covers in stretch fabric, which is the easiest way because the fabric molds to the shape of the shoe and you don't have to worry about closures. You can use a similar method for making non-stretch shoe covers, but instead of wrapping your shoe in fabric, you'll wrap it in plastic wrap and tape to create an exact mold of the shoe, much like the duct tape body form described in Chapter 4 (see page 80). Then, add seam lines until the pattern can be fully flattened, decide where to add the closure, and sew it up. For both styles of shoe covers, it's very important to make a mock-up or two to fine-tune the fit and shape.

TOOLS AND MATERIALS

▶ Sewing Essentials (see page 44)
▶ 1 yd (.9 m) of 60" (152 cm) wide four-way stretch spandex fabric (I used the same fabric as for the Superhero 3 costume.)
▶ Small piece (about 6" x 8"/15.2 x 20.3 cm) of rubberized non-slip fabric for the soles
▶ Small pieces of leftover stretch faux leather for trim
▶ Felt-tip marker
▶ 100% polyester all-purpose thread in a matching color

INSTRUCTIONS

1 Measure from your toes up your foot to the desired boot height, and around the widest part of your leg (**A**). Add at least 4" (10.2 cm) to both measurements and cut a rectangle of fabric to size.

2 While wearing the under shoe, wrap the spandex around your leg and pin along the bottom of the foot and back of the leg. Adjust and re-pin until it's smooth. You may need to clip into the rectangle near the heel to release the tension (**B**).

3 Use a felt tip marker to draw along the line of pins on both sides. If your shoes have heels, mark the line where the shoe joins the heel (see note below). Also mark the center front, following a straight line from your shinbone down to the point of the shoe (**C**).

4 Turn the shoe over and draw around the sole area. Place a piece of tracing paper on top and trace the outline of the sole (**D**). Wrap a separate small piece of spandex around the heel of the shoe and mark the center seam down the inside of the heel as well as the line where the heel joins the shoe (**E**).

5 Remove the pins and flatten out the cover. Copy your draped pattern (boot, heel, and sole) onto a piece of tracing paper and mark a ⅜" (1 cm) seam allowance all the way around each piece. Make sure to mark the center line, as this will help when aligning the shoe and sole and also for placing any centered embellishments. Make sure that the seam

NOTE

This method creates a shoe cover with a single seam down the back. It works best for shoes with a medium to high heel, as the angle between the foot and the leg isn't as sharp. Chunky heels are easiest to cover; for thin heels, you might want to just leave an opening to stick the heel through. While you can also use this method for flat shoes, you will end up with wrinkles at the front of the ankle unless you add a seam along the top of the foot or around the ankle. Sometimes this is okay, and the Superhero 2 booties (see page 162) were created in this way—they end right at the ankle and are finished with a simple band. In most cases, a yard of fabric will be enough to both drape the pattern (steps 1 through 4) and sew the final boot covers. If your fabric is limited, you may want to use four-way stretch scrap fabric for those steps.

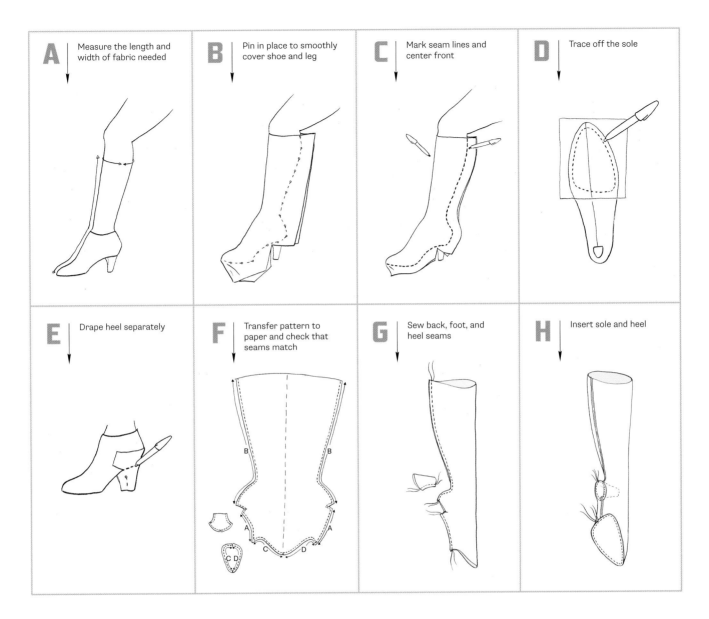

A | Measure the length and width of fabric needed

B | Pin in place to smoothly cover shoe and leg

C | Mark seam lines and center front

D | Trace off the sole

E | Drape heel separately

F | Transfer pattern to paper and check that seams match

G | Sew back, foot, and heel seams

H | Insert sole and heel

under the foot (a) and along the back of the leg (b) is the same length on both sides, even though they won't be exactly the same shape. The left and right toe curves (c) and (d) should be slightly shorter than the corresponding curves on the sole because the sole does not stretch. Also, check that your heel piece matches up with the corresponding opening (V-shaped notch) on each side of the main pattern piece, and make a small notch to help you line it up with the back seam (**F**).

6 Sew the seams along the bottom of the foot, the back of the leg, and the inside of the heel (**G**).

7 Sew the sole into the boot, stretching the spandex portion slightly to fit. Turn the heel right side out and stick it inside the heel opening, aligning the seam with the under-foot seam, and sew around the opening (**H**). Clip the corners of the heel opening up to the stitching to prevent them from binding. Finish the top edge of the boot covers with a facing (see page 66), with elastic (see page 68), or by joining them to a matching bodysuit. In this case, the faux leather accents are facings installed to turn to the outside, not the inside, with the edges turned under and edgestitched (see page 55) down.

SCI-FI JUMPSUIT

There's no doubt about it: jumpsuits are the uniform of the future. Everyone from dystopian drone to starship captain is wearing them, and this science-fictional style statement goes far beyond basic spandex. Texture, especially a mix of textures, is key to making these garments look more substantial and clothing-like. Think about layering fabrics—a sheer lace or mesh over a solid fabric—to get more depth and interesting color effects. Rib knits are another good option for adding texture, and their generous stretch can compensate for another fabric that's less flexible.

This costume is a new garment from the **Seamed Jumpsuit** pattern.

PATTERNS

▶ Seamed Jumpsuit, page 111

ACCESSORIES

▶ Wig
▶ Boots

TOOLS AND MATERIALS

▶ Sewing Essentials (see page 44)
▶ 1½ yds (1.4 m) of 60" (152 cm) wide matte moleskin spandex fabric (I used silver gray)
▶ 1 yd (.9 m) of 60" (152 cm) wide wet-look spandex fabric (I used turquoise)
▶ 1 yd (.9 m) of 60" (152 cm) wide four-way stretch mesh (I used navy)
▶ 1 yd (.9 m) of 60" (152 cm) wide four-way stretch spacer fabric (I used black)
▶ 10 yds (9 m) of 2 mm elastic cord
▶ 16" to 20" (40.6 to 50.8 cm) decorative zipper
▶ 100% polyester all-purpose thread in a matching color
▶ Stretch sewing machine needles (size 11/75 or 12/80)

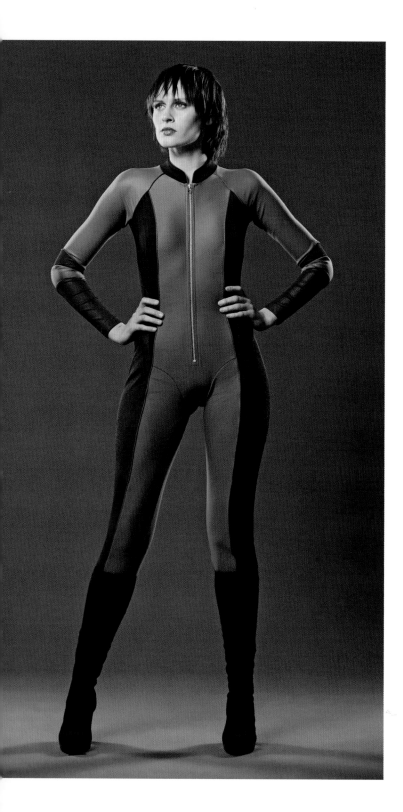

INSTRUCTIONS

1 Make stretch piping by cutting 1" (2.5 cm) cross-grain strips of thin spandex (like the turquoise wet-look fabric used here). Wrap the strips around the 2 mm elastic cord, and hold in place by hand basting or sewing with a stretch stitch and piping foot (a serger equipped with a piping foot can zip out as much custom stretch piping as you need in a matter of minutes).

2 Before you sew, add additional seams to the sleeve, side front, and side back pattern pieces to create the color blocking (**A**); see Adding Seams in Chapter 4 (see page 84). Construct the sleeve pieces, inserting piping (see page 92) between the seams. For the side panels and lower sleeves, cut each piece once in wet-look spandex and once from mesh for the overlay. Baste the layers together within the seam allowances to prevent them from shifting during construction, but remember to remove the basting after they're sewn so it doesn't interfere with the stretch. Sew the side panels to the upper side and lower leg pieces and assemble the sleeves.

3 Instead of inserting an invisible zipper in the back, stitch the entire seam and add an exposed zipper (see page 63) to the front.

NOTE

If you plan to combine multiple fabrics in your jumpsuit, think about choosing materials that are roughly compatible in weight. Sewing a very sheer mesh to a beefy doubleknit is sometimes unavoidable, but if you have flimsy faux leather and want to pair it with something bulkier, you may want to consider underlining it with another layer of fabric so you don't get a visible step in thickness at the seam line. Make sure all your materials give you enough stretch for comfort, and if the stretch is minimal, you may want to leave a little extra seam allowance at the side and princess seams to allow for adjustment once you've had a chance to try it on.

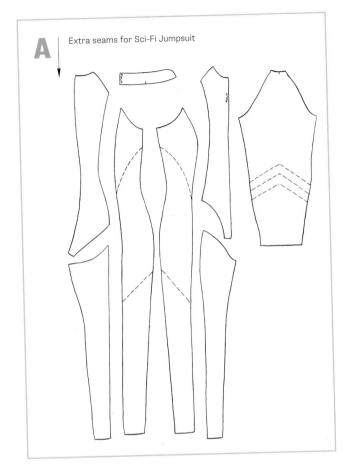

A | Extra seams for Sci-Fi Jumpsuit

Adding Texture

Once you've selected fabrics, there are still more opportunities to add texture, structure, and interest to your costume. Piping is a great way to highlight the seams. Topstitching helps to keep seam allowances flat and makes your jumpsuit look more thought-out and professional. You can also experiment with pleating, pintucks, and other fabric manipulation techniques to create various effects, especially with thinner materials that won't create a lot of bulk.

4 Construct the jumpsuit as in steps 2 through 7 (see page 112), inserting piping into the princess and raglan seams. Remove any basting.

5 Use the Front-Opening Collar for this costume. Sew the two collar pieces together around the top and sides, inserting piping if desired (it helps give the collar structure in addition to adding detail). With the bodysuit inside out, align the collar with the neckline, right sides together. Match the center point at the back and the front edges to the sides of the zipper, aligning the dots to the neckline edges. Serge the collar to the neckline, or sew through all layers with a stretch stitch, then again with a zigzag ⅛" (3mm) away, and trim the seam allowances to ¼" (6mm).

6 Finish the leg and sleeve openings with your preferred hem method.

CASUAL ELF

Simple and easy to sew, the tunic and leggings are both a great starting point for your sewing adventure and a mighty fine outfit to go adventuring in. Layer a mail shirt underneath when you're about serious business—mithril optional—and complete the picture with some leather boots, a shield, and a legendary sword. Or, if you're a more peaceable sort, accessorize with a magical flute and feathered hat. Up to you!

PATTERNS

▶ Tunic, page 121
▶ Leggings, page 103

ACCESSORIES

▶ Elf ears
▶ Leather belt
▶ Leather wristband
▶ Sword
▶ Suede boots

This costume is a combination of the example garments from the **Tunic** *and* **Leggings** *patterns.*

VARIATIONS

Pick casual, rustic-looking fabrics like linen or lightweight woolens for a convincingly rough-and-tumble tunic, but give it some texture and richness with a bit of embroidered trim or metallic braid. If you can find it, a brushed-finish knit can give you a convincing faux suede look for the leggings. Otherwise, look for matte-finish stretch fabrics like cotton/spandex jersey or even a lightweight sweater knit.

For a similar look in women's sizes, draft a similarly shaped neckline and facing onto the Blouse pattern (see page 131) and extend it to below hip length, then follow the tunic instructions for assembly. You can even make it without the side zipper, though you may want to go up a size or just add a little more room at the side seams so it's easier to pull over your head. Refer to Chapter 4, Alterations and Modifications, page 73, for details.

SEIFUKU

There are endless variations on the basic school uniform! Long sleeves, short sleeves, different color combinations for blouse and skirt, over-the-knee socks, tights, flats, Mary Janes—even weaponry can accessorize the simple top and skirt. When you combine the blouse and skirt to make a school uniform costume, you want to choose coordinating fabrics so they look like a matched set. If the blouse and skirt will be made from the same fabric, look for lightweight suiting materials with a bit of drape. Rayon blends are great. Avoid anything that seems like it would be scratchy or plasticky against your skin unless you plan on adding a lining. If the body of the blouse is in a different fabric, often the collar will be made from the same fabric as the skirt or it will be trimmed in a matching color. Go for it!

PATTERNS

▶ Pleated Skirt, page 125
▶ Blouse, page 131

ACCESSORIES

▶ Wig
▶ Satchel
▶ Shoes
▶ Scarf (To make your own, see instructions at right.)

This costume is a combination of the example garments from the Pleated Skirt and Blouse patterns.

INSTRUCTIONS (Scarf)

1 The school uniform is usually worn with a scarf, which is tied in a knot at the point of the collar or threaded through a decorative loop of fabric. The narrow scarf in this costume is cut about 10" (25.4 cm) wide and 50" (127 cm) long and sewn into a tube. Press the seam open and sew across both ends, straight or at an angle depending on your preference, leaving an opening of 2" (5 cm) or so to turn the scarf right side out. Sew the opening closed by hand, press, and you're ready to go.

2 For a different look, you can also make a square scarf by cutting a roughly 27" (68.6 cm) square from lightweight, drapey fabric like voile or charmeuse, and finish the edges with a narrow rolled hem sewn by hand or machine (see page 67). Fold the scarf along the diagonal, wrap it around your neck under the collar, and tie loosely.

VARIATION

For a summer variation of the school uniform, simply sew the blouse section from a crisp cotton shirting or sateen, cut the sleeves off at biceps level, and hem. The collar can be made in the same fabric as the skirt, or in white with trim to match the skirt, depending on your character.

ELF PRINCE

To turn the long coat into a robe fit for an elven lord, start with a spectacular fabric. Look for brocade or tapestry weaves with organic motifs, abstract geometric designs, or even paisley. Fibers like cotton, rayon, or silk will usually have a more natural sheen than the widely available polyester varieties, but keep an open mind to anything that has an appropriately regal look. Then pair your coat fabric with other interestingly textured fabrics and trims, so your costume looks richer and more detailed the closer you get. For this version, the outer fabric is a soft brocade with a pattern of leaves, paired with rayon satin pants. The pants are from the same basic pattern, but I extended them to full length instead of making cuffs.

PATTERNS

▶ Pants, page 137
▶ Coat, page 149

ACCESSORIES

▶ Wig (optional)
▶ Crown
▶ Staff
▶ Elf ears
▶ Brooch
▶ Boots

TOOLS AND MATERIALS

Pants:
▶ Sewing Essentials (page 44)
▶ 3½ yds (3.2 m) of 54" (137 cm) wide satin, crepe, or other fluid bottom-weight fabric (I picked a soft, drapey brown rayon satin to go with the coat.)
▶ 1¼ yds (1.1 m) of matching ribbon or cord for the back waistband lacing
▶ 1½ yd (1.4 m) of lightweight woven or weft-insertion interfacing for the waistband
▶ 6 metal eyelets, or heavy topstitching thread for hand-sewn eyelets
▶ Six ⅝" (1.5 cm) fabric-covered buttons for the center front fly
▶ All-purpose thread in a matching color

*This costume is a combination of the example garment from the **Coat** pattern and a new garment from the **Pants** pattern.*

INSTRUCTIONS (Pants)

1 Alter the length of the pants pattern as suggested in step 1 on page 139. I extended them about 21" (53.3 cm) to make them full length, including the hem allowance. Omit the cuffs when you cut out the fabric.

2 Construct the pants following steps 2 through 13, but don't gather the pant legs for cuffs in step 13. Add the back lacing tabs or not, as you prefer.

3 Hem as desired.

VARIATION

If you want pants you can tuck into close-fitting boots, use a lightweight material or consider gathering the fabric and attaching it to a simple cuff (maybe even one made of stretch fabric) to reduce bulk around your ankles.

MAGICAL GIRL

A great magical girl outfit is colorful, ruffled, and fluffy, with a touch of superhero swagger. The real joy of this kind of costume is in the details, but the basic pieces are actually very simple and easy to make, and infinitely customizable. This costume pairs the Dress with the High-Collar Variation of the Blouse to give it the right magical effect. Since the Blouse is meant to be worn underneath the dress, it's made in very light, slightly sheer double georgette to give it an airy feel.

PATTERNS

▶ Dress, page 143
▶ Blouse (High-Collar Variation), page 131

ACCESSORIES

▶ Wig
▶ Magic Wand
▶ Booties

TOOLS AND MATERIALS

Blouse:
▶ Sewing Essentials (see page 44)
▶ 1½ yds (1.4 m) of 45" (114 cm) wide lightweight blouse fabric in cotton, silk, or synthetics (I used a red silk double georgette.)
▶ ¼ yd (23 cm) of 45" (114 cm) wide blouse fabric in a contrasting color for the cuffs and tie (I used gold double georgette.)
▶ 12" (30 cm) invisible zipper
▶ All-purpose thread in a matching color

This costume is a combination of the existing garment from the Dress pattern and a new garment from the Blouse pattern.

INSTRUCTIONS (Blouse)

Follow the instructions for the High-Collar Blouse variation of the pattern. Use the contrasting fabric for the cuffs and for the tie; the latter is a simple fabric tube about 42" (107 cm) long, cut on the cross grain for fabric efficiency (though if you have extra fabric, cutting on the bias will give you a tube that's easier to turn out). See page 59 for directions on making tubes.

VARIATION

For more girly power, add some bows to the ends of the princess seams of the bodice. You can sew your own bows or add bows made of wide ribbon. If you want the bows to be easily removable so they aren't crushed when you launder the costume, attach them to snaps instead of sewing them on.

PIRATE

Pirate coats are just fun, okay? You get to pick gorgeous fabrics, pile on the trims and embellishments, and swoop around with a big, full hem. This version is based on the long Coat pattern, shortened to just below the knee and widened considerably at the hem. For a fantasy look, embellish your coat with lace appliqué, embroidery, or woven trims, as was done in this costume. If steampunk is more your thing, you may prefer to trim with leather, buckles and straps, chains, and so forth. Do your embellishment before assembling the coat if you want to do it by machine, but if you're adding stiff, delicate, or otherwise unwieldy trims, or if you intend to sew them by hand, you may wish to wait until the coat is complete so you don't have to deal with them during assembly.

This costume is a combination of the example garments from the **Tunic** and **Pants** patterns and a new garment from the **Coat** pattern.

PATTERNS

▶ Tunic, page 121
▶ Pants, page 137
▶ Coat, page 149 (see cutting layout on page 193)

ACCESSORIES

▶ Top hat
▶ Spyglass
▶ Walking stick
▶ Brooch
▶ High boots

TOOLS AND MATERIALS

▶ Sewing Essentials (see page 44)
▶ 5½ yds (5 m) of 45" (114 cm) wide velvet (I used deep blue.)
▶ 5½ yds (5 m) of 45" (114 cm) wide lining fabric (I used red.)
▶ 1 yd (.9 m) of 60" (152 cm) wide cotton twill or canvas for interfacing
▶ 4 yds (3.7 m) of 3" (7.6 cm- wide metallic lace or trim
▶ ⅔ yd (61 cm) of ⅛" (3 mm) ribbon to stabilize the neckline
▶ All-purpose thread in a matching color

INSTRUCTIONS

1 Make the following changes to the pattern when cutting out the coat:

Cut the front and front facing off at the center front line and add a ⅝" (1.5 cm) seam allowance.

Omit the collar pieces; instead, cut the back neckline facing piece (included on sheet 3) from the velvet.

Make a pattern for an extension as shown in (**A**); this is just the length of the side seam from the waist down swung out to create a wedge and added to the front, back seam of the side piece, and back as shown in (**B-D**). If adding pockets, adjust the placement to work with the new side seam shape (**C**).

NOTES

➤ The yardage on page 185 will make a knee-length coat with 12" (30.5 cm) extensions. If your fabric is wider than 45" (114 cm), you can make the wedge extension larger for even more volume.

➤ It's often easier to cut tricky fabrics like velvet in a single layer. It's also necessary in this costume because of the wide pieces, and as a bonus, it saves a lot of fabric.

➤ The pirate coat assembly is largely the same as the regular coat, but because the pirate coat is much fuller at the hem, you will find yourself with a lot of fabric to wrangle. Make sure you have plenty of workspace around your sewing machine to avoid bumping into things as you sew.

➤ If your character is less regal than this pirate and needs a grittier look, you can also weather the coat (see page 95).

➤ Depending on the fabric you use for the coat, it may be a good idea to finish the seam allowances, at least for the bottom half of the coat, as the lining is loose in this version.

➤ The whole torso is interfaced to support the soft velvet.

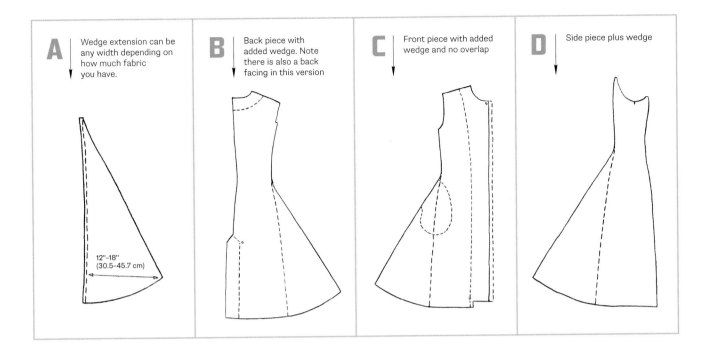

A Wedge extension can be any width depending on how much fabric you have.

12"–18" (30.5–45.7 cm)

B Back piece with added wedge. Note there is also a back facing in this version

C Front piece with added wedge and no overlap

D Side piece plus wedge

Cut the the pattern pieces off along the knee line, or at the desired length.

After cutting the coat and lining, cut the coat front, back, and side panel pattern pieces off at the waist and use them to cut the interfacing (you can tape the pattern back together when you're done if you like).

❷ Baste the interfacing pieces to the coat in the seam allowances, then assemble the outer shell and lining, following steps 1 through 5 for the Coat. Baste the back facing to the lining at the neckline, wrong side of facing to right side of lining. Turn the lower edges of the facing under, and edge-stitch or hand sew them to the lining. Pin the lining shoulder seams together.

❸ Let both coat and lining hang for 24 hours so the bias sections can drop. Trim the hems even before continuing; the lining should be 1¾" (4.4 cm) shorter than the coat.

❹ Follow step 6, but sew the coat hem at the top of the hem allowance instead of ¾" (1.9 cm) down. Use one of the hem finishes on page 67, as the coat hem may be exposed when the lining moves. Instead of folding the lining hem up as

at the end of step 6, press and sew a ⅞" (2.2 cm) double-fold hem (turn under ¼"/6 mm, then another ⅝"/1.5 cm).

❺ Do not sew the lining to the coat hem. Sew the facing to the front as described in step 7, but note that you are sewing up the center front line as there is no overlap.

❻ Continue with step 8. There will be no jump pleat as the lining is free, but the lining should overlap the coat hem by about ⅞" (2.2 cm), covering about half the hem allowance. After sewing the lining shoulder seams and setting the lining sleeves into the lining, match the coat and lining necklines up at the center back and shoulder seams and sew. You may want to incorporate a piece of ⅛" (3 mm) ribbon in this seam to prevent the neckline from stretching. Clip the seam allowances as needed so the curve will turn out smoothly.

❼ Turn the coat right side out through the opening at the hem, and proceed with steps 9 and 10 to finish the construction.

❽ Add trim around the sleeves and front edges of the coat. Depending on your chosen trim, it will probably be easiest to do this by hand.

HOW TO USE THIS BOOK

Pattern Sheet Guides

To use the patterns included in this book, first refer to the instructions for the garment you'd like to make, identify the pattern pieces required for the project you are making, and then use the Pattern Sheet Guide on page 194 for help locating which pattern sheet your pieces are on.

Cutting Layouts

Once you find those pieces on the pattern sheets, trace them using tracing paper, pattern paper, or tissue. Transfer all markings such as notches and darts. On pages 189-193, you will find Cutting Layouts, which will show you the best way to place your traced patterns on the fabric for cutting.

Choosing Your Size

Use the charts below to decide what size you need for the patterns in this book. The women's chart is used for the leotard, seamed bodysuit, blouse, and dress bodice patterns.

The men's chart is used for the leggings, seamless bodysuit, tunic, pants, and coat patterns. This is not to say that you can't make the coat for a woman or leotard for a man, but be aware that you may need to adjust the length and other proportions if you do. To make other fit adjustments, refer to page 74.

Use a freshly taken set of body measurements for the best results. (Don't just choose the size you usually wear.) See page 76 for more information on how to take your body measurements. All measurements should be snug against your skin, but not tight.

Fit is personal, and subject to your preferences, your build, and the materials you choose. You may need a different size than indicated if you prefer your clothes particularly loose or tight, or if your fabric has more or less stretch than the sample garments. If you're undecided, you may want to try measuring the pattern directly and comparing it to similar garments in your own closet.

SIZE CHARTS

MEN'S	x-small	small	medium	large	x-large
Chest	34" (86.4 cm)	37" (94 cm)	40" (101.6 cm)	44" (111.8 cm)	48" (121.9 cm)
Waist	28" (71.1 cm)	31" (78.7 cm)	34" (86.4 cm)	38" (96.5 cm)	42" (106.7 cm)
Hip	34" (86.4 m)	37" (94 cm)	40" (101.6 cm)	44" (111.8 cm)	48" (121.9 cm)
Torso Length	58"-61" (147.3 cm-154.9 cm)	60"-63" (152.4 cm-160 cm)	62"-65" (157.5 cm-165.1 cm)	65"-68" (165.1 cm-172.7 cm)	68"-71" (172.7 cm-180.3 cm)

* for height of about 5'10" (177.8 cm)

WOMEN'S	x-small	small	medium	large	x-large
Bust	33" (83.8 cm)	35" (88.9 cm)	37" (94 cm)	40" (101.6 cm)	43" (109.2 cm)
Waist	25" (63.5 cm)	27" (68.6 cm)	29" (73.7 cm)	32" (81.3 cm)	35" (88.9 cm)
Hip	35" (88.9 cm)	37" (94 cm)	39" (99.1 cm)	42" (106.7 cm)	45" (114.3 cm)
Torso Length	55.5"-58" (141 cm-147.3 cm)	56.5"-59.5" (143.5 cm-151.1 cm)	58"-61" (147.3 cm-154.9 cm)	59.5"-62.5" (151.1 cm-158.7 cm)	61"-64" (154.9 cm-162.6 cm)

* for height of about 5'5" (177.8 cm)

CUTTING LAYOUTS

CAPE

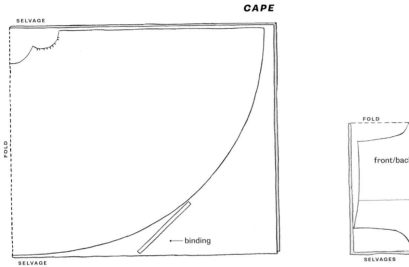

LEGGINGS

LEOTARD

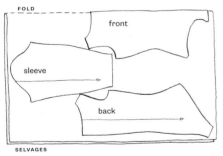

SEAMED JUMPSUIT

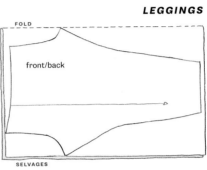

SEAMED JUMPSUIT - HALTER

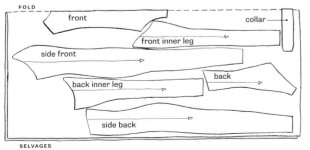

SEAMLESS SUPER-SUIT

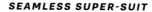

FOLD

front/back

sleeve

SELVAGES

TUNIC

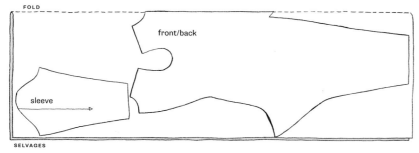

front facing

back facing

FOLD

FOLD

front

sleeve

back

SELVAGES

FOLD

BLOUSE

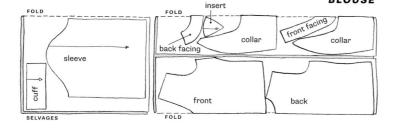

FOLD

insert

FOLD

sleeve

back facing

collar

front facing

collar

cuff

front

back

SELVAGES

FOLD

PLEATED SKIRT

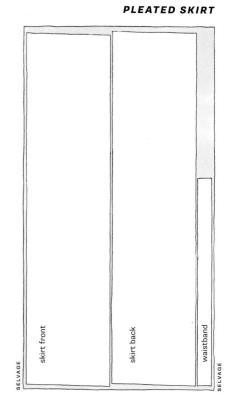

skirt front

skirt back

waistband

SELVAGE

SELVAGE

BLOUSE - STAND COLLAR

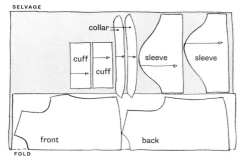

SELVAGE

collar

cuff

cuff

sleeve

sleeve

front

back

FOLD

PANTS

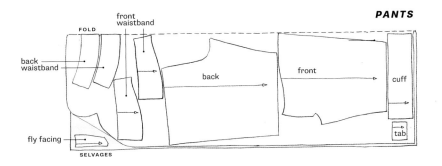

FOLD

back
waistband

front
waistband

back

front

cuff

tab

fly facing

SELVAGES

DRESS - TOP

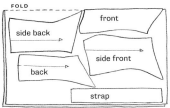

FOLD

side back

front

back

side front

strap

SELVAGES

DRESS - UNDER SKIRT

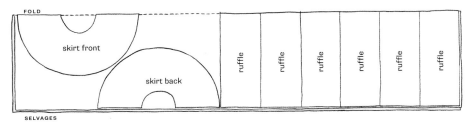

FOLD

skirt front

skirt back

ruffle

ruffle

ruffle

ruffle

ruffle

ruffle

SELVAGES

DRESS - UPPER SKIRT

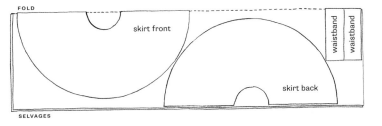

FOLD

skirt front

waistband

waistband

skirt back

SELVAGES

COAT

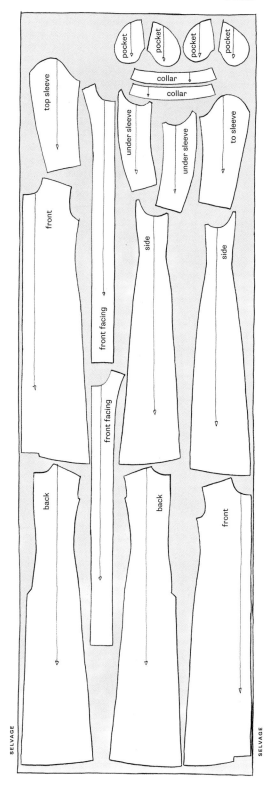

COAT - LINING

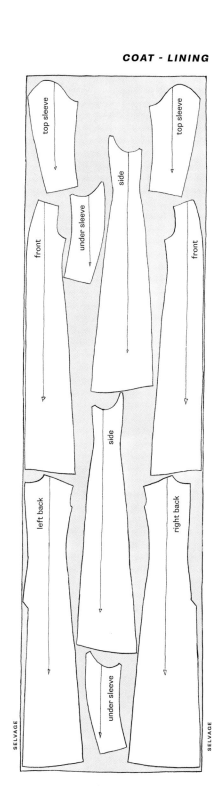

PIRATE COAT

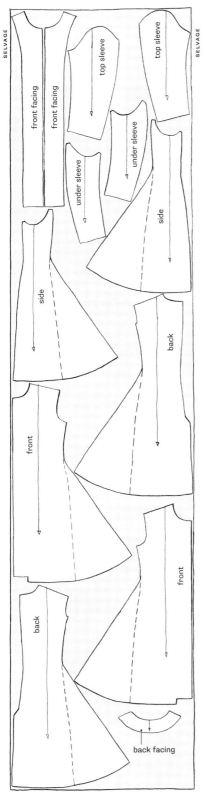

PIRATE COAT - LINING

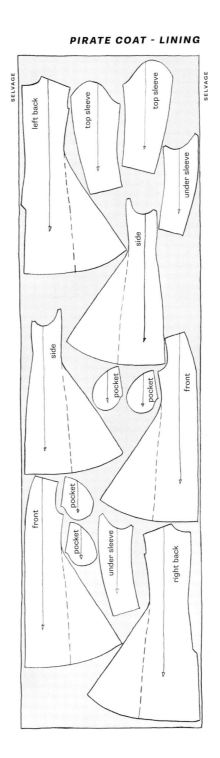

PATTERN SHEET GUIDE

Here is a list to help you locate the pattern pieces on the pattern sheets. The pattern sheets are inside the front and back covers of the book. Join lettered pieces into one piece, matching dots as indicated, before cutting fabric.

PATTERN SHEET 1
Leggings, page 103
▶ Leggings Front/Back (A, B)

Leotard, page 107
▶ Leotard Front
▶ Leotard Back
▶ Leotard Sleeve

Pants, page 137
▶ Pants Front
▶ Pants Fly Facing
▶ Pants Back
▶ Pants Front Waistband
▶ Pants Back Waistband
▶ Pants Cuff
▶ Pants Waistband Tab

Appliqués (shaded areas)
For use with Costume Warm-Up
(see page 157) and Superhero 1
(see page 159)

PATTERN SHEET 2
Seamed Jumpsuit, page 111
▶ Seamed Jumpsuit Front
▶ Seamed Jumpsuit Side Front (A, B)
▶ Seamed Jumpsuit Back
▶ Seamed Jumpsuit Side Back (A, B)
▶ Seamed Jumpsuit Front Inner Leg
▶ Seamed Jumpsuit Back Inner Leg
▶ Seamed Jumpsuit Sleeve
▶ Seamed Jumpsuit Back-Opening Collar
▶ Seamed Jumpsuit Halter Collar
▶ Seamed Jumpsuit Front-Opening Collar

Seamless Super-Suit, page 117
Note: Leggings Front/Back (A, B) can be substituted for Super-Suit Front/Back (B, C), if desired. You will need to add seam allowance to the center front of Super-Suit (A) as it will no longer be cut on the fold.
▶ Seamless Super-Suit Front/Back (A, B, C)
▶ Seamless Super-Suit Sleeve

PATTERN SHEET 3
Dress, page 143
▶ Dress Front
▶ Dress Side Front
▶ Dress Side Back
▶ Dress Back

Coat, page 149
▶ Coat Front (A, B, C; includes front lining and front facing)
▶ Coat Back (A, B, C; includes optional back facing)
▶ Coat Side (A, B)
▶ Coat Top Sleeve
▶ Coat Under Sleeve
▶ Coat Collar
▶ Coat Side Pocket

PATTERN SHEET 4
Cape, page 99
▶ Cape

Tunic, page 121
▶ Tunic Front (A, B)
▶ Tunic Back (A, B)
▶ Tunic Front Facing
▶ Tunic Back Facing
▶ Tunic Sleeve

Blouse, page 131
▶ Blouse Front
▶ Blouse Back
▶ Blouse Front Facing
▶ Blouse Back Facing
▶ Sailor Collar
▶ Blouse Sleeve
▶ Blouse Sleeve Cuff
▶ Blouse Neckline Insert
▶ Stand Collar

Superhero 3 Optional Details, page 167
▶ Upper Leg Appliqué
▶ Lower Leg Appliqué
▶ Halter Border

GLOSSARY

Appliqué A piece of fabric sewn on top of another fabric for decorative effect. In **reverse appliqué**, the decorative layer is sewn underneath, and the base fabric is then cut away to expose it.

Armscye The opening in a garment body where the sleeve is attached.

Basting Hand or machine stitching used to temporarily hold fabric in place.

Bias The diagonal direction 45° away from both warp and weft on a woven fabric. A **bias-cut** garment is laid out so the bias grain is perpendicular to the ground when worn.

Bias tape A strip of fabric cut along the bias and used for binding, narrow facings, or decorative techniques. Bias tape is preferred over straight-grain strips because it does not fray and molds smoothly around curves.

Binding A strip of fabric, often cut on the bias, that is folded around an edge and sewn in place. Used as a decorative finish for edges and openings.

Body A property of fabric that makes it stand up or out from the figure, forming wide folds or ripples.

Boning Strips of rigid or semi-rigid material inserted into a garment as a stiffener or support structure. May be inserted in a casing or sewn directly to the garment depending on type.

Casing A fabric tunnel created by sewing layers of fabric together or by applying a separate tape or ribbon; used to enclose elastic, drawstrings, or boning.

Clapper A block of hardwood used to flatten seams after pressing for a crisp finish.

Croquis A plain line drawing of a figure, used as a reference or starting point when sketching garments. A custom croquis, drawn to your personal shape, is most helpful in planning the proportions of a costume.

Dart A section of fabric that is folded together and sewn in place to add shape to a garment. Usually shaped like a wedge or diamond, sometimes curved for a smoother shape.

Dart-equivalent or **shaping seam** A seam that incorporates a curve or angle on one or both sides to add shape to a garment.

Directional fabric A fabric that cannot be rotated without changing its appearance, due to a nap, visibly asymmetrical design, or a motif with clear up and down. Most knits are also subtly directional. When working with these fabrics, all pattern pieces should be laid out with the same orientation.

Distressing (weathering) Any technique used to give new materials a worn or damaged appearance, including abrasion, stains, crumpling, etc.

Drape How a fabric hangs and folds. A drapey fabric flows and forms soft ripples; a crisp fabric forms sharp creases.

Enclosed seam A seam allowance that is concealed by lining or other fabric layers and not visible inside or outside a finished garment. Does not usually require finishing, but may need to be graded to prevent it from making a lump.

External facing A piece of fabric sewn to the inside of an opening and flipped to the outside, then sewn down to conceal the seam. Often piped, topstitched, or made from decorative contrasting fabric.

Give The natural extensibility of a fabric due to its fiber properties or weave. Even non-stretch fabrics usually have some give, if only along the bias.

Gathering A technique in which a long piece of fabric is bunched up in many small folds and sewn to a shorter length of fabric, usually by means of threads or cords sewn along the longer edge and pulled up like a drawstring.

Ease (noun) The difference in measurements between a garment and the body it is intended to fit. **Wearing ease** is the minimum ease required for comfort and mobility. **Design ease** is additional ease added to create a specific fit or silhouette. **Negative ease**, when the garment measures smaller than the body, is sometimes used for stretch fabrics and in body-compressing garments like corsets.

Ease (verb) To reduce a fabric's length by compressing the weave, so that it can be sewn to a shorter length of fabric.

Facing A band of fabric sewn to an edge or opening and turned to the inside of the garment, concealing the cut edges between the layers. Often used as a finish for necklines, pocket openings, cutouts, shaped hems, etc.

Feed dogs The set of oscillating claws in the bed of a sewing machine that grip the fabric and move it under the needle.

Finish To secure or enclose the cut edge of the fabric at a seam or garment edge to prevent it from unraveling.

Flange A flap or extension along the length of a seam or trim. On piping, it is the flat part that is caught in the seam.

Flat-applied sleeve A sleeve that is joined to the front and back body after the shoulder seam is sewn, but before sewing the under-sleeve seam or side seam.

Flounce A curved or circular panel of fabric attached along its concave edge so the longer convex edge falls in loose ripples. It can be used decoratively or as a main garment piece.

Four-way stretch A fabric with considerable stretch and recovery in all directions. Garments such as leotards require four-way stretch for fit and mobility. These definitions are often used inconsistently: some retailers may use two-way and four-way stretch interchangeably, but if you need four-way it is safer to ascertain the actual stretch percentage in each direction.

Fusible interfacing or web A heat-activated adhesive product typically applied with an iron.

Godet A wedge-shaped panel of fabric sewn into a seam or notch to create a flared shape. Most often used to add fullness to a hem.

Gore A tapered or flared panel sewn together in multiples to create a 3-D structure. On a beach ball, the gores come to a point at both ends, while a trumpet skirt uses gores that are narrow at the top and abruptly widen near the hem.

Grade To trim seam allowances or other enclosed fabric layers at different widths, creating a gradual transition in thickness and preventing the appearance of a visible ridge on the outside of the garment.

Grain The direction of threads in a length of fabric. The **straight grain** runs in the direction of the warp threads, parallel to the selvage. The **cross grain** is the direction of the weft, parallel to the cut edge. Unless otherwise indicated, garments are cut so that the straight grain is perpendicular to the ground when worn.

Gusset A small panel of fabric inserted to add ease or improve range of motion in high-stress garment areas like the crotch or underarm.

Horsehair braid A flat braid made from thin, wiry strands of nylon or polyester, ranging in width from a ¼" (6 mm) up to 6" (15.2 cm) or more. Used as a support material, especially to add body and stiffness to a hem.

In-seam pocket A bag-shaped pocket inserted into a seam of a garment.

Interfacing A material used in specific areas to reinforce an outer fabric or add body. May be fusible (adhered directly to the fabric) or sewn in.

Jump pleat A small fold at the hemline of a lined jacket or other garment, to allow vertical ease in the lining. Prevents the lining fabric from pulling or puckering the outer fabric.

Knit fabric A material created from a continuous thread or threads arranged in interlocking loops.

Miter A short, angled seam or pleat that creates a neat corner finish. Often used for corners in hems, bindings, and trims.

Muslin A mock-up or trial run of a pattern in inexpensive fabric; named for the unbleached cotton fabric often used for this purpose. Also called a **toile**.

Nap Surface fibers or pile that has a predominant direction on the fabric.

Natural fiber A fiber derived from plant or animal sources, such as cotton, linen, silk, or wool.

Nonwoven textile A material created by bonding fibers together in a continuous sheet with no obvious grain.

Patch pocket A pocket sewn to the outside of a garment.

Pile Short fibers that extend perpendicular to a fabric surface, as in fur or velvet.

Piping A trim consisting of a narrow strip of fabric inserted in a seam or at a garment edge. It is usually filled out by a cord.

Pleat A fold that is permanently sewn or creased into the fabric, used decoratively or to add shape.

Press To iron with an up-and-down motion instead of sweeping side to side. Used in sewing to flatten seams, apply interfacing, form pleats, etc.

Princess seam A vertical shaping seam. Usually originates at the shoulder or armhole seam and extends down to the hem.

Raglan sleeve A sleeve that extends past the shoulder to the neckline and is joined on by diagonal seams in front and back. In woven fabrics, usually requires a seam or dart on top of the shoulder for shaping.

Recovery A fabric's ability to spring back after being stretched. Can be mechanical but more often requires the presence of spandex or other elastic fibers. Fabrics with poor recovery will tend to sag, but can sometimes be restored by washing or steaming.

Right side The side of the fabric that will be visible when worn; this can be either side of the fabric but should be consistent throughout the garment.

Ruching A panel of fabric that is gathered and secured along both edges to create a draped or textured effect.

Ruffle A length of fabric gathered and sewn in place along one edge as a decorative feature.

Selvage The tightly woven border that prevents a fabric from unraveling along each edge. It is sometimes a different color than the rest of the fabric, and may contain woven-in or printed information about the fabric's manufacturer.

Set-in sleeve A sleeve that is assembled before it is attached to the garment and joined on by a seam at the end of the shoulder. The **sleeve cap** (rounded upper portion) is often eased to help it curve over the shoulder.

Sheer Describes a fabric that is transparent or see-through.

Shirring A panel featuring many regularly spaced rows of gathering that create a deeply textured surface. The effect is often created with elastic to make stretchy areas in an otherwise non-stretch garment.

Stretch When a fabric can extend significantly beyond its basic length, as a result of the fabric structure (sometimes called **mechanical stretch**) or the inclusion of extensible fibers such as spandex. Usually measured as a percent difference between the relaxed and fully extended lengths.

Stabilize To temporarily or permanently prevent a fabric from stretching or distorting by securing it to a rigid material. Necklines and shoulder seams are sometimes stabilized to prevent stretching or sagging, and temporary stabilizers are often used to support a fabric while embellishing.

Staystitch To sew a line of stitches, typically within the seam allowance, in order to prevent the fabric from stretching or distorting before it is permanently sewn.

Structure The inherent shape of the garment, created with the use of darts or shaping seams.

Synthetic fiber A fiber manufactured from raw materials, such as polyester or nylon.

Tailor's ham A hard pillow stuffed with sawdust, used to support the fabric when pressing curved seams and darts.

Topstitching Stitching intended to be visible and executed from the right side of the garment.

True To correct a seam after making an alteration, e.g. redrawing a curve to remove jagged edges, or reshaping the end of a dart so that it can be caught in the seam.

Two-way stretch A fabric with at least some stretch in both horizontal and vertical directions. Usually, one direction stretches more than the other.

Underlining A material used to support the outer fabric or make it more opaque. Typically cut from the same pattern as the outer fabric, sewn together, and treated as a single layer.

Understitching Stitching that joins a lining or facing layer to the seam allowance without passing through the outer fabric; prevents the understitched layer from rolling to the outside of the garment.

Wrong side The side of the fabric that faces the inside of the garment. If the difference between the right and wrong side is not readily apparent, use chalk or adhesive tape to mark the wrong side to avoid confusion.

Walking a seam The process of matching up the pattern pieces on each side of a seam to ensure that they are the same length and any markings align correctly.

Warp The strong threads oriented along a woven fabric's length, parallel to the selvage. When weaving, the warp threads are held taut on the loom and the weft worked back and forth between them.

Weft The threads oriented across a woven fabric, perpendicular to the selvage.

Woven fabric A material created by interlacing warp and weft threads at right angles to each other.

Yoke A smooth horizontal panel of fabric in the chest, upper back, or hip area, usually incorporating shaped seams to replace one or more darts and sometimes used to anchor a gathered or pleated section.

GLOSSARY OF STYLE ELEMENTS

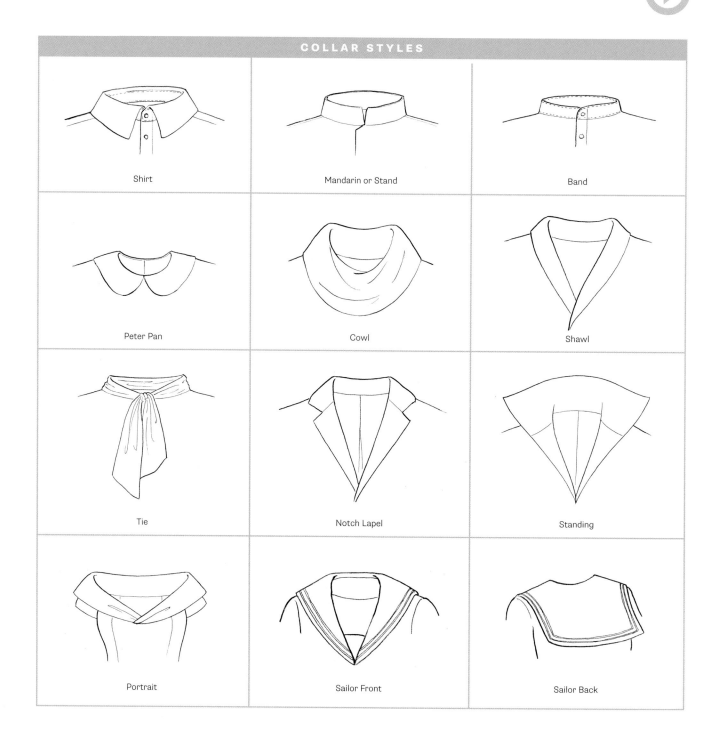

COLLAR STYLES

Shirt

Mandarin or Stand

Band

Peter Pan

Cowl

Shawl

Tie

Notch Lapel

Standing

Portrait

Sailor Front

Sailor Back

Jewel

Scoop

V

Boat

Square

Strapless

Halter

Draped/Cowl

Sweetheart

Funnel

Asymmetrical

Surplice

Plunge

Keyhole

Off-shoulder

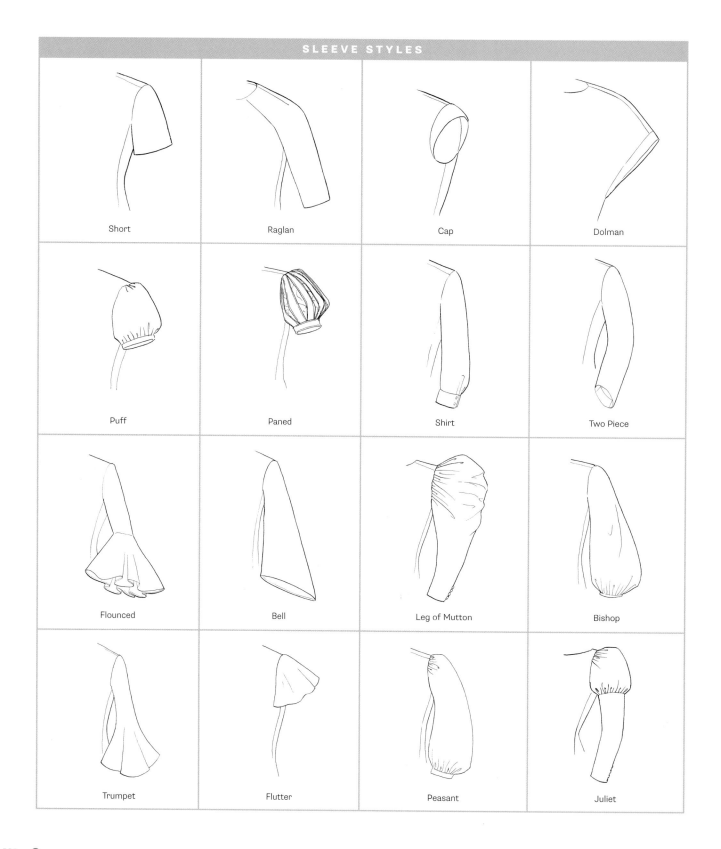

Short

Raglan

Cap

Dolman

Puff

Paned

Shirt

Two Piece

Flounced

Bell

Leg of Mutton

Bishop

Trumpet

Flutter

Peasant

Juliet

SKIRT STYLES

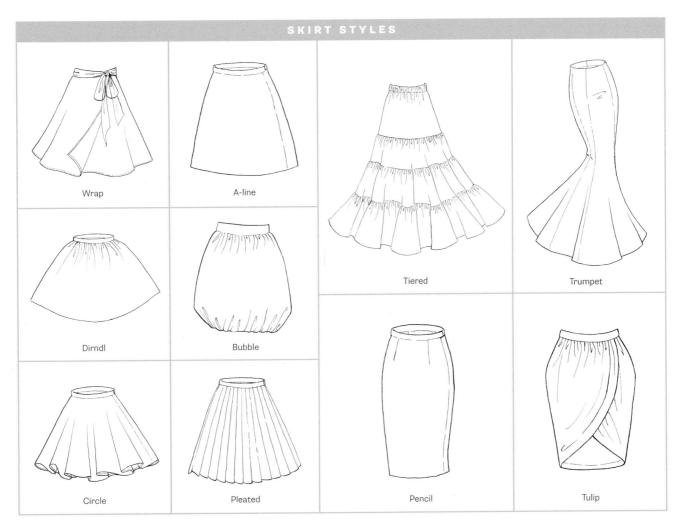

Wrap

A-line

Tiered

Trumpet

Dirndl

Bubble

Pencil

Tulip

Circle

Pleated

PANT STYLES

Leggings

Trousers

Wide-leg

Drawstring

Dropcrotch

Sheath

Shift

Fit and Flare

Empire

Slip

Body Conscious

A- Line

Bustier

Ballgown

Mermaid

RESOURCES

Additional Reading

The Art of Manipulating Fabric
by Colette Wolff
All kinds of fabric manipulation techniques, from ruffles to pleats to smocking. Great for adding texture and detail to your costumes.

Couture Sewing Techniques
by Claire B. Shaeffer
Detailed information on hand and machine sewing techniques used in high-end clothing.

Fabric for Fashion: The Complete Guide by Clive Hallett and Amanda Johnston
Covers various types of fabrics and their design applications. Illustrated with fashion examples, so you can see how the materials behave in real life.

Fitting & Pattern Alteration by Elizabeth Liechty, Judith Rasband, Della Pottberg-Steineckert
Exhaustive reference on fit problems and solutions. Especially handy if you plan to sew for other people.

How to Use, Adapt, and Design Sewing Patterns by Lee Hollahan
Good pattern alteration resource for beginners, including alterations for both fit and style.

Pattern Magic (series)
by Tomoko Nakamichi
Creative pattern alterations for unusual and sculptural designs. Best if you already have basic construction skills.

Successful Serging by Beth Baumgartel
Basic and decorative serger techniques, including stitch settings, handling, and troubleshooting.

Tailoring: The Classic Guide to Sewing the Perfect Jacket
by the editors of Creative Publishing International
Jacket and coat tailoring including interfacings and how/where to use them; construction of pockets, linings, collars, and sleeves; how to build in shape with padstitching and/or fusibles.

Vogue Sewing
Broad introduction to sewing techniques, including construction, fitting, and how to work with various fabrics.

Fabric, Notions, and Other Supplies

Clover
clover-usa.com
Notions, marking supplies, pressing accessories, bias tape maker tools.

CorsetMaking
corsetmakingsupplies.com
Boning, busks and other fasteners, corsetry tools, grommets, corset fabrics.

Dharma Trading
dharmatrading.com
Dyes, dye-ready fabrics in various fibers, inexpensive silks, fabric paints. Also has extensive resource section on dyes and dye methods.

Fabric.com
fabric.com
All kinds of garment, quilting, and decorating fabrics; faux fur.

Fashion Sewing Supply
fashionsewingsupply.com
All types of sew-in and fusible interfacing, buttons, elastics.

Manhattan Wardrobe Supply
wardrobesupplies.com
Pressing tools, dyes and weathering supplies, professional hair and makeup products.

Pacific Trimming
pacifictrimming.com
Trims, buckles and fasteners, hardware, notions, elastic and elastic cord (great for piping).

Spandex World and Spandex House
spandexworld.com and spandexhouse.com
Nylon/spandex in all weights and finishes, novelty spandex, ponte knit, spacer fabric, faux leather, stretch mesh, and powermesh.

Spoonflower and Fabric on Demand
spoonflower.com and fabricondemand.com
Custom printing on various fabric substrates.

Tandy Leather
tandyleather.com
Leather and leather tools, rivets and grommets, buckles and hardware.

Wawak Sewing Supplies
wawak.com
Bulk fasteners and thread, zippers, lining and interfacing, tools and notions, patternmaking rulers.

Useful Websites

Craftsy
craftsy.com
Video classes on innumerable art and craft topics, including extensive offerings on sewing and fitting.

Foundations Revealed
foundationsrevealed.com
Subscription site all about corsetry.

Mary Corbet's Needle 'n' Thread
needlenthread.com
Great starting point for hand embroidery; has a huge library of tutorials as well as embroidery book reviews.

The RPF
therpf.com
Message board for costume and prop making enthusiasts.

ACKNOWLEDGMENTS

Where to begin? Thank you to Andrea Somberg, who saw the potential in this book and kept me afloat with relentless enthusiasm. Thank you to my editor, Cristina Garces, for boundless patience, reassurance, and emergency button sewing. Thanks also to Valerie Shrader, technical editor extraordinaire, who found all the squishy parts of the manuscript and prodded them into shape. And thanks to Susi Oberhelman for taking all my bits and pieces and corralling them into gorgeous pages.

Thanks to all the people who showed up on photoshoot day and made my crazy outfits look fantastic: photographer Karen Pearson and assistant Zomnia Vasquez, stylist Alethia Weingarten, and hair and makeup artist Stacy Beneke, as well as the spectacular models Anne Winsland, David Emmanuel, and Kimberly Maldonado. You all made magic.

My parents, Mark and Carolyn Conahan, planted the seeds for my love of cosplay with handmade Halloween costumes back in the day. I owe them for creative skills, design sense, and endless encouragement, but also for concrete advice on ink, paper, and drawing implements, and for the nitty-gritty process stuff. Thanks for teaching me about adjustment layers, Dad. And I would not be the sewist I am today without Grandma Su, who taught me how to finish seams and (I'm convinced) gave me the fabric hoarding gene.

Endless gratitude as well to Allison Jamieson-Lucy, who swooped to the rescue more than once when I hit my sample sewing limit. She also provided color theory expertise, consultation on art supplies and technique, and much-needed moral support.

Thanks to Renée Miller, who got me started on hand sewing twenty-odd years ago, and to Sharon Blair and Portland Sewing for a solid foundation in pattern drafting. Thanks also to Kathy Marrone and all my colleagues at the McCall Pattern Company for education, support, and enthusiasm throughout this process.

My sister Kathleen was an invaluable sounding board in the early stages of the book, and helped to test the patterns. Conversations with Natalie Scott, Gareth Hauser, and Kenrick Vezina were also pivotal in the development of this book.

Finally, thank you to Seth for ten amazing and transformative years, and for letting me take over the entire apartment with my crafty shenanigans. Now that's dedication.

INDEX

Note: Page numbers in *italics* indicate specific patterns and costumes. Page numbers in **bold** indicate glossary definitions. Page numbers *P-1, P-2, P-3, P-4* refer to the four pattern sheets.

Editor: Cristina Garces
Designer: Susi Oberhelman
Production Manager: Kathleen Gaffney

Library of Congress Control Number: 2016945899
ISBN: 978-1-4197-2396-4

Printed and bound in China
10 9 8 7 6 5 4 3 2 1

Abrams books are available at special discounts when purchased in quantity for premiums
and promotions as well as fundraising or educational use. Special editions can also be created to
specification. For details, contact specialsales@abramsbooks.com or the address below.

ABRAMS The Art of Books
115 West 18th Street, New York, NY 10011
abramsbooks.com